Y0-COS-532

WITHDRAWN

THE EXILE OF THE SOUL

THE EXILE OF THE SOUL

By Roy Mitchell

The case for two souls in the constitution of every man

Edited by John L. Davenport

Buffalo, New York

Acknowledgement: The selection on pp. 312-14 is from *The Inner Game of Tennis,* by W. Timothy Gallway. Copyright ©1974 by W. Timothy Gallwey. Reprinted by permission of Random House, Inc.

BP
573
M3
M58
1983

Copyright 1983 by John L. Davenport
All rights reserved.

Published 1983 by Prometheus Books
700 East Amherst Street, Buffalo, NY 14215

Library of Congress catalog card number: 83-62528

ISBN: 0-87975-232-7 cloth
0-87975-233-5 paper

Printed in the United States of America

CONTENTS

Part III B

FOREWORD

I take great pleasure in writing a foreword to this book and in introducing the editor to the reader.

John L. Davenport was born in Hamilton, Ontario, Canada, in 1906 and was trained as a chemical engineer at the University of Toronto. After graduating he joined in 1929 the chemical manufacturing firm, Pfizer Inc., of Brooklyn, New York. He soon rose to senior positions and stayed with the company until 1967.

Early in his career he made decisive improvements in practical methods for the fermentation and recovery of citric acid from the mold Aspergillus niger. Originally Pfizer made citric acid from Italian cull lemons, but after the discovery by Currie that a carefully cultured mold of Aspergillus could produce citric acid from cane sugar, the Pfizer company developed an industrial process which eventually yielded citric acid far more economically than lemons. This development took place in the 1920's and 30's.

A second major achievement was the industrial production of penicillin. This came about when Florey, Chain and Heatley were told that it would be impossible to produce this new and promising drug commercially in wartime England. They therefore contacted American chemical manufacturers with a view to developing the laboratory process for large-scale production.

Pfizer's ingenious skills in handling molds on a large scale were the prime factor that soon put them far in the lead in the production of penicillin at a time in World War II when it was so desperately needed. Davenport was one of the leaders of a team that accomplished this work.

Very soon this pioneering achievement led the pharmaceutical industry to the large-scale production of a variety of antibiotics—an inestimable boon to mankind. It brought under control many of the bacterial infections, such as sepsis, pneumonia, tuberculosis and venereal diseases, which in the past had been appalling health hazards.

For his contributions Davenport was promoted to the position of superintendent of the Brooklyn plant and then successively became a director of the company, secretary, vice president of production, executive vice president and chairman of the executive committee.

In 1957 he decided to give up his executive work and go back into research—this time cancer. For the last ten years of his association with the company he was director of the John L. Smith (a former president who died of cancer) Memorial for Cancer Research which worked in close collaboration with the National Cancer Institute in Bethesda. This unit included over 200 people with an annual budget of over $3 million.

When in 1967 John Davenport offered to take a rather early retirement he did so in order to devote his time to his many other major interests.

In 1940 as a hobby he made practical improvements in the techniques of photography by combining brightness range, exposure and development of negatives into numbers that achieved consistently high-quality prints. This work has been acknowledged in *The History of Photography,* by Newhall.

Love of the ocean shores where he lived turned into a book on unique methods for the protection and preservation of ocean beaches.

Starting with a humble hand-set type press he began in 1955 to print and publish small fine books principally in the field of philosophy, a subject which ever since his teens had been an absorbing hobby of his.

Davenport's interests in matters philosophical were kindled early by a family friend, Roy Mitchell. Mitchell was an outstanding person, and above all a tireless student of comparative religion and philosophy. He did much to raise the standard of the theatre in North America. A book he wrote about the theatre was widely studied and praised.

Mitchell was particularly intrigued by the dual nature of

man, an ancient problem discussed often since the early Eastern religions and the classical Greek period. The Jekyll and Hyde idea is an example from more modern times.

Mitchell died in 1944, and he left a number of unpublished papers on the subject matter to John Davenport which in this book are now made available to a wider public. Comments on the dual nature of man usually include a mystical element, often clad in poetic form. I am myself too much of a scientist to be attracted by mysticism. I accept of course that mysticism has always played an important part in people's religious and artistic experiences.

One of my own interests is in the origin and cause of delinquency—especially in the appalling recent increases among juveniles. In this context, the dual nature of man with its noble and evil elements, to which John Davenport refers in an early part of this book, is of much concern to me. How should we go about, I ask myself, helping the noble to get the better of the evil? Here is a link between my thoughts and the world of Roy Mitchell.

Hans Krebs

Oxford
May, 1981

TWO SOULS, ALAS, ARE DWELLING IN MY BREAST.

Faust, Goethe

Part I

WHITHER

Most thoughtful men are aware of a certain dual nature within them. They observe their conscious mind or ego arguing with another voice—a voice sometimes subtle, sometimes brash, but one which invariably argues for selfish aims, personal comfort and lazy solutions to problems. It conjures up fears and emotions which block action on the problem at hand. It is ever ready to complain. In its milder departure from the disciplines of the ego, its desires extend to the pleasures of life. In its worst forms it crushes the ego and dominates the man with ugly moods, emotional disturbances, cruelty or addictions to alcohol and drugs. Misfortunes follow the man who heeds the advice of the other voice.

This duality has been studied for centuries by philosophers, religions, and more recently by the psychologists.

It is the concern of this book to explore this other voice because it carries with it a nagging question. Why must man be bound to this distracting entity? The answer to this question leads to the most important question a man can ask. What is our purpose here on earth?

One might inquire,"Well if man is divided into two parts, maybe he is divided into three or four or more." As a matter of fact the ancient sages of the Eastern religions have advanced a good case for seven parts in the constitution of man. They are not as easy to prove as the two parts. For instance, men of high spiritual attainment are well aware of a noble part, a spark of the divine also known as the field of archetypal knowledge. This book would not be complete without such inquiries.

The best answers to these questions are to be found

in a little known book by Roy Mitchell, *The Exile of the Soul.* Rather than try to paraphrase what Mitchell has said, it was obvious that he should speak for himself. So we have here a book within a book. The first part consists of introductory comments, the second is *The Exile of the Soul,* and the third is a collection of references and fragments pertaining to these questions.

Mitchell draws such startling conclusions the reader will want to know who else entertained such ideas. His studies brought forth an abundance of confirming data from widely different sources. To these have been added a variety of supportive evidence by the editor over a period of 50 years.

Roy Mitchell (1884 – 1944) was a man of extraordinary talents who lived in relative obscurity in Toronto and New York. From the University of Toronto his work was first in newspapers and then in development of the little theatre. In 1929 he published *Creative Theatre* a superb volume on its basic principles. His knowledge of philosophy, comparative religion and mysticism was profound. Led by an intuitive curiosity, he devoted most of his life to piecing together the facts of dualism and the constitution of man in order to establish his main idea—that a man has not one but two souls.

Mitchell's framework on which life is based is set forth as follows: A high race of souls, to whom we belong, had progressed far beyond the stature of man. They were sent to earth by a universal law of brotherhood to redeem a lower race of souls who in their evolutionary journey had fallen into an iniquitous disaster. The higher soul is thus an exile from his own sphere, slowly trying to bring order out of chaos in the irrational or animal soul he was sent here to redeem. The higher souls who are succeeding in their mission are our sages, heroes, poets and saints.

Picture each of us as a Jekyll and Hyde as in the enduring story of Robert Louis Stevenson* which, of course, is an exaggeration of the struggle which goes on within most of us.

Emerson, whose pivotal theme was the dualism in man put it so well when he said, "The soul says, eat; the body would feast. The soul says, the man and woman shall be one flesh and one soul; the body would join the flesh only. The soul says, have dominance over all things to the ends of virtue; the body would have the power over things to its own ends."

When Emerson said "body" he did not mean the physical stuff of which the body is made. It is obvious from his definitions that he meant a desire entity which selfishly contends for its own comforts, fears, anger, passions and gratifications. Who has not heard this contentious voice in almost continual colloquy with the conscious mind always striving for dominance? Through the ages men have described in detail the characteristics of that part of man which is selfish, base and brutal. They have called it a part, an aspect, sometimes a principle of man. Only rarely have they called it what it really is—an active, separate, lower entity, an animal soul—called by Plato the irrational soul, called by Jung the "shadow."

The task of the conscious mind (the ego) linked with the higher soul is to channel the marvellous energies of the animal soul into useful labor and calm behavior,

*There is no doubt that R. L. S. was a strong believer in the dual nature of man. It is said the plot for his story came to him in a dream. He wrote an essay, *Books Which Have Influenced Me,* which appeared in *British Weekly* (1887) in which he said: "Biography usually so false to its office, does here for once perform for us some of the work of fiction, reminding us, that is, of the truly mingled tissue of man's nature and how huge faults and shining virtues cohabit and persevere in the same character."

teaching it the great skills of which it is capable. It is the conflicts of these two souls that the psychiatrists and psychologists endeavor to resolve.

To accomplish its Great Task, the ego (or conscious mind) must be able to discriminate between the demands of the lower soul and the higher powers of his own being. For instance he may lend his imaginative powers to the lower soul who will use them for selfish degrading purposes or he may use them for high constructive purposes. The task is not one of exterminating the lower soul but one of disciplining and putting it to work much as you would a child.

For most people it is hard to discriminate because there can be a confusion between what is lower and what higher. In *The Exile of the Soul* and another work *Through Temple Doors,* Roy Mitchell has delineated the characteristics of the higher and lower souls. A collection of these has been made in the collectanea, see Part III B, p. 249 of this book. It will enable anyone to clarify which voice is speaking.

The struggle between the higher and lower souls is not something that lasts a brief 70 years, but one that goes on for thousands of years. This of course, requires that the soul has been on this earth many times in the past and will return here many times in the future. It is one of the oldest beliefs of man. It is a central theme of all Eastern religions, the ancient Egyptians, the Greeks and the Alexandrian Neoplatonists. Christianity had it in the early days when the church fathers, St. Clement and Origen, were closely connected with the Alexandrian Neoplatonists but the later church suppressed the idea. However, even in our Western civilization countless wise men have stoutly put forth their thoughts on the continual return of the soul to earth. A splendid book* has

**Reincarnation in World Thought* compiled and edited by Joseph Head and S. L. Cranston, Julian Press, New York, 1967.

detailed who they were and their intuitive and rational declarations.

In the *Dialogues of Plato* when a discussion came to an impasse, Socrates used the device of introducing ideas from mystical sources such as Diotima in *The Banquet* and the divine sources in *The Meno*. His approach would be: let us see if this will help us to resolve the questions we have raised. This is the method of Roy Mitchell.

These refreshing concepts which at last clarify the meaning of our sojourn here on earth will open up new rational vistas for the mind to ponder. The disappointments, sufferings and despairs of mankind take on a new perspective as the disciplined lower soul goes to work and a certain *joie de vivre* takes over. Hope takes on new meaning. It can no longer be viewed with cynicism.

In a most remarkable way, Roy Mitchell shows how the interactions of these two souls fit into biology, psychology, hypnosis, mathematics, philosophy, theology, mythology, ethics and humanism.

> Here is realization.
> Here is a man tallied—he realizes here
> what he has in him, . . .
>
> To know the universe itself as a road, as many roads,
> as roads for travelling souls.
>
> All parts away for the progress of souls,
> All religion, all solid things, arts, governments—
> all that was or is apparent upon this globe, or any
> globe, falls into niches and corners before the
> procession of souls along the grand roads of
> the universe.
>
> Walt Whitman

John L. Davenport

THE EXILE OF THE SOUL

BY

ROY MITCHELL

First published in serial form in the 1920s for
the *Canadian Theosophist* periodical and for lecture
material. First published in book form posthumously
in 1949 by the Blavatsky Institute of Canada,
2307 Sovereign Crescent SW, Calgary, Alberta, Canada.

CONTENTS

BIOGRAPHICAL NOTE

Roy Mitchell was born in Fort Gratiot, Michigan, in 1884, of Canadian parents, and was educated in Canadian schools and at the University of Toronto (1902–1904). He spent thirteen years in newspaper work in various cities in Canada and the U.S. During this time he was constantly in and around the theatres as press agent, dramatic critic, and dramatic editor. In 1908 he became interested in experimental little theatres, and for the next seven years he carried on such activity under the auspices of the Arts and Letters Club in Toronto. In 1916 he went to New York City to study theatrical design. He became technical director of the Greenwich Village Theatre during its first year (1917–1918). In 1918 he went to Ottawa as Director of Motion Pictures for the Dept. of Public Information, and from there to Hart House Theatre, University of Toronto, as its first Director (1919-1921). Hart House Theatre was an ideal laboratory to test his theories of motion, mutable settings and color systems described in the final chapters of *Creative Theatre*, a book he wrote which has received high acclaim for its basic knowledge of the theatre. In 1926 he was married to Margaret C. (Jocelyn) Taylor, an artist and sculptor, who was a worthy partner in his work. In 1927 Mitchell returned to New York City where he engaged in production, writing and lecturing. In 1930 he became Professor of Dramatic Art at New York University. While there he developed a type of group singing based on phonetics, so that folk songs of all nations could be presented in the native language, although his superb Consort singers did not speak the languages.

From the time he was a young man Mitchell became intensely interested in philosophy, comparative religion and the mystical meanings of mythology. Through the Theosophical Society in Toronto he studied these subjects in great depth, linking fragments from all sources to give him an understanding that is so well expressed in *The Exile of the Soul*. He was an outstanding lecturer on these subjects. This activity and the people it brought around him was his labor of love. He died on July 27, 1944 while on a sabbatical leave from the university.

THE EXILE OF THE SOUL

1. THE BIOLOGICAL PROBLEM

Biology, ancient as well as modern, has taken count of three classes of phenomena. The first are the phenomena of the thinking soul. These are the noetic functions. The fact that modern biological writers call them psychic should deceive nobody. It only means that some writer looking in a lexicon for a Greek word for soul took the first word he found, "psyche", regardless of its suitability. If he had been a better thinker he would have kept on until he found the word "nous" which means thinking or rational soul. Psyche means the animal or irrational soul. The second class of phenomena are those of animate nature. Just where animate nature ends and inanimate nature begins is still a matter of doubt to biologists. By animate they describe whatever lies between noetic and physico-chemical phenomena. In the best terminology these functions would be called psychic. The biologist, a little off key as usual, calls them vital. Vital is a word that, as we shall see, has other connotations. It is however, the accepted name for a series of phenomena, and, in the form "vitalist", stands for a school of opinion, and I shall have to use it. The third class of phenomena are the physico-chemical ones of the so-called inanimate nature.

Biologists, ancient and modern, are regimented according to the way in which they view these classes, the way in which they group them and the relative importance they assign to them.

Animists are those who give first importance to the intelligent soul but deny the separate existence of the psychic or vital functions. These latter they say are no more than lower, unconscious functions of the noetic power. Recognizing thus only soul and body they declare that the body is directly guided and controlled by the thinking soul. As a scientific theory of life animism is comparatively recent. Its great exponent was the German physiologist Stahl (1660-1734). After his death it was continued by some of his pupils and had a revival in the last century under E. Chauffard. It is the theory of life most easily aligned with theology, and has been largely influenced by theological considerations.

Monism is the opposite pole. It is like animism in that noetic and psychic functions are confused and identified. It differs from animism in that its followers give first importance to the body. Monists in addition to confusing thought and feeling, commit the further error of assimilating all phenomena, psychic and noetic, to general forces in nature which govern plants and animals. They tend to deny the existence of individual souls. In the beginning of modern science the monistic or mechanistic biologists saw the body as a complex of chemical apparatus, of pipes, pumps, retorts, levers, etc., etc., and interpreted soul as an illusion growing out of the activity of these. They have gradually approximated more closely to vitalism with the difference that they call the vital factors directional ones, and deny them actual entity. Monism corresponds to the Charvaka school of ancient and modern India. Biological monism is a reaction from theology.

The third possible position is called vitalism. It takes count of the three classes of phenomena, noetic, psychic and physico-chemical, as entitled to separate consideration. It says there is a vital (or psychic factor) between the thinking soul and the physical body by means of which the body is governed and directed.

In modern times vitalism arose out of the obvious failure of the animistic doctrine of Stahl, and has numbered among its exponents Bordeu, Grimaud, Barthez, Johannes Muller, Liebig, Candolle the botanist, Flourens and Dressel. Its origin, however, as a theory of life goes back into furthest antiquity. It is the doctrine of the oldest occult schools, of religions at their inception, of the mystery systems, and is taught by Pythagoras, Empedocles, Plato, Aristotle, the Neo-Platonists, Galen, Paracelsus, Van Helmont, Agrippa and others. Vitalism is neither a leaning towards nor a reaction from theology but has maintained its course regardless of current fashion.

The great objection the vitalists bring against animism is the philosophical one that animism requires the impossible conception of the thinking soul acting directly on the material body. Vitalists argue that the functions of the soul are reflective, volitional and conscious whereas the phenomena of the body are automatic, involuntary and unconscious. The only means of communication, they declare, can be through a vital principle which is distinct from thought.

Although the intentions of the animists and the monists are diametrically opposed, say the vitalists, their conclusions are particularly identical. The animist throws down all barriers between thinking and feeling. The monist destroys the barriers between feeling and physiological action. The animist posits a soul that performs all functions from the highest intuitional ones down to the lowest gleam of consciousness observable in plant and animal life. The monist posits a body that can by physico-chemical action explain all functions from the simplest chemical ones up to (and for some monists including) the functions of thought. They both—excluding the utter mechanists of course—

have a spiritual principle which animates all living creatures and both schools have a body which is purely materialistic. The dispute between them is which is the cause and which the effect. Does the thinking soul of man merely clothe itself with a body it does not understand, or does the body generate a kind of motion which is to be understood as mind?

Neither, says the vitalist. Pythagoras taught that between *nous*, the thinking soul, and *soma*, the body, there is a feeling or sensitive soul which he called *psyche.* Plato says there can be no understanding of man until we have made the difference between the divine rational soul which is immortal and the irrational soul which is mortal. Aristotle enunciating the ideas of his time took count of *nous*, the intellectual soul, and *psyche*, the irrational or vegetative soul. The Egyptian priests had a passional or desire soul which they called *ab-hati* standing between the immortal soul, the *ba,* and the body or *chat.* The Hindu schools have a thinking soul, *Jivatma* (the living, divine principle) or *antah-karana* (the cognitive soul) and a body called *Sthula sharira.* Between the soul and body they have an animal soul called *Kamarupa.* Their symbol for the thinking soul is Vishnu and for the animal soul, Shiva.

Galen, physician to Marcus Aurelius, and the medical writer whose system continued in Europe until the Renaissance, took count of (1) mind, (2) what he called animal, vital and natural spirits, and (3) body. Paracelsus, the reformer of mediaeval medicine taught the existence of a (1) thinking soul, (2) the Olympic spirits or vital forces of animal life, and (3) the body. Van Helmont the alchemist, physician and philosopher was a vitalist and refused to admit that the soul directly directs the body. The gap between soul and body he filled with a sensitive or feeling soul ruling a hierarchy of entities that correspond to the animal-vital natural series of Galen and to the Olympic spirits of Paracelsus.

In the ranks of modern biologists, the monists, whose great emphasis is on body and bodily function are vastly in the majority. The animists have dwindled to a mere handful. The vitalists remain but are widely different in their allegiances. At one pole are those who maintain an animistic vitalism that almost loses the vital principle in the thinking soul. At the other are those who maintain a monistic vitalism which almost loses the vital principle in the physiological processes.

The steady trend of modern biology is, however, in the direction of vitalism and as experimentation goes on there are increasing analogies for, and demonstrations of, the existence of a lesser soul and of whole ranges of souls inferior to that again, as the occultists have always contended. In common with the other sciences which are gradually turning back to the older philosophies and vindicating occult theories, biology is returning to a vitalist theory of man through what is called pluri-vitalism.

Pluri-vitalism is the secondary doctrine we saw in Galen, Paracelsus and Van Helmont. These occultists argued that the functions of the body are governed by a multitude of lives, cellular, corpuscular and organic. Galen's doctrine of three kinds of spirits was that the animal spirits preside over the nervous system, the vital spirits govern most of the other functions and that the natural spirits regulate the liver and can be incorporated thus in the blood. Paracelsus' Olympic spirits, which, as we shall see, derive their names from the earth gods of the Greek Olympus, are forces peculiarly of this earth stream of evolution, and control the functions of the liver, heart and brain. They exist also, says Paracelsus, in all other living forms of nature. Van Helmont, in placing below the thinking immortal soul a sensitive mortal soul, gave the sensitive soul as its agent an *aura vitalis* or principal *archaeus* (the Hindu *prana*, and the true vital element). This latter he says has its seat at the pylorus, or orifice that empties the stomach. Below this again Van Helmont placed the lesser individual lives he called *blas* or *vulcans* in each organ. The Kabbalists, the Egyptians, the Alchemists and all ancient schools placed the seat of the true psyche or feeling soul in the heart and said that its fluid vehicle, by which it pervades the body, is the blood. This is, by the way, the reason for the Jewish practice of slaughtering a food animal in such a way as to bleed it.

It was the fashion a generation ago to ridicule these classifications. Experiment has shown, however, that they are a valid terminology for phenomena since demonstrated. It has long been known that the lowest creatures are complete lives in their various parts. Plants propagated by cuttings have all the qualities of their parental stock. Worms cut into many parts complete themselves. In 1901 at Turin the biologist Locke kept the heart of a rabbit alive for several hours. Since then the heart of a man has been kept beating eighteen hours after the man's death. The experiments have been continued with muscles, glands, cells, tissues, nerves, the brain itself, demonstrating the old belief that each organ and each lesser centre of life has a separate existence. In the phrase of the Montpellier vitalist, Bordeu, each part of the body is "an animal in an animal."

The body of man is therefore the field of activity of a vast number of beings of whom the soul is only one—albeit the highest and capable of becoming the governing one. The thinking soul is the potential ruler of a great colony of entities extending from a sensitive soul or psyche down to the lowest cell life. The mechanistic biologist is loath to call these lesser lives entities. The furthest he will go is to call them vital properties, but the march of discovery is forcing him back to the idea that each, as a spiritual entity—however low its manifestation—is a fiery life. Moreover he is being driven by analogous advances in psychology and physics to realize that the co-ordination of these—so frequently inimical to each other—is not the work of the thinking soul but of a soul below the level of our consciousness. The present fashion in biology is to refuse to consider the vital soul as an active agent. A trifle afraid of each other, biologists take refuge in evasive sayings. They say it is a directional factor, an "ideal plan in the process of being carried out". Which of course entails the concept of an Ideal Planner, a sort of diffuse and non-individualized God, who only enters His plan as a vague force or energy. They argue that the vital properties in each organ are modes of activity inherent in the living substance and that these modes are derived from the arrangement of the molecules of the substance. Whether the arrangement is fortuitous, as the chemists have held, or is the careful work of the divine Molecule-Arranger they cannot agree. That the Planner and Molecule-Arranger might enter His plan as many individual souls—however humble—would be mythological and pagan. It might land them before their university senates on charges of pantheism or even witchcraft.

It will be observed in all the foregoing, the confusion arises out of the problem of the thinking soul. Thousands of phenomena show that it is not the efficient governor of the body. It knows nothing of the normal functioning of the organs. The beating of the heart, the coursing of blood, the chemistry of the conversion of food into renewed tissue, the expansion and contraction of the lungs, the processes of glandular secretion, the peristaltic action of the intestines, all go on without us. If the noetic soul were the direct ruler and knower of these functions we should have no occasion for debate about them. The proof that the thinking soul is external to these activities is to be found in the fact that it is unconscious of them.

Even the phenomena of death do not, for the vitalist, require the soul. Death for the animist is the withdrawal of the thinking soul. Death for the monist is the break-down of the machine. For the vitalist death is the with-drawal of the animal entity, Withdrawal of the noetic soul alone, while the psychic entity survives, is insanity.

Man minus a thinking soul would be a problem completely assimilable to all the problems of animal life. His introduction into the animal scheme renders the latter abnormal. The early animists, when pressed for an explanation of the fact that the soul could do so little with the physical functions, borrowed from theology a reply which theology had long ago borrowed from occult philosophy and said,"The soul is prevented by the consequences of original sin from guiding and directing the body."

Despite the ridicule the answer it elicited contained a clue to the solution of the problem. The animal order to which the human body belongs is a symmetrical and ordered whole—a stream of lives proceeding according to a plan. The thinking soul is the anomaly. It is the governor who does not govern. It is the deluded being who does not know the nature of its own forces. It is the thinker that now identifies itself with governance and now realizes its impotence. It is the thinker that cannot determine between these three—the soul as the director of the body, the body as the creator of the soul, or the soul as the co-inhabitor with a lower entity of a body which is itself the creation of a great number of still lower lives. The whole confusion is brought about, seemingly, by the effort of the thinker to identify himself with an order of beings to which he does not belong.

When we understand the thinker in man as an onlooker, and the real present ruler of the body as a sensitive and passional soul, the confusion begins to clear.

2. THE PSYCHOLOGICAL PROBLEM

The science of psychology, whose function it is to describe and explain the states of consciousness, has the same problem of the dual soul of man as that which confronts the biologist. The nature of the psychologist's research, however, requires him to approach it from another side.

Psychology was once a branch of philosophy and proceeded by introspective and philosophical methods. It was given its present name by a writer named Goelemus who is not distinguished in its annals except for the fact that it fell to his lot to go to the Greek lexicon for the word meaning "the lore of the thinking soul" and to come back with a word meaning "the lore of the unthinking soul". As we shall see, Goelemus was more fortunate than were those biologists who were similarly careless with their Greek.

Modern psychology was drawn into the field of science at the time when materialistic scientists were greatly in the ascendant and were most sure that the explanation of all the phenomena of consciousness could be found in the nature of physical matter. The natural sciences of astronomy, geology, physics, chemistry and biology all proceed on the assumption that the phenomenal universe is a reality which can be understood without reference to life or consciousness. The special concern of modern science is with a realm of effects. It may assume that these effects are causes and succeed in gaining a wide knowledge of them. An hypothesis may be intrinsically wrong and still be valid for working purposes. Chemistry proceeded in its routine operations under Dalton's atomic hypothesis and can continue to do so in spite of the fact that a few years ago the atomic theory had to be replaced by the electronic. So also, physics proceeded successfully for two hundred years on Newton's gravitational theory only to be advised a few days ago that its basis has to be thrown into the discard. Psychology has not fared quite so well. When it took on the scientific method it could not as the physicist does, for instance, relate all things to energy and matter. Energy and matter are part of the spectacle and can be viewed apart from life. Psychology, however, assumed the task of using the limited means of science in order to view the spectator himself.

So it has hung between sky and earth, refusing to be considered a branch of metaphysics and never quite gaining respect as an exact science. The most materialistic of its apostles have undertaken again and again and in a variety of ways to align it with chemistry and explain consciousness by the qualities of matter—saying that consciousness is a derivative of matter. Unhappily, however, for all their endeavours they have never produced a working hypothesis that covers the whole field of their science as Newton's did for physics or Dalton's for chemistry. The psychological theories work admirably for certain limited groups of facts but fail hopelessly to solve quite as important groups. The failure is due to the fact that psychologists are undertaking to prove the functions of the spectator by the functions of the spectator—to prove something by itself. A philosopher can, within the terms of his method, succeed in this; a scientist never can.

Thus it happens that Professor William James, leader of the physical school of psychologists, summing up the advances of psychology as a science says:

"Psychology is but a string of raw facts, a little gossip and wrangle about opinions, a little classification and generalization on the merely descriptive level, a strong prejudice that we have states of mind and that our brain conditions them, but not a single law in the sense that physics shows us laws." This in 1892 and, except for a greater quantity of descriptive material, psychology has scarcely moved since then.

It is still engaged in warfare over its basic definitions. What is consciousness? The majority of psychologists say "mind", and refuse to admit that there can be any other form of consciousness than mind. Their chief reason for declaring that consciousness is mind is that nothing can be known to them until it becomes a thought. Which is the equivalent of telling a physicist that there can be nothing but mental matter and energy because energy and matter have to be imaged in mind before they can be examined. This adherence to the dogma of the necessary identity of consciousness and mind has sterilized the entire research and leaders among the psychologists have not been slow to tell their fellows so. Professor Edward Montgomery says:

"Psychology as a science of self-originated and self-acting conscious existence . . . can only lead to nihilistic results; such a science constructed without reference to an abiding *extra-conscious* source of actuation and emanation will end in vacancy." And Montgomery goes on to argue that the states outside the conscious mind are not necessarily mind at all.

This is why, when the student tries to arrive at a general idea of current psychological theory he comes constantly on the use of the word "mind" as describing factors that have no place in mind.

Broadly speaking, modern psychology agrees (or disagrees) on the following classification of the levels of consciousness. Above conscious mind is one group of phenomena. Then comes conscious mind. Then below it two groups. Let us examine them in this order.

Above mind, what is called supraliminal mind, or

supra-conscious mind. The existence of this as a separate group is in dispute. It is the field of intuitions, of conscience and of the recognition of duty. Some psychologists see it as the connecting link between the Ego and the God, the field of our conceptions of eternal verity and the means of our power to know verity. Other psychologists repudiate it altogether. They do not believe in intuitions, forgetting that all the basic assumptions of science itself rest on intuition. All mathematical assumptions are intuitions. The idea that consciousness exists in all persons is an intuition. With the means at his disposal the scientist cannot prove scientifically that consciousness exists in any other person than himself. This realm above conscious mind is the world of archetypes in the older philosophers. I shall return to it in later articles. The Eastern philosopher calls it Buddhi-Manas.

Then comes conscious mind. It is called sometimes "the lighted circle". Thomson Jay Hudson named it "objective mind" and said some wise and a great many foolish things about it. It is the realm of mental awareness, and is that part of mind in which the consciousness or Ego is normally focussed. Any image in it may depart from it—slip out of it—any time. The Hindus call this Manas and never make the mistake of confusing it with consciousness. It is matter in its own plane and only one of the grades of matter in which consciousness can manifest itself.

Below conscious mind is that which is commonly called the sub-conscious mind. Myers called it the subliminal consciousness. Hudson called it subjective but confused it with so many other qualities as to make his description unserviceable. It is the plane of half-forgotten fragments of thought, of lost (but recoverable) memories, of characteristic impulses, of what are modernly called complexes (called by the Buddhist skandhas or confections). It is the plane also of emotions which are hybrid unions of thought and passion, the desire-saturated odds and ends of past thoughts which are the principal creators of moods. The Eastern philosopher calls this twilight plane Kama-Manas. In occult science the combination of all its elements is called personality, the mask through which Egos on earth see each other.

Below the level of sub-conscious mind is a fourth division which links the three levels of mind with the forces of the body. It is the plane of instinct, of reflexes and of automatic and involuntary function. It is also the repository of muscular and functional habits that have been acquired consciously at some time in the past, and the method of their acquirement forgotten. The Eastern philosopher calls this level Kama. Some psychologists have called it "unconscious mind." Psychologists themselves are at war over it, and in it is the whole crux of modern psychology.

Some psychologists, Ladd for instance, while admitting the factors of consciousness it describes, ridicule the name. They say there can be no such thing as unconscious mind. It is a contradiction in terms. To talk of unconscious mind is to talk of unconscious consciousness or of non-existent existence. It is inconceivable, they say.

And so it is in the sense in which its inventors use it. None the less there are such functions as are thus described, and of them the Ego is undoubtedly unconscious. What active and efficient consciousness can exist in a man of which he is not conscious? The inevitable answer stares the psychologists in the face, but they will not accept it for the same reason that the biologists would not accept vitalism. This lower consciousness that stands between Ego and body is one of which the Ego is unconscious because *it is not his consciousness.* It is the consciousness of a separate and lower entity.

Modern psychologists are facing the same old *impasse* that Stahl faced two hundred years ago, when he ascribed all human functions above the chemico-physical ones to the thinking soul of man, and Bordeu laughed his theory into oblivion. Stahl tried to stretch the concept of soul beyond its workable limits. The psychologists are stretching their concept of mind to an extent which makes their research sterile, as Montgomery assured them they would. The instinctive activities below mind are undoubtedly forms of consciousness but they are not mental consciousness.

This was the doctrine of the older philosophers. Pythagoras, Empedocles, Plato and Plotinus taught it. So did the Church Fathers, Clement, Origen and Tatian. It was the doctrine also of Emanuel Swedenborg, who declared that man is a trinity, that there is an internal man who is celestial, a reasoning man who is spiritual and an external man who is the natural entity—natural because he is a part of nature. The distinction between the Ego and the lower entity or animal soul has been testified to many times by scientists like Wigan, Brown-Sequard, Proctor and by Carl Du Prel in his *Philosophy of Mysticism.*

This idea of a duality is the very foundation of the most fertile of all psychological departments of research—hypnotism. In no other field can the psychologist gather the unequivocal data he does in hypnotic experiment—ugly and all as it is in its method. It is now an axiom of hypnotism that the one essential characteristic of hypnotic states is that the Ego must be unconscious of what is occurring. That is, after the somnambulistic period he should have no memory of what has occurred. The only possible explanation of all the phenomena of such conditions is that the conscious Ego, by consent, surrenders the entity of whose activities he is unconscious, to the will of the operator. He does not merely surrender himself. If he did he would be conscious of it and would prove that consciousness by retaining a memory of it. Neither does the Ego merely surrender the body. The subject in a hypnotic state is a going organism possessed of all automatic and involuntary functions, all reflexes and all instincts. For the duration of the trance state this lower entity obeys the operator as he would his own Ego. Perhaps a little better.

We come now on a curious thing. It is as illuminating for the occult student as it is confusing for the scientist. The entity whom the hypnotist controls possesses mind. Not all functions of mind. There are certain ones it does not possess, but on the other hand it uses those it does possess to a higher degree of efficiency than is manifested by the subject of the experiment in his normal state.

Because the subject under hypnotic influence exhibits mental powers, the psychologist assumes that in some mysterious way only the memory of the Ego has been inhibited and that everything else remains. But an examination of the kind of mind manifested by hypnotized subjects shows that it lacks precisely that kind of mind which is peculiarly the mental characteristic of the Ego. The entity under the control of the hypnotist is unable to discriminate. It is unable to observe a series of facts and draw a general conclusion from them. It does not, in other words, manifest inductive reason. The mind which the controlled entity exhibits is entirely reproductive and recollective. The subject cannot think what the Ego has not thought before. It can draw on the storehouse of thoughts, words and actions existing in the subconscious mind above it, the submerged rubbish-heap of bygone intellection, but it cannot invent new things. It cannot initiate. Invention is done for it by the hypnotist who has taken the place of its normal inventor, the Ego. A hypnotized subject will get drunk on water because he is told it is alcohol, and will sober up on brandy because he is told it is an antidote to alcohol. If the Ego is musical the subject of a hypnotic trance will be musical; if the Ego is philosophical the subject will be philosophical—not otherwise.

It would seem therefore as if the sub-conscious mind can be drawn upon by either of two beings, the Ego who created it, or the animal soul for whose use and endowment, according to the old philosophers, the thoughts were made.

So much for the demonstrations contained in hypnotic suggestion. The hypothesis of unconscious mind as a lower entity is also the explanation of auto-suggestion in its forms of Christian Science, faith-healing, habit-curing and mental therapeutics. The reason why the hypnotist is more successful than the Ego himself in making the lower being do what he is told, is that the hypnotist is detached and has no sentimental or habitual misgivings. He is a successful hypnotist because he does not change his mind.

It is the explanation—and H. P. Blavatsky offered it half a century ago—of the phenomena of the seance room. The lower entity—the elemental or animal soul—is, in the vast majority of cases, the visitant who floods pyschic literature with his puerile recollections of earth and his ante-mortem theories of post-mortem states. Just as we saw him in the hypnotist's laboratory, he cannot, after death, reason inductively. He can offer fragmentary memories or corroborate what the sitters put into his mind. This is why a *revenant* can create the externals of a disembodied entity but can so rarely transcend the automatisms of earth life. He is the animated *bhuta* or *pisacha* of Eastern occultism, the shell of Theosophical literature.

Freud's psychoanalytic system, which owes far more to mediaeval and Renaissance occultists than its author might care to admit, offers valuable testimony to the independent existence of the lower soul, and the active part it plays in demanding from the Ego the intellectual reinforcement it needs for the fulfilment of its desires. The Ego—Freud's "censor"—is not only the creator of ideas for his own use, but he is also most frequently the creator of ideas that have no other purpose than the satisfaction of the desires of the lower being. This is the reason for the desire-saturation of the elements in the sub-conscious realm of mind, the ideas that have slipped out of the Ego's field of conscious knowledge and form the reservoir of animal mind in man. The fact that Freud, misreading his data, proposed an animal ethic for the divine soul, only demonstrated that psychologists, like other men, do not know what to do with facts when they get them.

Behaviourism, the *enfant terrible* of modern psychology, is for the most part a study of the relation of the animal soul to the body. It disagrees with occult science in the same way that all materialistic science does, and proceeds on the assumption that bodies are real and soul is not. It says that the body of man by its muscular reflexes and visceral twitchings begets the illusion of all higher faculties. Even misinterpreted thus, the Behaviourist data are valuable to the student. Watson's identification of emotions and powers with specific centres in the body is a restoration of the ancient doctrine of the body as a mirror of soul-function. Like so many other schools of psychology, however, Behaviourism survives by denying the existence of phenomena its theory will not explain. It offers a plausible theory of living persons but it gets into trouble when it is confronted with the problems of dead persons, and with the other psychological phenomena of seance rooms. Behaviourists know they will never persuade anybody that visceral twitchings in the present body can continue in an after world after the physical viscera have ceased to twitch. Neither can it say with authority that visceral twitchings in the medium enable her to know that somebody's deceased mother's cousin was named Edward. Nobody wants to be a failure, so, rather than fail, Behaviourism repudiates psychic phenomena altogether.

It has become apparent to the student of occult philosophy that the principal cause of the psychologist's quandary is his refusal to admit the materiality of any other planes than the physical. The Eastern psychologist has no such problem. For him the world of desire or *Kama* is a definite realm of matter interior to and interpenetrating the highest state of physical matter as water interpenetrates a solid. His world of mind or *manas* is a still subtler plane interior to the plane of desire and interpenetrating it and the physical planes as air interpenetrates liquids and solids. Interior to all these is a still subtler plane of radiant matter called *Buddhi*, that stands in the same relation to the three below it as light does to gases, liquids and solids. A soul in Eastern psychology is an essence, a *Jiva*, as immaterial as the Western scientist would ask, but possessed of the power of manifesting in any of the planes—in the radiant world of Buddhi as a cognitive spiritual being, in manas as an intellective, form-making creator, in kama as a sensitive, feeling soul, as the souls of animals are. The fundamental fact about him is that he is not the plane in which he operates. He is spirit; it is matter. In all of which the Eastern psychologist may be as wrong as Newton and Dalton were and still he might supply Western psychology with a working hypothesis.

The identification of consciousness or awareness exclusively with mind is an absurdity and responsible for the absurdities in which psychology is enmeshed. The Ego is obviously a being making forms in mind. Quite as obviously the lower entity is another being living a passional life in the realm below mind and borrowing his intellectual elements from a Jiva who is for some reason his instructor. The sodden, forgotten world between the two is the debris of lives of incompetent and misused instruction. Sub-conscious mentality is a disorderly tangle of forms on which Ego and animal draw at will. When years ago Dr. Maudsley reproved science for forgetting that all external objects are really seen within us, he voiced his celebrated witticism, "A thing is a think." Psychology will get out on to *terra firma* again when it learns to say "A think is also a thing."

In the meantime Goelemus the unskilful word-searcher is being justified. Psychologists are devoting themselves less and less to the thinking soul which must ever elude materialistic science, and are resigning its study to the metaphysicians. More and more they are devoting their inquiries to the feeling soul—the true psyche—which because it is external to man is capable of being studied in the objective manner of science. Gradually they are isolating it, describing it and revealing it as conformable to the animal world from which occult science says the Ego has lifted it. At the same time the true Ego withdraws and day by day becomes more definitely the anomaly he is—a visitor in a world that is not his own. The question is, "What is his true world?"

3. THE MATHEMATICAL PROBLEM

Something peculiarly enlightening for the student of the occult sciences has occurred in these recent years of the steady materialization of thought under the influence of positive science. There has been a revolution against materialism and strangely enough the rebel has been the most exact of all scientists—indeed the only scientist who has never had a doubt cast upon his exactitude—the mathematician.

The mathematician has been the factotum of his fellow, and less scientific, scientists. They brought him their sums to do. They enlisted him to work out their formulae. They engaged him to impart to their young men enough of his science to enable them to carry on the simpler operations of their own. He was a sort of slave-pedagogue, regarded as vague and unpractical in his preoccupations but none the less useful.

The mathematician has always been more or less of a mystic. He is constantly engaged in meditation on abstractions like those archetypal ideas of Plato's. The nature of his work compels him to remember what less scientific inquirers forget, that all the major assumptions of scientific research are intuitions and are unprovable by mental process. He is used to remembering that the mind of the seeker, while it is an instrument, is none the less in itself a severe limitation. The mathematician knows that you can never have a science until you have posited a number of things you are entirely incapable of proving. These he calls axioms. If he is a bit shaky about whether his intuition is accurate he is honest and calls them postulates. Consciousness, for example, is an axiom. Space is only a postulate. So is time. Matter is only a postulate, Motion is a postulate. The mathematician is strict. If he is not it is bound to show in his result.

I have said the exponents of positive science bring their formulae to the mathematician for solution, and like the good auditor he is, he reproves the evils of their book-keeping. He objects, for instance, to their trick of trying to explain one unknown by another. When, to take a classical example, they say motion is change in the relations of matter, and when they are then asked what matter is, they say matter is the field in which motion makes changes, the mathematician is reproachful. He reminds them that they cannot define one postulate by another.

They can get nowhere, he has reminded them, until they make up their minds on the whole subject of knowledge. What is knowable? What is not knowable? How is anything knowable? He does not demand with Berkeley that they believe only in consciousness and deny that anything has actual existence outside of the spectator's idea of it. Neither would he let them take their stand with Buchner and Haeckel and go to the extreme of saying that matter and motion are the only truth and that consciousness is merely a sensation arising out of their operation.

The mathematician votes with Kant. He says the only sound position is the critical one—that each of us is a consciousness, that there exists outside of us a world of causes. A tree is something that causes me to think of a tree, but a real tree is vastly different from what I think it is and if I do not know all about a tree, it is because I have not brought to bear on it an adequate perceptive equipment. Or as the occultist would say, I am not seeing the tree on a high enough plane to know its high plane truths. Or as Ouspensky has stated it in his *Tertium Organum*, it is not because I have a confused perception of a real world, but because I have a very acute perception of an entirely unreal world. Or again, as Hinton would have said it, I am not seeing a real tree but the thinnest possible three-dimensional section of a real tree. Or as Kant would have said, the space-sense I bring to bear on the tree is inadequate: it is a limitation of my mind. In the far older *Voice of the Silence* the parallel saying is, "Mind is the great slayer of the real."

The modern restoration of the idea that our sense of a three-dimensional world is not ultimate, begins with Kant. His philosophical successors promptly lost the idea or never knew he had it. His mystical successors carried it on. The academic philosopher's ideas only have to be accurate enough to get into a book or a student's notes. The mathematician's and the mystic's ideas have to work. K. F. Gauss and N. I. Lobachevsky were the first continuators of Kant's idea. Then came C. H. Hinton, who in a remarkable series of works developed a mechanism of cubes for the education of the space-sense. He declared that diagrams on paper were quite useless because the solid itself being a symbol, the diagram is a symbol of a symbol. His mechanism is an equipment of coloured cubes by which to make the transition from three-space into four-space perceptions. After Hinton the most notable figure in the same phase of the inquiry has been the Russian P. D. Ouspensky who has worked out a remarkable relation of the ideas of two-, three-, and four-space consciousness to mysticism and occultism. More recently and in the field of physics, Einstein, Eddington and their group have made the mathematical formulae that demonstrate the concept of time as being a limited understanding of a fourth way in space. They have also developed Kant's relation of the observer to the object observed into their theory of relativity.

For my present purpose I require only the straightest way through the subject.

The line represents one-dimensional space. It is generated by the motion of a point. It has no "up or down" and no "across." It has only "along." A line moved in a direction at right angles to its length generates a surface. It has the dimensions of length and breadth but no "up and down," no thickness. This is two-space. A surface moved in a direction and breadth generates a solid. This is three-space. Can this solid—imagine it a cube—be moved in a fourth direction which is none of the three others but perpendicular to all of them and thus generate a four-space shape—a tesseract?

Mind cannot grasp it. The positive scientist says emphatically, "No." Mathematicians say "Yes, it is puzzling and paradoxical but we must say it can." There is a dimension of space (perhaps several) that eludes our mental space-sense but is none the less real on that account. It is probably more real than our limited mental concept."

The mathematician has a constantly recurring problem. When a physicist, let us say, brings the mathematician a sum to do, and it is one that involves linear dimensions carried into surfaces, the mathematician writes alongside and above the quantity a little 2–x^2—meaning the quantity is to be squared. If it is a problem running into solids, the mathematician writes x^3. But occasions arise when he must write x^4. You can imagine a colloquy between the mathematician and his client. The physicist says:

"But there is no such thing as four ways in space."

"I am sorry," says the mathematician, "but there are the processes. I'd like to make the result easier for you but I cannot tell a lie."

"But I cannot imagine such a thing."

"That is a defect certainly," says the mathematician, "but it is your own defect. The calculation is all right."

Which is precisely what Kant said. Mind shackles us to an adequate concept of the world and therefore precludes our knowing the truth about it.

Hinton said that by observation and reflection we can know three dimensions. By intuition we can know four dimensions. This intuition he called direct apprehension. It has been called by the occultist direct cognition, and is said to be an attribute of Buddhi, the fourth level of the manifested world, and the plane next above Manas or mind, which is the third. In his posthumous book, *A New Era of Thought*, Hinton has, curiously enough, related this direct apprehension of four-space to love and sympathy and brotherhood which are also attributes of Buddhi and the indications are that his realization of the relation arose out of his own experience as he developed by means of his cubes the power of seeing the tesseract.

After Hinton came Ouspensky who built on Hinton, but carried the experiments into many other fields. The phase of his research that means most to us at the present moment is that which has to do with the higher animals. Ouspensky says the dog and the horse, for instance, have no consciousness of three-space. All their actions in and reactions to the world around them show that they are under a two-space limitation. They see the same objects—or causes—as we do but they cannot convert what they see into three dimensions. He advances a great many demonstrations of this. For most of them I must refer the reader to his *Tertium Organum.*

Ouspensky's work stirred resentment and unbelief among some lovers of animals. They were chiefly the people who anthropomorphize their pets and attribute to animals thought processes like their own. They believed it involved some degradation of the animal to impute to it a limited space sense. The better animal lovers welcomed a profound insight into age-old problems of animal behaviour. It offered the explanation of why a dog, going round an unfamiliar tree, for example, is startled when he sees a previously unseen branch and swerves as if the tree had thrust an arm out at him suddenly in hostile demonstration. His master knowing a third dimension of trees knows that the branch extends another way in space and has been there all the time. Ouspensky offers the only valid explanation of dogs barking at the turning wheels of vehicles in the notion that they are alive. He explains also the animal's inability to use the principle of the lever, a fundamental mechanism of all three dimensional concepts.

Occult science offers a continuation of Ouspensky's thesis. It says that the Ego is living in the body of an animal and is compelled to see the world through the sensory and sensational mechanism of an animal. It will be unnecessary, therefore, to go to the dog and the horse for assurance of the two-dimensionality of animal consciousness. If what Ouspensky says is true, the whole series of phenomena will be observable in the complex of organisms which we call man. If all knowledge of the physical world must pass to the Ego through the eyes and consciousness of an animal nature, there must be a stage in every percept when it will be two dimensional.

And is it not so? The reader must test it for himself. Our first view of everything is two dimensional. We see a surface. Depth, the third dimension, has to be reasoned out by an effort of thought. Look at the moulding on the door or window before you. It appears as a flat surface with light and shade. You examine it more carefully and analyze the shadows into a third dimension, saying, "It goes back there, it comes forward here, it curves towards, it curves away." Pick up a perspective drawing in, let us say, a text book of solid geometry, or look at a mechanical drawing in line. It presents itself at first as an arrangement of lines on a surface. Then you reason it out, setting back this plane and advancing that one, recognizing this as receding, that as approaching, this plane as foreground, that as middle ground, a third as distance. Or wake up in an unfamiliar or half lighted room and watch the tricks your animal vision will play on you before you resolve the flat impressions into their successive planes by effort of will. Or, come around the corner and see unexpectedly a coat thrown over a chair and observe how you start like the dog did as he ran around the tree, until your mind asserts itself and assures you there is nothing hostile in what at first seemed so. You say in such cases that you got a start. Of course you did not. The animal got a start.

Evidently Hinton left out a step. His formula should have been: By observation we know two-space; by reflection we know three-space; by direct apprehension we know four-space.

Let us return now to the direct apprehension of four-dimensionality. Is it a function of a higher soul than the thinking soul we identify with ourselves, or is it a higher function of the thinking soul? Hinton's experiments prove conclusively, and so do Ouspensky's, as also do those of Einstein, that the apprehension of objects in their four-dimensionality is the removal of a limitation. It is a function of the soul in a level just above mind. When Hinton sets about his space-education discipline, he shows that the vision comes first in glimpses that can be made increasingly permanent. Each time he wants to make the transition into four-space, he starts by making the transition from two-space to three-space as a means of knowing what the three—to four—transition would be. The two-space to three-space transition is easy because we make it more or less unconsciously every minute of the day. Since the transition from two—to three—is a resumption each time of a power of thought we have long possessed, the transition from three—to four—is similarly a *resumption.* It is not a new acquirement but a renewal of an old power.

We are back again with the occultists! Occult science takes count of seven dimensions in space, of which The Divine Ego, by virtue of evolution in past world periods has made himself master of four. In his present anomalous state of limitation and bewilderment he has "fallen" from his four-dimensional consciousness into a three-dimensional one. Presently, the occult traditions say, unless he consolidates his forces and reasserts his divinity he can fall another stage and come under the limitation of two-dimensionality.

Two dimensions mark the present apex of the evolution of the animal soul. The dog cannot himself make the transition from two to three. Two are for him what four seem to be for us. (I offer here because it will come up later, the suggestion that the Ego has really touched a fifth dimension in his past but has not fully mastered it.) Our task, the occult tradition would indicate, is to help the animal soul to make his necessary transition into the three-space consciousness of mind. We must first recover our own apex and then lift him. We cannot stand still. If we will not go up we must go down. The descent into Avernus manifests itself in its incipient stages as psychism, which, unless it is resisted, must degenerate into two-space consciousness. The psychic is one who cannot resolve his perceptions into their necessary planes, either of time or of space. With this process of degeneration I shall deal more fully later in the series.

Here then is another contribution to the necessary picture of the Exile in his relation to the worlds above and below him. Again his position is anomalous. He sees surfaces, he thinks them into solids. He could go on and resolve them into vastly more potent four-space forms but he faints and grows weary. He is the user of a power of vision above that of the animal in which he dwells and is the possessor of a dormant power of vision higher than that he uses. Resumption of his high vision does not seem to wait on evolution or any cyclic process. It seems to be available when the Ego wills it. The animal soul, on the other hand, is a creature of cycles. It is evolving. Is this perhaps what the *Secret Doctrine* means when it says the Ego is not evolving; it has emanated?

4. THE PHILOSOPHICAL PROBLEM

We have seen how, in the latter half of the nineteenth century, psychology, attracted by the glittering beginnings of scientific research, deserted the field of philosophy for that of positive science and came thereby under limitations that have made it almost unworkable. The other branches of philosophy could not so readily change to a materialistic basis and they have remained more or less in their original field of subjective research, but they too have been affected by the scientific fashion. They have assumed the name of "the philosophical sciences". They define their province as the co-ordination and synthesis of the results of scientific research. That is, they have been persuaded that the interior or subjective method is no longer good enough, because reality lies outside us. They become, therefore, the servants of external reality. The modern philosopher proudly calls himself the "critic of the sciences," and, as inevitably happens when a man devotes himself exclusively to the criticism of the product of others, he ceases to produce in his own right.

The philosopher's position would be superb if he could sit in state and have the scientist bring results to him for criticism. But a scientist does not quite see the necessity for a philosopher at all. The scientist is quite confident he can do his own criticizing. And so, within the rules of his enquiry, he can. At last with no business coming in, the philosopher goes looking for business and ends up in the orbit of a scientist who has his eye fixed to the end of a microscope. When a few philosophers, all in quest of business, have gathered, they find nothing to talk about but whether the microscope-man can believe his eye. The idealistic monists contend that what he sees is all in his mind.

The materialistic monists ask, "What is he himself but the sort of thing he sees under the microscope?" The reality is in the object. The seer is an illusion arising out of the motion of the parts of the object. The critical realists, who as we have seen before have a high position—Kant's—if they wish to take it, content themselves with a compromise and try to steer a peaceable middle course.

Am I flippant about it? Here is a modern philosopher stating it in more dignified terms. It is Professor A. S. Pringle-Pattison speaking:

"Subject-object, knowledge, or, more widely, self-consciousness and its implicates—this unity in duality—is the ultimate aspect which duality presents. It has generally been considered, therefore, as constituting in a special sense the problem of philosophy. Philosophy may be said to be the explication of what is involved in this relation."

This is the present state of the art of Pythagoras and Plato, of Kapila, of Sankaracharya, of Nagarjuna, of Aryasangha, of Plotinus, of Kant, and all the line of the lovers of wisdom. It has been said, not once but many times, these recent years, that formal philosophy has reached the most arid, unserviceable and generally contemptible era in its history.

Professor Pringle-Pattison's definition of the crux of modern philosophy is the sterile modern form of what once was the great fertile problem of epistemology, the theory of knowledge. The ancient philosopher asked, "How does knowledge come into the world?" The immediate and inferior answer is, "Through the senses." Such an answer will not stand the test of the commonest experience. We are all conscious of knowledge not traceable to what we have seen or heard. Apart from visions in dreams, which might be recollections of something we have seen but have forgotten, we have tendencies, aptitudes, capacities which are themselves a sublimated form of knowledge. If playing the piano after long training is an earned aptitude, the capacity to play the piano without any training in this life can only be an earned aptitude. Precocious genius is a kind of knowledge not traceable to known experience. So the philosopher, articled to the scientist, who is in his turn articled to the doctrine of the exclusive reality of an outside world, falls back on the idea of heredity and says some ancestor earned the aptitude. These knowledge-powers, he says, are transmitted from generation to generation. This is the Plan of the Universe.

It may be true, but at the best it is an inefficient Plan, and in nowise to be compared to the other processes of nature. For one thing, too many of the wisest of mankind do not transmit at all, and when they do so it is with the poorest results. Almost all of mankind transmit at a time when they would seem to have the least worth transmitting. The valuable experience of all of them is at its greatest worth long after they have ceased transmitting. Too many make no use of what has been transmitted, and too many destroy it with counteractive energies. Added to which the scientist is now satisfied that acquired characteristics cannot be transmitted anyway. What escaped these abysses of inadvertence is called heredity. This seems to be the Plan. A more incompetent one could scarcely have been conceived. A Greek or Hindu philosopher would be ashamed to entertain it even for a moment. It neglects the one factor of which the philosopher—or anybody else for that matter—can be sure, the factor of soul. But this man of ours, having become a critic of the revelations of microscopes can only admit what microscopes reveal, and they are not equipped to reveal souls.

For a statement of the problem in terms of souls, therefore, we must take the whole inquiry to the older philosophers. Plato is nearest to hand and easiest for my reader to examine for himself. It comes up in the *Phaedo.* There, in the last talk between Socrates and the Thebans, Simmias and Cebes, Socrates raises the whole question of knowledge. Whence comes it?

Socrates wastes little time on the possibility of attaining pure knowledge through the senses. Even seeing and hearing, the best of the senses, are not accurate or exact. What then of the inferior senses of smell, taste and touch? Certainly the body is of little assistance. On the contrary it contaminates truth. It keeps man busy finding sustenance for it. Its diseases hinder the pursuit of truth; it begets passions, desires, fancies and foolishness, and so constantly does it break in on study that the Ego finds it almost impossible during life to think at all.

But man, Socrates argues, has interior standards of truth, and the perceptions of this world fall short of them. Two objects, for example are almost equal. They just fall short of a perfect, abstract equality which man can entertain although he has never seen perfect equality on this earth. So it is, Socrates argues, with every other external fact we contemplate. We measure it against an abstract perfection which cannot have arisen out of earth experience. We look at a triangle. It is not a perfect triangle. How do we know? We have never on earth seen a perfect triangle. Neither have we ever seen perfectly parallel lines but we persist in thinking of them. So also with a point which we cannot ever have known on earth, and a line, and all the posited ideas of geometry. We have abstract perfect criteria for goodness, truth, beauty, love, justice.

None the less these perfections we cannot quite bring to earth. They are vague and fragmentary, now in our effort to realize them, stronger; and since obviously they are not of this human state, in which such perfections are nowhere evident outside of us, there is only one possible explanation of them. They are recollections. They are the earned aptitudes of a half-remembered past. Of what past?

The scientist recognizes interior recollections that have no counterparts in this life. He says they are inherited and has erected about them a doctrine of racial memory, but that will not explain their perfection. His race is evolving. Its ancient memories cannot be of things more perfect than anything in its present state. If so the race is degenerating.

There is also a school of pietists who deny the interior ideas as memories, preferring to think of them as divine intimations of the future. Socrates has a quick answer for these!

"If a man, when he has heard or seen or in any other way perceived a thing, knows not only that thing, but also has perception of some other thing, the knowledge of which is not the same but different, are we not right in saying that he *recollects* the thing of which he has the perception? . . . As when one sees Simmias, one often remembers Cebes."

What other solutions are there? That we got the perfections in this life? Obviously not. That we got them at the instant of birth and lost them in the same instant? This is ridiculous. Did we get them in a previous life on this earth? There could be nothing more perfect in a previous human life than in this one. Whence then?

From a state that preceded the human one, when, before we were human beings, we were in a state higher than the one in which we now find outselves. Our present earth life and the earth lives preceding it are to be thought of, not as our proper place in a scheme of soul evolution at all. If so we are degenerating. The old philosophers called our present state a temporary obscuration and the result of some offence of ours against divine law. It is an obscuration that has brought about a condition of amnesia. Thus only can we explain the high memory that is evoked by the imperfect perceptions of this earth life.

The problem is the central one in Plato. In Socrates' discussion with Meno, the whole dialogue turns on this theory of knowledge. If Meno knows the whole of anything he need not ask about it. If, on the other hand, he knows nothing about it, he can neither ask nor learn. The only possible condition under which he can know enough to ask, and little enough to profit by being told, is that he possess a fragmentary recollection of it. This fragment is his fragment of crystal. The instruction enables him to restore it to its original completeness. One man cannot teach another unless by virtue of the fact that the other has a partial recollection of the truth to be taught.

Socrates, in Meno's presence, demonstrates the truth of his doctrine, when he calls in a slave-boy and, first, by letting the boy discover his own ignorance, then by asking him questions to elicit his memory, leads him through the geometrical problems of the duplication of the square.

This is the central doctrine in the greatest of the lovers of wisdom. It is Empedocles' doctrine of the fall into the dark meadow of Ate. It is Plotinus' doctrine of the restoration of the Divine Intelligence and the return to the One. It is the basis of the Taraka Raja Yoga system which proceeds by an exercise of reminiscence identical with Plato's dialectic or "choosing through." It is the basis of the many mnemonic systems occultists have used as an aid to meditation, those curious arrangements of questions and the philosophical categories placed on revolving discs such as the one Raymond Lully invented and Giordano Bruno used. It is the basis of the lamasery wheels of which the exoteric "praying wheels" are the distorted form, the discs of the Tibetan mystics called *chakravartins* or wheelturners. It is the explanation also of the effort of the older philosophers to arrange knowledge in categories. It is the only valid theory of meditation itself as the process of stilling the body and steadying the mind in order to elicit from the archetypal memory what the Ego has known but has forgotten.

This is the only fertile mode in philosophy. The narrow treadmill of subject-object must always be sterile, must always contradict itself, must always fail of what it undertakes to do. We can only know the higher truth of a thing by rising into a higher plane of being.

What then must we do? Await the slow crawl of the evolution of the soul until we evolve those higher powers? Maybe we can try to hasten evolution. We had better save ourselves so vain an effort. We would be trying to hasten that which cannot by its very nature be hastened.

It is not a problem of evolution that faces the soul, and still less a problem of hastening evolution. It is a problem of *resumption,* of recovery of atrophied powers long since evolved and now forgotten.

This is the testimony of the sages and seers. They do not offer it as a guess. They offer it as a demonstrable fact which every man, by virtue of his dormant divinity, may know for himself by examining his intuitional memory.

Clearly it is not a current problem in academic philosophy. Philosophers of our time have forsaken intuitional memory and devoted themselves to the inferior reports of the senses. And, as we have seen, fertile philosophy has tended these recent years to pass over to the mathematicians for whom the senses matter less and the intuitions more.

For the purposes of this series, the problem of the theory of knowledge offers us another picture of the Ego, bewildered and stripped in a strange world which he sees through senses which are not his own, in a body that limits the use of the mind. He is the possessor of a high reality which he neglects for an illusory appearance he has lost the power to interpret.

5. THE MYSTICAL PROBLEM

We come now upon another phase of the same problem of consciousness—that presented by the phenomena of mystical experience. I use the word mystical in its modern sense as describing an interior revelation that can be had independently of the senses and of the reasoning processes.

Needless to say, this idea that there can be a transcendental knowledge superior to ordinary processes is one of the most ancient in the history of mankind. It is to be found at the origin of all religious systems, and indeed, as we shall see, all religion is to a lesser or greater degree a distortion of it. The possibility of this interior experience has been asserted by the greatest philosophers, by the saints and sages, and is in a sense the one ever-present and enduring thought in religion. It is also the idea around which the fiercest struggles have raged and against which the bitterest persecution has been directed.

Although an enormous literature has arisen out of mysticism, only recently—in this era at least—have we had a comparative examination of its phenomena. The first notable one is by the Canadian psychologist Richard Maurice Bucke who in his *Cosmic Consciousness* assembled and examined a large number of cases of the direct illumination commonly described as mystical.

It is outside of my purpose in this article to make a complete examination of Dr. Bucke's material and results, but to deal with certain special aspects of it. Drawing largely from biography and autobiography, he cites many remarkable cases of illumination in the lives of Jesus, Buddha, Walt Whitman, Jacob Boehme, Francis Bacon, Plotinos and other historical figures.

These he supplements with modern cases of interior experience drawn from among his friends and patients.

The records thus gathered present certain common factors. One is a more or less definite sense of "lighting up" and is frequently accompanied by an objective luminosity, when the subject finds himself bathed in light. Another is the descent upon the subject of an ineffable peace likened to the "peace that passeth all understanding" in the Christian Testament. A third is that of possessing a direct apprehension of fact, a means of knowledge that is best described as the mystics described it, as transcending reasoning processes altogether. A less common, though no less marked, experience, in the cases where it is recorded, is the modification or complete elimination of the sense of time, as if time were merged or lost in another way in space. The German Theosophist, Jacob Boehme, says he saw the "signatures of things" and that he saw the grass growing.

More important than any of these is the realization by the subject of a communion between the members of the human race and an actual sense of being in a realm of consciousness where all separation and longing are at an end. It is an entry into a one-consciousness, seemingly without loss of individuality, and a kind of all inclusiveness in which the person experiencing the new state takes the rest of the race into his being.

Walt Whitman in *Song of Myself* describes it thus:

"Swiftly arose and spread around me the peace and knowledge that pass all argument of the earth,
And I know that the hand of God is the promise of my own,
And I know that the spirit of God is the brother of my own,

And that all the men ever born are also my brothers,
  and the women my sisters and lovers,
And that a kelson of the creation is love,
And limitless are leaves stiff or drooping in the
  fields,
And brown ants in the little wells beneath them,
And mossy scabs of the worm fence, heap'd stones,
  elder, mullein and pokeweed."

Dr. Bucke in his analysis of the cases came to several interesting conclusions which, while they will not satisfy all the demands of occult philosophy, represent nevertheless a great advance in the scientific study of mystical experience. He divides consciousness into three great grades or successive divisions. The lowest of these, representing sub-human levels, as of the animal, he calls "Simple Consciousness." The reasoning consciousness of men and women, limited as it is by a sense of separateness, he calls "self consciousness." The illuminated state, in which separateness disappears, he calls cosmic consciousness, a level transcending the mental state as much as mind transcends the instinctual consciousness of the animal. Issue has been taken with him on the use of the word "cosmic" as describing too high a level, but nobody has yet suggested a more satisfactory term.

Since Dr. Bucke's time there have been numerous other inquiries and, although it is not a popular subject with academic psychologists because it makes trouble with theologians with whom they have to live, it has had a considerable share of attention from the more independent writers. The general disposition has been to regard the superior consciousness as one into which the human race will eventually evolve, and to look on those who have had intimations of it as forerunners of the rest of mankind.

When this theory goes hand in hand with the idea of physical evolution or race-evolution, as it sometimes does, and there is no element of the immortality of the individual soul implied in it, it means that succeeding generations of men and women begotten of the present ones will have an increasing number of cosmically conscious persons among them, cosmic consciousness becomes the general and finally the universal condition.

This is a cold idea. It offers the present generation the comfortless theory that all our striving and suffering is for the purpose of transmitting to other entities in a distant future powers and blessings they have not earned. To complete the anomaly, experimental science has now reached a position where it declares that all our striving will not and cannot transmit its fruit anyway. So poorly do the facts of interior illumination consort with the Darwinian theory of evolution that it is little wonder the psychologists are not fond of the subject.

When the theory of cosmic consciousness goes hand in hand with the idea of the survival of the soul of man after death and the passage of the soul into higher realms of consciousness, a heaven-world or whatever, the disposition of writers—mostly theologians—is to treat the experience as a passing intimation of the after-death states, a sort of foretaste of heaven vouchsafed by God to saintly persons during their earth life. The exponents of this theory are in grave difficulties. The chief one arises out of the fact that the experience is not confined to saintly persons but sometimes happens to persons whose lives are to say the least heretical and sometimes markedly irreligious in any sense that would please the orthodox God. Conversely many persons of saintly conduct do not achieve any such foretaste of the hereafter. The ironical commentary on this theory is that the cosmic vision has been frequent among those whom the Church found necessary to burn at the stake. In fact the church has had a definite antipathy to persons who had a foretaste of its own Heaven. It may have feared that some visionary would blurt out the truth.

A much better theory of it is the Hindu one—that the soul is engaged in a pilgrimage of experience which requires a long series of lives on this earth, in the course of which it evolves successive powers. Having passed through an arc of descent from spirit to matter and having turned at the mineral on its way back to a vastly enriched spiritual existence, the soul, they teach, has had successively the consciousness of the mineral, the plant and the animal, and is now passing through the mental state of consciousness as man. Beyond the mental state is a state of direct cognition or awakening into reality, which they call Buddhi. This has been attained by the leaders of mankind and into it all men will in due time enter. Those who have experienced it partially are our vanguard on the long path of the evolution of the soul. This is the opinion commonly offered today as Theosophy. In point of fact it is orthodox Brahminism and is, in its own way, scarcely less a distortion of Theosophy than is orthodox Christianity.

The fatal defect of the Brahmin explanation of the data of cosmic consciousness is identical with the defect of the Christian explanation of the ecstasies of the saints as an advance knowledge of the hereafter. Both religions assume that those who have a touch of cosmic consciousness are of great mental and spiritual stature.

The facts show that they are not. While many who experience the higher vision are, like Jesus and Buddha, beings of transcendent spirituality, and some, like

Bacon, are giants of intellect, many of the recorded cases are of very simple, often ignorant and frequently anything but blameless people. The experience is nothing if not sporadic and obeys a law of its own nature. The Christian, finding no rule for it, attributes the whole thing to the pleasure of God. The Brahmin, whose theory of gradual advance would require that before going on with a realm above mind, a man should have exhausted the development of mind, has no adequate explanation to offer.

This curious illumination strikes like lightning. While it does favour the saint, it does not neglect the sinner. It comes very often to the sick, to the drunkard and the epileptic. Remarkable cases of conversion (literally, together-turning) as in the cases of Raymond Lully, John Bunyan and others, show that it can come even to men plunged in vice.

The learned, the ignorant, the devoted, the austere, the sodden, the well, the sick, the vicious, the nearly mad–these are not categories of leadership. Half of them give the lie to the other half. Nor did Jesus seem to expect that leaders would be the readiest to receive his message of liberation. He tended to pass over acknowledged leaders and to devote himself to those who by reason of misery and suffering on earth were best able to understand a doctrine of transcending earth and entering into a Kingdom of Heaven that he declared awaited them. Gautama did not confine himself to leaders among men. He found great men as did Jesus but his doctrine was as readily applicable to the vicious as to the austere. The *Dhammapada* shows him going to young men mired in their vices and bidding them turn. When they did they became Arhats.

That the manifestation in man of a power above

the level of mind is the experience of men and women whose intellectual powers are not equal to the task of explaining it, is evidenced by the fact that mystics themselves differ widely in their explanations.

Mystics with an inclination for orthodox Christianity, for example, say the illumination flows into the soul by a supernatural channel. For the Roman Catholic Church the Church itself is such a channel. So are the sacraments. For mystics of Protestant sects, the Bible is a magical channel.

Quietistic cults like the Friends and the followers of the Abbe Fenelon and Madame Guyon ascribe the results to direct Divine intervention. They say that, in answer to aspiration, God himself acts immediately upon the mind of the devotee. Jacob Boehme held this theory of his own remarkable experiences. He declared that in his vision he saw God. H. P. Blavatsky remarks drily that what he saw was his Divine Ego, as all aspirants eventually see it.

More valid than either of these is the Platonist theory maintained by the most philosophical of the mystics. They say that the illumination comes by faith or intuition resident in the higher consciousness of the soul itself, and that there can be direct attainment of truth by virtue of the fact that man possesses from a previous world-period an inheritance of wisdom which he now neglects, but which he may at any time recover. A momentary return of it may be experienced under special conditions.

Obviously the cosmic consciousness is not, then, a *latent* thing, in the sense that it is still to be developed. It is a *dormant* thing in the sense that it has been developed and lost temporarily. It is not a potentiality to be realized in a distant future. It is an ever-present knowledge which the vast majority of men cannot use because it is overlaid by mental and emotional confusions. When such a power can be aroused by aspiration, the following of intuitions, or by austerity, it is sufficiently explained as an intimation of a new power. When, however, it comes direct out of intense suffering, out of turning from vice, or out of disturbed physical conditions, we need a wider formula than either the Brahmin or Christian one. We need a formula that will reconcile the contradictions. The old occult formula, the only one that will serve the unbiased inquirer, is that cosmic consciousness is an old, hard-earned power, lost and in these cases for a brief time recovered. The Christian formula for it, as the words were originally understood, is that in the parable of the prodigal, "This my son was dead and is alive again; he was lost and is found."

The implication in the highest mystical and occult schools–indeed the explicit statement many times repeated–is that we thinking souls are all prodigals, alienated from a divine unified consciousness which the *New Testament* calls *ho theos*, the god. That consciousness we have as a dim, flickering, inward light.

This aspect of it as a unified whole is important for purposes of the present study. The universal characteristic of all true experiences of cosmic consciousness is an immeasurably quickened sense of unity with the rest of mankind. This is variously described. Sometimes it is a flooding of the nature of the subject with a great love. Sometimes it presents itself as a sense of peace resultant on the passing away of the sense of separateness. It has also been described as an attainment of the centre of a wheel where stillness prevails and the stress of earth life, even of mental life, vanishes. It is the place of stillness that the Chinese called *Tao,* and the Buddhists call *Alaya.* "Alas, alas, that all men should possess *Alaya,*" says *The Voice of the Silence,* "and that possessing it *Alaya* should so little avail them."

All these descriptions bear out the old idea that the world above mind is the Oneness towards which At-one-ment tends, and that we only lose our way in a too far removed and unserviceable notion when we talk of being merged in Ultimate Deity. The Unity to which we are now returning is the rest of our race —the divine exiles here on earth.

This seems to be the reason why persons who have had a touch of cosmic consciousness show a prevailing impulse for the rest of their lives to make mankind the object of their devotion, to see God as it were in their brothers' faces. All true humanism has arisen primarily out of this mystical vision and has taken its stand against the worship of a personal God. The older humanists called the Divine Communion, in whose body we are all atoms, Osiris, and symbolized the present partition of mankind into scattered and confused souls as the dismemberment of Osiris, the fragments of whose body must again be assembled. It is to the assembling of the fragments that the Masters are pledged.

Damascius says of this resurrection of the dismembered Osiris, or return to the higher consciousness, that it "should be a mingling with the God, an all-perfect at-one-ment, a return upwards of our souls to the divine".

So we have again, in another problem of modern science which is compelling the attention of students, a picture of the soul of man which can transcend mind under conditions so contradictory as to preclude the idea that the soul is slowly evolving into the transcendent state. We must decide whether we will take our stand with the Church mystics and the Quietists and say it is the fantastic gift of a personal God, or with H. P. Blavatsky and the occultists who say it is the renewal, brief or enduring, of an ancient power of entering a common consciousness we have forgotten.

6. THE THEOLOGICAL PROBLEM

Within recent years theological problems presented in the theologian's manner have ceased to be matters of great importance to thinking people. They are survivals of a gloomy interval in the history of mankind and do not conform to a free habit of thought. Emancipated thinking must be based on verifiable experience that can be correlated and made to yield laws. While the proper correlation may be greatly assisted by the records of previous enquiry and by intuitional processes, it is none the less necessary that the whole inquiry have its roots in physical, emotional and mental phenomena.

Instead of proceeding from fact on any of these three planes, theologians demand that you proceed from imputed fact—dogma. This dogma, which we now know derives from an ancient, symbolical guide to the intuitions, has been so badly mutilated that it will no longer interpret fact. The theologian is in a quandary. Lacking the ability to impose it by force, he must discard it altogether or thump a desk and assert that it is fact.

The primary material of Christian theology—all other theologies embody the same principle but manifest it variously—instead of being made up of data of experience, is a body of tradition or fable, handed down from generation to generation, and, as I have suggested, badly distorted in its many transfers. In its starkest form the tradition is as follows:

That the universe and all its creatures are the product of an omnipotent, omniscient and omnipresent, but none the less personal God, who is moved by anger, jealousy, unwillingness to forgive and by preferences for one of His creatures over another. That the first human beings He created in His own image proved a disappointment and plunged themselves and all their physical descendants into a state of alienation from the omniscient God who must have known perfectly well what they intended to do, but was none the less angry with them for what He permitted them to do. So unrelenting was He, or so incompetent at finding a way out of His mistake that it was a trifle over four thousand years before He executed a scheme of redemption by which He incarnated on earth as His own Son. Those who would or could thereafter believe such a relief measure was actually the work of the same One Cause, who kept the stars in their courses, ordered the minerals and plants and animals with all their myriad intricacies and ramifications, could at death go to eternal happiness. Those who for some defect could not, were condemned for eternity to an inferior state, if not to a state of actual torment.

Most theologians, for reasons of common sense, would repudiate so bare a statement. They avoid bare statements of their dogma because without theological adornment and a thick mist of words it is too terrible for acceptance. Rarely does any of them dare to state it even in full. They devote their lives to special and less contradictory aspects of it.

None the less, what I have given is a map of the theological theatre of war, and all the great battles of theology have been settled or are still raging within its boundaries.

The profound controversy between theists and deists is between those who think that a personal God, having made the world, remains in touch with all His creatures to hear their prayers and importunities, and those who think that having made it, the personal God is now beyond reach and is no longer bothering about it. The deists are called rational theologians.

The intricate trinitarian dispute turns on whether God incarnated Himself as His Son, or whether He made for the occasion a Son of superior quality but separate from Himself.

The struggles over original sin are also within the map. They have to do with the mystery of that first offence which God must have anticipated but which so gravely annoyed him when it occurred. They have to do with the precise nature of the offence, the extent of the alienation, and the justice of the inheritance of the penalty by souls who had nothing to do with the offence and do not even know what it was.

The famous, but never finished, war between the Traducians and the Creationists is a dispute about the origin of the individual soul and started as a skirmish in the fight about original sin. The Traducians declared that souls are generated at the same time and in the same manner as bodies, by sexual union. Thus only, the Traducians said, could there be any transmission of the original sin by inheritance. The Creationists insisted that whenever two bodies came together and made a third, God hurriedly created a soul to thrust into it. Although Traducianism is the only theory (within the map) that will validate original sin, it is now rarely held. The Creationist picture of a God of love making an innocent new soul to accommodate the amours of a drunkard and a harlot, who will later instruct it in their arts and send it bowling along to hell, has evidently proven more attractive to the theologians. Perhaps it is another mystery into which you must not peer—or you may laugh.

The unending controversy between the exponents of free-will and those of predestination with all the rarefied subtleties that have gone into it, is a war to decide, within the boundaries I have outlined, whether, because God knows everything in advance—as would become an omniscient deity—all events are therefore fixed, or whether one of God's creatures can decide of his own free will to do something God knows in advance he will not do or something God had not foreseen. Predestination destroys the whole point of the redemptive system, because whether an individual will be saved or not is all fixed in advance. Free will, on the other hand, makes God less than omniscient. If the Predestinarian is right, God knows in advance every time he makes a soul for eternal torment, but seemingly He continues to do so because He is bound by a law manifested in the sexual proclivities of His creatures. In which case again He is not only less than omnipotent but is a servant of sex.

The wars over the true apostolic succession are no more than commercial wars about the authorized agency for the redemption brought to earth by Incarnate God. The apostolic successors would argue that in addition to making an inefficient scheme of salvation, God further vitiates its efficiency by permitting a monopoly of it instead of using every agency to further it. They have this in their favour of course, that the God who would work out such a system of salvation would be just the one to limit its use. He is that kind of a God.

The controversy over the actuality of the eternal torment for those who rejected or missed redemption are wars of method. They are between those who believe in scaring men into the arms of a loving Father, and those who would lure men into the arms of an angry one. Or the other way about. It does not make much difference.

These are the great wars. There are numberless little ones. Does the power of the Incarnated God to absolve from sin continue in his human self-elected successors and exponents? Does an infant who dies without doing wrong suffer eternally for the sin of those first parents to whom he is in no way spiritually related except through the Loving God who made all three? Can a ritual of admission to a Church save such an infant from the penalties for sins he never committed? Has God made any provision or amnesty for those who missed redemption because God made them before it came into effect? Has He made any provision or amnesty for those who miss it or have missed it for geographical reasons–being born in an unfavourable place? Has He made any provision for those who refused the whole doctrine because they sincerely believed they had a better one, or because the men who tried to persuade them by argument or force were notoriously debauched or dishonest or cruel? If God has made any or all of these provisions is it not a much less advantageous thing for a man to hear of redemption than to live in ignorance where the responsibility is not so great? Was not the whole redemptive scheme, therefore, a further cruelty in that it put on some a responsibility it did not put on others? Who is to be held responsible, the Congo native who dies in ignorance of redemption for lack of a visit from the missionary, or the missionary who went to a garden-party instead of carrying the message to the native? Or does God personally adjust these lesser inadvertences at the last day? Since all cases contain inadvertences, might He not merely adjust each case as it comes up without any redemptive complications at all? Is redemption to be considered the reward of godlike acts, or is it the reward of simple belief in the scheme? If it is the reward of acts, what point would there be in redeeming a dying man already bankrupted by his sins? If this is the reward of faith the sooner a man dies after his redemption the better. This, incidentally, was the position of the Chicago clergyman who, having reconciled a murderer with his God, opposed a commutation of the death penalty, for fear his convert, if permitted to live, would fall again from grace. The clergyman was strictly logical within the theologian's scheme. If other clergymen were as logical, and were devoted enough, they would first save and then shoot their converts.

These are a few of the crucial issues of Christian theology. They fill the dusty tomes of those great and good men whose books we see but so rarely read. Stripped of their latinity and reduced to everyday language these are the subjects theologians debate. They are at great pains, however, not to let the contradictions get into one sentence where they will become too evident. As long as they are carefully compartmented they are impressive. If perchance the contradictions become evident the theologian says, "That is a great mystery, and it does not do to pry into the inscrutable will of God. It unsettles the faith." What he means is that such enquiry unsettles theology. People will reject his system as valid theory and his revelation as fact.

You will observe that for the theologian his dogma presents many problems. For the person no longer persuaded that the Creator of the universe can be so incompetent and ridiculous a personage as the theologian makes him, there can be only one problem—a psychological one:

How has such a farrago of nonsense maintained the tenacious hold it has upon the minds of men?

There are several reasons, some lesser, and one, I believe, the great central reason. One reason is to be found in human laziness, the willingness to let men whose trade it is argue these problems. Another reason is human fear—the fear of going in the face of bigotry. Another and more important reason is that the flower of the teaching of Jesus, regeneration through love, has so commended itself to good men and women that they have accepted for its sake the tangle of degradations the theologians have permitted to grow up around it. Another reason is that, aided by the forces of bigotry and frightened compliance, theologians of a certain type have, wherever they could, destroyed the traces of efforts men have made to purify and cleanse it.

Beyond all these, the great reason for its persistence is that, concealed within its misshapen form, there is just enough of the element of truth to arouse in men the vague memory of a truth they once held but have forgotten and cannot quite recall. Deformed as the fable is, it has still the discernible shape of an age-old wisdom about the origin of man and of his relation to earth. The dogma has the power to stir the ancient memory without reviving it, and men cling to the distorted formula in dread that if they lose it they will have no clue at all. The more they dread the loss of the clue the more frantic and bigoted they become.

There is no absolute untruth in the world. The grossest superstitions are divine visions reflected in the waters of man's desires, and the more disturbed the waters, the more hideous the reflections. The Kabbalist says, "Demon deus inversus est—the evil principle is only the godlike principle upside down."

For the student of occultism every distorted image is a divine image he must restore. Every myth, every fanaticism, every broken fragment of unclean magic, has somewhere at the heart of it a clue to a divine function. Man does not make new ideas of religion; he gets old ideas wrong.

Let us see if we can find what was in the minds of the first progenitors of the fable, who possessed their memory of the ancient truth, and see then how the theologian has reflected it in the waters of his own desire. In order to do so we must now go outside the Christian field because although all theologies are distorted, the distortion varies with the religion.

By putting fragments together and comparing one with another we discover the original formula to have been something like this:

That from an Absolute Divinity, an Unmanifest, have emerged wave upon wave of beings, no less divine than their ineffable source but limited by their conceptions of themselves. That in long process of ages they have proceeded through experience to more and more extended consciousness, presenting in the aggregate the picture of a great army of journeying souls stretched out along a road, none less divine than any other, but differentiated by their consciousness of divinity. That not only do they advance but they are bound by the law of their being to preserve the unity of the whole by transmitting, each to the orders below it, in a kind of cosmic link-motion, the spiritual forces received from the orders of beings beyond. That, being each a first cause in his own right, they have the same free will that inheres in the great First Cause, and can manifest it in the measure that they have realized divinity. That in the chain, however it came about, a race, identified with this earth before the thinking Egos touched it, broke down, and whether by the exercise of its own will or by the failure of the will of the regents who guided it, became distorted. That another race beyond these—our own—whose duty it was to transmit higher powers to the lower race, refused to accept responsibility for the misshapen creatures, or to enter into them. That at last under cosmic law the higher race was compelled to do so, was drawn down into the sphere of earth, where its individuals dwell now, embodying themselves as rarely as cosmic law will permit, in the misshapen bodies of the beings they have to redeem. That by their rebellion they have lost a great measure of the powers they first brought to earth, and instead of being the Unity they once were, are a scattered and terrified host. That if they take thought and renew their lost powers they can return to that comparatively high wisdom from which they fell. That if they do not they must inevitably be drawn down into the creatures they despise. That from time to time one of the unwilling becomes willing, performs his task, returns to the Unity with his brothers–the God of which he is a part–and knowing the truth pledges himself to work for the restoration of it among his exiled brethren here upon earth. That such liberated ones work without ceasing, relying upon each other for support, and creating a unified body of doctrine which they renew from century to century as the activities of theology vitiate it. That the liberated one stands in the relation of exemplar and friend to the rest of mankind, and that it is the Ego who is, himself, the redeemer and potential Son of the Unity or God he has forgotten. That the original sin which taints us all refers therefore to the refusal and that it is carried from incarnation to incarnation by each Ego and not from father to child by generation.

At first glance it seems as fantastic a formula, perhaps, as the other. It has this difference, however, that it is capable of proof by phenomena on all planes. It is the key to comparative religion and it agrees with the findings of philosophy and the sciences as far as they have gone. Often, as I have shown, it solves what they cannot.

Let us see now how the theologians vitiated the age-old formula–in what desires they let it reflect itself.

Their first destructive step was when they desired that their God should be more important and all-inclusive than the gods of their rival religions. They expanded the phrase "the God" in the books they had inherited. "The God" was evidently what the Eastern religious teachers called Atma. It is our Unity or Oversoul and functions in a realm immediately superior to mind. Between it and the First Cause are vast ranges of consciousness which will be beyond our ken for untold ages. As soon as the theologians of those early years said "Our God is the All-God" they started at once a series of destructive contradictions, and they had to give attributes to an Absolute Unmanifest who cannot have attributes.

The next distortion arising out of their desires was when they made their teacher Jesus the one and unique Son of their Absolute God. This required that they wipe out all traces of previous teachers who were also Sons of "the God". It required also that they destroy the symbolic and exemplary relation of Jesus to all Egos and have it in the special and historical relation of the pseudo-deity Jesus to all mankind. It was Sanchoniathon who said of the Egyptians that "they corrupted their mysteries by cosmical and historical affections," which is precisely what these early Christians did. They made "the God" cosmic in his scope, and the Son who was the symbol of each Ego they reduced to a historical incident.

When you have told one lie you must either acknowledge it or tell another. No falsehood ever stood alone. In order to validate their cosmic Father and His unique Son they had to wipe out also that which had been explicit in early Christianity, as it is in all religions at the beginning, the doctrine of the rebirth of the soul. If the Omnipotent Creator after a long interval begets His one and only Son, it is essential for a belief in it that the souls who are to be saved shall come only once to earth. If they have come many times before and are to come again and again thereafter as a means of working out their own destiny, the one and only appearance of the Saviour must be only a trifling incident in their lives. Furthermore if you admit the principle of coming again and again, the first thing you know you will have the necessary idea of a Saviour coming again and again, which of course plays the mischief with the unique redeemer idea. People will shop around and go where they like the theology best. It also arouses the suspicion that the pagan redeemers whose cults surrounded early Christianity might have been similarly Sons of God. Buddha might have been a redeemer, and Krishna, and Dionysos, and Attis, and Hercules, and Horus, and Baldur. So, abolishing reincarnation from their formula, the early Christian theologians had to fall back upon the alternative of souls begetting souls by sex or of God creating souls to order.

Another distortion of the ancient truth must necessarily follow. If the soul has not lived before, it cannot have shared in an offence that alienated it from the God. Therefore the very evident state of alienation that exists must have been inherited in some obscure way or must arise out of God's annoyance at the behaviour of Adam and Eve.

The old universal saying is that the soul alone is responsible. What it has sown, that also must it reap. The degraded formula says, "By a special act of clemency on God's part, the soul may sow a great evil and reap a great good, or may sow a little good but for lack of having taken part in God's clemency, may reap a great evil." Exact justice thus becomes a farce. When the Church Fathers had extracted the last comic element out of it in this form, their Latin successors developed new comic values by remitting evil themselves. Then they spun out the doctrine to permit of the issue of coupons that would remit sins even before they were committed.

It is easy, therefore, to see how men who take such a doctrine and by falsifying the idea of "the God" so necessary to its usefulness, by removing the idea that each soul is a redeemer of a fallen being, by vesting the redemptive power in one personage, by throwing away the necessary idea of the pre-existence of the soul, and by making justice the whim of deity, must come out with a monstrous caricature of the old idea.

They have had hundreds of chances to amend. They had a choice between Plato who knew it and Aristotle who did not. They wiped out the Platonists and clung to Aristotle. Origen knew and taught it and they put him under anathema. In 1400 it was a punishable offence on the part of Pico della Mirandola even to offer to debate whether Origen was in hell. Paul knew the old tradition and for centuries the Latin theologians would willingly have left him out of the New Testament. They laboured to supplant him with their favourite Peter through whom they had exclusive salesrights on salvation. The Mithraists knew it and the Holy fathers crushed them. The Manicheans knew it and a hundred thousand were put to death with torture. Basilides knew it and his books were burned. The Cathars and Albigenses knew it and were mercilessly destroyed even though the south of France had to be devastated. The troubadours knew it and paid with their lives. Lully knew it and was locked up as mad. Dante knew it and was an exile all his life. Roger Bacon knew it and was kept under lock and key. Bruno knew it and was burned to death.

Since the Renaissance the burnings have been less frequent. The bigots have been forced to use persecutions of a lesser sort, obscurantism, tampering with books, and fulminations from their pulpits.

There has never been but one heresy—the effort to restore the old doctrine of the exile of the soul and to restate the means by which each man must find his way back into the widom of the God.

7. THE MYTHOLOGICAL PROBLEM

In the preceding article I have offered a brief version of an ancient formula as an approximation to the truth underlying Christian theological distortions of the tradition of the fall and redemption. I have claimed for the formula that it is a key, not only to the understanding of the Christian mythos, but to the interpretation of all other mythological systems. I am now under obligation to demonstrate that it is as I have said.

It should require no great space to prove that Christianity, however bitterly theologians argue for its historicity, is a mythos like all the others. It is true that for many centuries, during which there was a poverty of comparative data, the theologians had little difficulty in persuading men that the miraculous birth, the escape from slaughter in infancy, the baptism by the forerunner, the transfiguration on the mount, the temptation, the crucifixion, and ascension of Jesus were unique in religion, and were celebrations on the part of God of His special paternity of the Judean redeemer. Neither was it difficult in those days to argue that the sayings of Jesus embody a truth and ethic previously unattained by any sage or prophet among men.

A better informed generation knows now, from archaeological research and the inflow of Eastern scriptural writings, that every religion has had its virgin mothers, most religions several of them. Virgin birth is now recognized to be much more a spiritual than a physical fact. Better philosophers than ours find something ridiculous in our Christian insistence on a foolish and unnecessary trick by which a God would distinguish this unique Son from the multitudes of other ordinary sons. The slaughter of the innocents by Herod has never been taken as fact except by the credulous. So wholesale a massacre would have been corroborated by a dozen classical historians. Now we know that an identical legend forms part of the symbolic story of every avatar in his infancy. Buddhist Gautama, Hindu Krishna, Egyptian Horus, all had similar escapes from the powers of evil, and in the Egyptian mythos, the jealous ruler was actually called Herrut, the "slayer of the youngling in the egg." Even Herod seems to have been used mythically. All religions have the illustration as a symbol of the passing under the waters, or plunging in the waters of desire. Most religions have a transfiguration on the mount, and of some of these other transfigurations, notably the Buddhist and Egyptian, ours is only an attenuated shadow. Even our cherished cross is a universal glyph of the process by which a superman sacrifices himself for an erring race, and is the symbol of the means by which, having done it, he re-joins the Oversoul. Gautama Buddha is marked with a cross on his forehead; Krishna is transfixed to a tree by an arrow in a cruciform attitude; Horus is crucified on an orb between two trees or "breathers"; Bacab in ancient Yucatan is crucified between two revilers in Tzonpantli, the place of the skull. All redeemers ascend to heaven after their work is done and take their place with the Father. The husband of the Virgin of the world is always an artificer, Vulcan, mate of Venus Urania; Joseph of Mary; Seb of Isis; Brihaspati of Soma. The secret teaching is invariably given on mounts of vision; the twelve apostles have their parallels in the twelve labours, the twelve adversaries of Buddha, twelve initiations, twelve Zodiacal signs and the twelve powers in the body along the girdle of the beast. The avatars are always fishers of men, or shepherds of men, or both. There is always an adversary who has been cast out in some fabulous war in heaven.

Even the *Logia* or sayings of Jesus, clung to so desperately by men whose business it is to prove that they are selling an exclusive line of goods, are not original with the Christian scriptures. They all have their earlier parallels, often richer and fuller than the fragments which survived our era of patristic bigotry. The Sermon on the Mount is age-old and was never spoken extemporaneously. It was obviously written. The Lord's Prayer has earlier parallels for every phrase, so also have the parables. The whole story of Jesus from Gethsemane to the end is not a historical narrative. It is a scenario for the secret mystery drama of the early Christians, that drama to which St. Paul refers when he says: "O foolish Galatians, who hath bewitched you, that ye should not obey the truth, before whose eyes Jesus Christ hath been evidently set forth, crucified among you?"

To the kind of man for whom there is more virtue in a story if it be given time and place and if all the events in it are actual, this passing of the treasured marvels of the historical life of Jesus into spiritual myth is a desecration. To the thinking man such a spiritualization opens a door into wisdom. History, he knows, is shadow; myth is the effort of the creative mind to explain the truth behind shadow. A historical event is over and done with; a myth is ongoing and eternal. Sallustius, the Neo-Platonist said of Greek myths—and of all myths: "These things never were; *they always are.*"

As the Christian fable resumes its place among the cosmic stories of the world, it takes on dignity. The tradition, once frankly allegorical, then reduced for so many centuries to the imbecility of unrelated fact, stands again abreast of the great spiritual dramas of the race, and may be interpreted by means of its parallels.

There are three kinds of modern writers about mythology. The first are the few who see in it a secret tradition passing from generation to generation, kept always in the world for returning and returning souls as they become in time pure and intuitive enough to receive it. They interpret the parallels of religion and myth as meaning that all systems emanate from the one body of truth available to all sages. These myth-interpreters have their reward in the wisdom that comes of discerning similarities and in the power that comes of teaching.

The second are the mythologists who with a great parade of scholarship and scientific method, but with a definite intention, none the less, to bring in a verdict for the uniqueness of Christianity, plunge into the subject and emerge presently with a book that proves, by disparaging all other faiths, that Christianity is the sole and effulgent light of the world. These get their reward in professorships, curatorships of museums, editorships of safe books and occasionally a bishopric. They produce many books but are not extensively read. Their celebrity arises chiefly from the fact that they quote each other approvingly. It is very doubtful, for instance, that you have ever read a book by J. Estlin Carpenter, or Professor Grant Showerman or Dr. Pfleiderer, but if you have ever read any book in this class, you are sure they are great men.

Third are the mythologists who, having observed the success in our time of the materialistic doctrine of evolution, have endeavoured to interpret mythology along lines parallel to it. They decide that myths evolved with man. All religious fables, they say, arose out of primitive misapprehension and superstitution, and all religion is the philosophization of the errors of savage belief. These mythologists try, according to various formulae, to probe the benighted mind for the influences–hunger, fear, cruelty, and lust–that were the first parents of religious belief. If they are consistent in their theory, of course, they have to find that Christianity is similarly a collection of rationalized outcroppings of savagery, but their art and usually their fame is in the measure of their skill in not saying so in a manner that will give offence. Most of them make a slight, but still discernible, genuflexion as they pass the altar. They have their reward in being acclaimed as very scientific and uncompromising, and are said to be abreast of modern culture. They produce many books and are most widely read of the three classes. None the less they are a puzzled lot.

Their first difficulty arises out of the fact that none of them has ever succeeded in proving that a religion evolves, or even improves as time goes by. Like the Christian apologist whose business requires him to demonstrate the superiority of Christianity, they have carried a partial conclusion into their impartial enquiry.

Every datum of religion indicates that a religious system does not evolve. It always degenerates. It is never born of human ignorance, but of human vision. The normal habit of mankind is not to enrich the lucubrations of the village idiot, but to cheapen and miss the point of the sentences of the village wise man. The best Christian to date has been the inspirer, whoever he was, of the Christian renewal of the wisdom tradition. No Christian would contend for a moment that the founder of Christianity had been surpassed or improved on. The best Buddhist so far, and the wisest, has been Gautama Buddha. The best exponent of Bhagavad Gita has been the teacher who uttered it. There has been no Platonist greater than Plato, no teacher of Yoga greater than

Patanjali, no exponent of Veda greater than Veda Vyasa, no Hermetist greater than Hermes, no Zoroastrian greater than Zoroaster, nor any Vedantin greater than Sankara. A stream does not rise higher than its source. What student would be so foolish as to read the five thousand words of Lao-Tsze and then examining modern Taoism with its devils and its shamanism, declare that the present form had evolved? A garment evolves? It evolves tatters and filth.

We have no trouble demonstrating the degeneration of living religions, where we can find something of the personality of the prophetic founder and his apostles. Why then should we suppose that a different law supervenes when the personalities of the founders are missing? Or should we, having a system, refuse to believe there was a founder? Whatever is true of religions whose whole duration falls within the historical period is true also of those whose start was prehistoric. Why accept a Jesus or a Lao-Tsze or a Buddha and reject an Orpheus or a Hermes? And finding the degraded fragments of an older faith why should we suppose them to have had an origin different from that of the degraded fragments of a younger one?

If the older forms are more corrupt it is not because they have had a different kind of origin, but obviously because they are older, and more thousands of misunderstanders of the first ideal have had a chance to corrupt them. One selfish or stupid man can defile a whole sect; he can disgust the more intelligent members of it with his distortions of truth until, when they go elsewhere, he can have only the people foolish enough to perpetuate his follies. How great then can be the destructive effect on a religion of the entry into it of thousands of self-seeking and inferior men who make filthy its first intent. With such a destructive process in mind it is not hard to foresee the time, for instance, when the selfishness and bigotry of the followers of Christianity encrusting it with their dogmas of papal infallibility, of sacraments that are pure whether the priest is or not, of plenary absolutions, of indulgences, of extreme unctions, of assumptions of Mary; their fetichisms of sacred hearts, of charms and amulets and scapulars, of magical waters, of reproduced stigmata, and bones and nails and bits of wood, of Veronica's napkins, will make Christianity no longer fit for the use of the higher kind of intelligent humans and will hasten it down the long road to voodoo and tribal magic.

In the meantime thinking souls will have enlisted under other and newer teachers, no more inspired than the Christian and no less Sons of the God, but with a restored and cleaner magic. If in lives to come one of our present Christians happens on broken shards of the Christian vessel and thinks of them as born of the mistakes of savage minds, he will be making the same error about the Nazarene that our mythologists make about the forgotten northern sage whose wisdom remains to us in the Elder Edda, or about that Thoth-Hermes whose vision became the hocus-pocus of a thousand Egyptian cemeteries.

This is the prime reason why the evolutionary mythologists are puzzled. If you are quite sure that nine-tenths of the material of your study is nonsense, it will be fatally easy—for reasons of mental laziness alone—to give up your effort to understand a difficult problem, and assign the whole thing to the nonsense division. The man who is satisfied that the earth is flat and that the sun goes over and under it, can never become a distinguished interpreter of Copernicus, nor will any man who thinks compassion a waste of time make much of the sayings of Gautama Buddha. Neither will anyone who is sure the science of philology was invented yesterday have the patience to unriddle the *Cratylus* of Plato. Instead you will find him saying, "Plato, so intelligent about other matters, was ignorant and credulous in his tracing of the origins of Greek words, and his *Cratylus* has no scientific value." Which is to say that the clear-eyed Plato, in spite of the strictest habit of examination of any philosopher we have ever known, in spite of a lifetime in the use of Greek, in spite of association with the greatest trained minds of the golden age of Athens, in spite of an intimate knowledge of the several dialects and related languages, the possession of dictionaries that have disappeared, for all he pondered words and was the greatest classical user of them, for all he was the avowed continuer of the then-extant lore of Orpheus, Onomacritus, Pherecydes, Aglaophamus, Homer, Pythagoras and Pindar, word makers and users, knew less of these things than a foggy-minded English or German curate.

Similarly you will find such a Gradgrind writing, "The Greek mind, of course, was incapable of understanding such and such a thing" or, "It never occurred to the ancient Egyptian that ——", or "The Hindu could not conceive of ——", or when Homer does not specifically mention something, saying "It is certain that Homer knew nothing of ——." Sometimes you will find one of these omniscient gentlemen writing this kind of nonsense; "The figure of the infant Horus with his finger upon his lips was long considered a symbol of secrecy, and was used as such by Egyptian, Greek, and Roman secret societies. Modern research shows that it meant nothing of the sort; that it was merely a sign of childish innocence." That is to say, the societies that *used* it and the sculptors who *made* it with such a use in mind, as a sign of the inviolability of a mystery cult, did not know why they used it or why they made it. What is one to do with minds like these? Yet such are the constant processes of argument brought to bear on the modern interpretation of myth. These are the absurdities inseparable from an evolutionary theory of religion.

With this habit to defeat their best endeavours it is easy to see why our interpreters of religious fable do not penetrate far into the mystery. They have in recent years worked out a definition of myth on which most of them agree. In the version of W. Sherwood Fox it is as follows:

"A myth is a statement, or virtual statement as implied in a symbol, an attribute, or an epithet, accepted as true by its original maker and his hearers, and referring to the eternal nature and past acts of beings greater than man, and frequently to circumstances which to us are improbable or impossible."

It is the requirement of this school of thinking that the phrase "accepted as true by its original maker and his hearers," should mean that it was accepted as literally true, or if some element of symbol did enter in, it must be such a symbol as could be easily grasped by child-like minds. If one suggests that it may have been offered as philosophical or mythical allegory, these mythologists reply that being born of savagery it could have had only a trifling interpretation. Under no circumstances must you attribute a high meaning to it although it is permissible to attribute ever so far-fetched a low one. Their dogma is that because it originated early in the history it must have a less profound value than if it had appeared later. Which is the same as saying that all later poets must be superior to all earlier ones, that all later philosophers must be wiser than all earlier philosophers and all later teachers more profound than all earlier ones. Which of course is nonsense.

The outstanding fact about human thought is that

wisdom is where you find it and you are more likely to find it in a document of tradition that has had the power to move many persons over a long period of time. The great myths may easily have been—indeed the mass of evidence is in favour of their having been—the symbolical expression of ideas from which we are excluded because of materialistic prejudices. The same Sallustius I quoted before had another wise saying about which is a key to the art of myth reading. It was that when the events of a myth become improbable or impossible as literal fact it became the duty of the student to look for a spiritual fact. Only an evolutionary mythologist can assume that these early poets and seers must have been fools offering impossibilities to credulous listeners. By the rules of his game he must think Keats a fool for telling people that jocund day ever stood tiptoe upon a misty mountain-top.

The central clause is valid enough but it is insufficient to account for the facts. He says that myth refers to "the eternal nature and past acts of beings greater than man." What is needed to complete it is an idea, as easily available to Dr. Fox as it is to any other reader. It is to be found throughout the pages of the best and wisest teachers of the various systems—that most of the beings greater than man, whose eternal nature and past acts form the body of myth, *are none other than man himself.* The rest are man's adversaries here upon earth.

Pythagoras is clear upon the point so far as Greek myth is concerned. So is Empedocles and so is Plato. So also are Plotinus, Plutarch, Iamblichus and Proclus. Hermes Trismegistus, the Egyptian, leaves no doubt of his belief that men are fallen divinities. The Hindu sages, Krishna, Gautama, and Sankara, taught it. So did the Chinese Lao-Tsze, Lieh-Tsze, Chuang-Tsze, Confucius, Chu-Hse, and Wang Yang Ming. No one can read the

Gathas without recognizing it as fundamental in Zoroastrian belief; the Sufis taught it, and so did the Christian Gnostics. It is in the Eddas, the Quran, and the Kabbalah. It is in our Christian tradition.

Why then, if it is so evident that all the myths deal with a golden age before the descent of the Divine Egoes, a bondage or enchantment here in the hands of the adversaries, and a return again to our earlier home, do not modern mythologists accept it?

Because they do not want it. And honest use of their scientific method would dictate that they report the phenomena as they find them saying, these are the beliefs and although we do not hold them, these foolish and credulous people did. They are not so honest; they repudiate the philosophy that accompanies the stories and assign meanings they themselves can believe. The only reason for thinking an ancient Mayan could possibly believe the ocean swallowed the sun at night and disgorged it in the morning is that Sir Bertram Windle had the kind of mind that permitted him to believe the Mayan could.

Just as surely as the Christian apologists are pledged to the belief that Christianity is the true light, so the evolutionary mythologists are pledged to the idea that evolution is the only true theory of man on earth, and no matter what the facts, they will bring in their predetermined verdict. That man was once higher than he is and is now below his true place is a defiance of Darwin and Haeckel and although you may say what you please about God, Darwin and Haeckel are sacred. Too many men have invested their reputations in them.

Meanwhile, the contradictions involved in the life, let us say of Dionysos, the heights from which he has come, the degradations to which he has fallen and the heights to which he will again ascend, clear enough as

Proclus explains him, must be modernly interpreted as the sap in the grape-vine. Prometheus, the god who fell into the bondage of the earth forces, so revealing a figure in Aeschylus, must remain a primitive savage who discovered fire; the Kumaras or celibate youths who descended into half animal bodies to redeem them, must have their interpretation in sex magic and taboo; the Chinese men of old time who knew the Tao and lost it, must be understood as skin-clad barbarians of a pastoral age. The key that would reconcile the contradictions and thus lead to a useful conclusion, these mythologists reject because they do not want the conclusion.

The fables of redeemers, understood in all the older faiths as types and exemplars of man himself, of the ego of each of us, are to these interpreters, "culture-heroes" and no more. The fables of Orpheus who came down into this place of shades for Eurydice, of Persephone drawn down into the realm of Pluto, of Herakles who toiled for the liberation of men, of Perseus who freed Andromeda from the sea-monster, of Theseus who defeated the minotaur, of Apollo who slew Typhoeus, of dismembered Osiris assembled and raised again, of the Greek Sons of the Sun besieging the stronghold of the Sons of the Moon to free Helen, Rama the Son of the Sun freeing Sita from the moon host, Arjuna and his four brothers all the Sons of the Sun defeating the Kurus or Sons of the Moon. Vainamoinen defeating the evil magician Lemminkainen, the Volsungs toiling to save a lower race, are nothing but childish efforts of the dawn of human intellect to celebrate their tribal strong men? It doesn't seem reasonable. There is too much power in the stories. They have moved too many wise men of vision. If they do not move mythologists to vision the implication is plain.

8. THE ETHICAL PROBLEM

We get our word 'ethics' (through the latin *ethicus*) from the Greek *ethikos,* that which pertains to *ethos,* character. With the Greeks the word *ethos* had other connotations. It meant custom, usage, native habit, and in its original sense contained also the idea of an accustomed seat or place, a habitat, or primal abode.

As a branch of philosophy ethics concerns itself with the meaning and scope of the words "good" and "bad", "right and wrong", as applied to character and to conduct. The first phase of its enquiry is descriptive. It endeavours to classify thoughts, moods, and actions according to their goodness or badness. In its second phase it determines, if possible, whether the common ideas of goodness and badness and right and wrong reveal any absolute standards of action, or point to any cosmic laws that govern the issues of conduct.

After many centuries during which ethics had been looked upon as purely philosophical in its subject matter and method, enthusiastic scientists of the nineteenth century made an effort to bring it into the fashionable field of positive science, but without notable success.

It should have been evident to the biologists who made the effort that it must end in failure. It inevitably ends in a ring-around-a-rosy. A science is necessarily experimental. Since the results of right and wrong action could be understood only by the experimenter and in his own person—to anyone else or in anyone else they would be mere opinion—he must be, therefore, not only his own laboratory but also his own judge of results, and he must judge by means of his ethical judgment which is the subject of his experiment.

Worse than this for practical purposes, it is the great

defect of all attempts at ethical experiment that the observable consequences of actions are too far removed from their causes in point of time. Indeed the cycle of most important moral operations does not fall within a single lifetime. This makes a positive science of ethics quite impossible for a materialist or a theologian. If the experimenter is a materialist he can have no assurance that the results will show at all before the soul that produced the causes is resolved again into the life force from which it came. The results of most of his experiments must therefore be lost entirely or must be seen in physical descendants, in which case the whole problem is transferred to the field of heredity. An action that will only have its effect in a man's remote descendant is not a matter of active ethical interest, especially if he does not expect to have a descendant. If the experimenter has a predisposition for Christian dogma he is in an equally bad fix. The results of most experiments will only become evident in Heaven or Hell and will not be natural effects on the doer but merely effects manifested in the approval or annoyance of God. The only possible scientific experimenter in ethics would be the theosophist who believes in reincarnation, and he would expect the results to show in a subsequent life and would regard effects in this life as arising out of experimental conduct in previous ones. He would then have two courses of procedure. One would be to set up a cause and wait patiently for its result with the certainty that by the time he reached his result he would have mislaid his memoranda of the cause. The other would be to develop his memory of the specific causes in previous lives that have given rise to present results. As we shall see there is a simpler method.

It is now generally agreed that ethics had better remain a branch of philosophy.

Philosophy has been defined as "a process of reflection upon the presuppositions involved in unreflective thought." In other words the philosopher turns his attention upon himself to discover how and why his mind does what it does and what are the elements he has all along carried in his mind without thinking of them. He does not deal with new things but with old and previously unobserved things. He sets his own precepts, concepts and processes in new lights and examines them. He seeks merely to become more fully aware of himself.

In logic he examines the processes of reasoning. In epistemology he seeks a theory of knowledge, endeavouring to know how he knows and whence come his ideas. In metaphysics he examines his apprehensions and his conceptions of space, cause, time, and substance. This is the enquiry into what the Greeks called the True —*aletheia,* the unforgettable. In aesthetics he examines his ideas of the Beautiful—*kalos,* excellence of form and motion as embodying interior spiritual function. In ethics he examines his ideas of the Good—*agathon,* that which is firm and secure.

In its first stages ethics is not a philosophy at all. It deals with specific problems such as any man might face in his daily life. "What would be just in this case?" "What, in that case, would excuse one from responsibility?" The power to answer such questions is present with every Ego however little it may have been exercised. The power grows with use. Presently the first philosophical phases of the subject arise. "Why, given similar cases, should there be so great difference in the answers given by different men?" "Why should the answers vary at all?" "Or, why, indeed, should men, having found an answer to a question, proceed to do something contrary to that which they have decided?"

"Why should men, desirous of following a certain wrong line of conduct justify their actions by casting doubt upon the authority of the ethical judgment?"

Thus, out of its own contradictions and difficulties, arise ethics as a philosophy. After all it is natural that it should so arise. Ethical philosophy is born of its own disabilities as certainly as a study of health is born of the fact of illness.

All ethical systems belong broadly to two groups. There are those who maintain that the intuitive power of judgment possessed by man is supreme, and a supreme guide to conduct. The others maintain, on one ground or another, that man's ethical judgment is not final but that there are other and external considerations which must guide his actions. These external standards vary. Herbert Spencer tried to erect standards on biological data and failed egregiously. Christian theologians have tried to base standards on an imputed revelation of the dictates of a personal God. Various writers have tried to found systems based on what they claim to be the universal acceptance of certain judgments, social, legal, or political. In view of the fact, however, that each of these systems is finally tested by the author's own ethical judgment and is addressed to the ethical judgment of those who read or study it, we are forced to conclude at last that there is only one valid basis for ethics, that of supreme power of the soul of man to decide between right and wrong. If a soul deciding for itself addresses to souls deciding for themselves a system of ethics which declares that souls do not decide for themselves, there is something wrong with the system.

One of the great controversies in ethics has revolved around hedonism. The hedonist bases his contention that pleasure is the end of all human effort upon the universally experienced feeling that for a "good" to be good it must in some sense be "my good." The anti-hedonist offers the fulfilment of duty as the true end of effort, arguing that the pleasure of the individual can never be complete in himself.

A multitude of controversies have arisen also out of theology and the effort to place the ideas of an omniscient God above man's interior judgment. The first fallacy of such an external standard for conduct lies in the fact that the ethical judgment is itself superior to the idea of God. Man has never been willing to worship a God who does not fulfil his moral requirements. God is therefore inferior to whatever it is in man that makes ethical judgments. The folly of thinking of a God greater than the maker of Him has led to innumerable contradictions. The most noticeable in its effect on ethics has been that dispute to which I have referred before in these articles, the one about free will and predestination. It is a dispute that never could arise in the realm of pure ethics at all because all the ideas of ethics have to do with free choice between right and wrong and the inalienable right of man to will his own destiny. It is only when theologians have managed to persuade men of the existence of a personal deity who knows everything in advance that anyone will consider even for a moment the soul as bound to a routine laid in the mind-made God's foreknowledge.

The central problem of ethics, and the one with which I am especially interested in this series of articles, is a mystical one. It is the problem of the nature of that mysterious quality in man that makes him the sole and final arbiter of his relation to earth. The primary manifestation of the quality is the operation of Will. The soul of man acts, it refrains from action. It approves, it disapproves. It judges. It may judge rightly or wrongly in any given case but it reserves, for some high reason it does not itself understand, the right to will and to judge.

Emerson's schoolboy with his book of history is in no awe of Napoleon or of Alexander. He arraigns them for every thought, word and deed, he praises, he condemns serenely and without passion. He is their equal, not of this earth but of a higher world than this from which they all three have come. He is one soul appraising another and deciding what he would do—nay, will do—in like case, trying them by a higher criterion than they or he can bring to actuality. So he judges all kings and saints and heroes. His judgments of the event may be faulty, desires may disturb his calm; anger may sweep over him or a chill of fear; his understanding may limp but from his height he decides. He and they are beings superior to earth, walking about fitfully and dimly remembering how Gods should walk.

Plato, in common with all the great occult philosophers, found in this high assumption a demonstration of the state of the soul prior to its original descent into the bondage of earth. Lest I be accused of twisting Plato's doctrine to my needs, let me offer a summary in the words of the late Dr. Henry Sidgwick:

". . . If the objects of abstract thought constitute the real world, of which this world of individual things is but a shadow, it is plain that the highest, most real life *must lie in the former region and not in the latter.* It is in contemplating the abstract reality which concrete things obscurely exhibit, the type or ideal which they imperfectly imitate, that the true life of the mind in man must consist; and as man is most truly man in proportion as he is mind, the desire of one's own good, which Plato, following Socrates, held to be permanent and essential in every living thing, becomes in its highest form the philosophical yearning for knowledge. This yearning, he held, springs—like more sensual impulses—from a sense of *want of something formerly possessed, of which there remains a latent memory in the soul,* strong in its proportion to its philosophic capacity; hence it is that in learning any abstract truth by scientific demonstration, we merely make explicit what we already know; we bring into clear consciousness hidden memories of a state in which the soul looked upon Reality and Good face to face, *before the lapse that imprisoned her in an alien body,* and mingled her true nature with fleshly feelings and impulses."

Sidgwick gives here the impression, frequent in modern philosophical writing, that Plato's Reality and Good are the ultimate Reality and Good. It is evident from Plato himself and from the Neo-Platonists that they were only comparative and that they do not in any sense embrace the entire scale of knowledge, but only an octave above and beyond the present octave of mind, namely, that subtle but none the less material plane the Eastern writers call Buddhi. It was the realm of the Christos in the Gnostic systems. This interior world which the soul has lost, Plato and his followers regarded as one in which our now separated souls must be reintegrated into a unity we once enjoyed but have lost owing to the delusions of earth. The re-awakening of the soul of man is for Platonists, a return to that Unity. This is the One of Plotinos, and as I have already suggested, it is the One which Christian theologians disfigured into their ultimate and all-knowing God.

Conceiving the race of men here upon earth as disintegrated and scattered fragments of that Unity, but essentially bound, each to the others, we have a clue to the truth about that other great crux of ethics—duty. This is the one which Kant called the greatest of mysteries. It is the ethical factor we saw the hedonist rejecting when he said, "That is not good which is not *my* good." The exponent of duty is a believer, however dimly he may see it, in the lost Unity, and he says, "Good can only be *our* good." There can be no good which omits any of the exiled race. They must go through together.

The concept of duty—that which one owes—is, then, a blurred recollection of the essential fact of existence in the One. This is the only valid explanation of the constantly recurring intuition that can impel a man to an act of sacrifice which he cannot justify by any process of mind. Hedonism is of the mind; duty is a reminiscence of the lost world beyond mind, and mind has been called always the great slayer of the real. The concept of justice is an archetypal idea from that lost world, as are the concepts of love, philosophy, mathematics and the yearning for beauty.

The differences between the souls of men in this world are not, therefore, to be explained as differences of development or as varying accretions of powers. They can only be explained as varying degrees of loss of divine self-consciousness. This is the only adequate explanation of the differences in the clarity of ethical judgment. Failure of judgment does not come of inadequate development but of over-clouding. The will to act, the arrogation of the right to decide are of the divine soul and are common to all men. The failure to judge wisely comes of the obscuring forces of an alien earth.

9. THE HUMANIST PROBLEM

The magnificent old word "humanist" is one which has known many vicissitudes and if the rising fashion is any index, it is likely soon to know a few more.

In its broadest and most general sense humanism denotes a greater preoccupation with the welfare of man than with the glory of God. It implies a realization that whatever God's glory may be will be most efficiently enhanced by the service of God's creatures. Humanism is therefore an emphasis and an approach rather than a theory, and is polar to theology and sacerdotalism, which tend to emphasize man's duty to an extra-human and highly hypothetical Deity and to ascribe human joys and sorrows to the operation of His inscrutable will.

Of course humanism is as old as the human love which motivates it, but in periods of priestly ascendancy it is forced to flow underground. In Europe it has several times welled up into a visible stream, once with Plato, once with the Neoplatonists, once with the Arabian philosophers who came into Europe with the Saracen invasion, and once with the rebirth of Platonism at the Renaissance of the fifteenth century. It is with this last that the word is specially identified, but like so many other words it has been parcelled out among the seers of the parts of things and has been used in limited senses. It is widely used to refer to the cultivation of classical (profane or non-Christian) literature; sometimes to mean any kind of secular learning. More recently Comte and his followers arrogated it as a name for the Positive philosophy. R.B. Haldane and others have used it to describe modern scientific advance. Professors Irving Babbitt, Paul Elmer More and Norman Foerster have revived it as a name of their kind of addiction to "polite letters" and abstention from anything that seems too modern, and have used it to describe a cold, intellectual gentility which they pretend derives from Plato. In the past year or so it has become a cult name and seems to be in for a vogue that will defile it, just as the word "Theosophy" has been defiled. It will then have to go back to the limbo of soiled words to be reissued when men have forgotten the follies associated with it. To date, however, it is a clean, noble word.

Each of the great humanistic movements in Europe in history has had a direct theosophical origin. It has been the projection into philosophy, religion, the arts, philanthropy and government of an idea which is fundamental in all theosophies—the idea of the essential unity of mankind and the consequent necessity for brotherhood as a means of awakening the intuitions of interior divinity which are the central object of effort in every theosophical system. This is the idea bound up in the word "Theosophy" itself. It is not, as so frequently interpreted, merely Divine Wisdom. Any religious system purports to be that, and saying that theosophy is especially so is no more than vociferation. It is "the wisdom of the god", that wisdom which man may make manifest by virtue of the fact that he has in the past attained to a far higher measure of divinity than he now displays. Or in another symbol, it is the Sophia, lost since our entry into this sublunary sphere.

It is easily demonstrable that no theology (Christian or other) can generate a vigorous humanism. Although Jesus, for example, is a humanist of the first order, engaged in his lifetime in the task of humanizing Jewish dogma, the theological accretions that have gathered about his doctrine have inevitably destroyed the spirit of his work. The dogma concerning Jesus is that a Father in Heaven, of whom he is the extraordinary son and we the step-children, has sent us all into the world and has known in advance the outcome of His action and ours. Nevertheless this God requires of us that we make a series of choices that His own foreknowledge renders impossible. Theology argues also that we can repair wrong choices by an implicit belief in the disparity between us and Jesus. It says that the outcome of this brief and futile period of choice–in which there is obviously no choice–is a return to the Father, Who will in Justice and Mercy, (not manifested up to date) straighten out the whole intolerable tangle. With so muddled a theory of life and so optimistic a theory of death it is not marvellous that the central hope of theology will be a return to the Father. The more contradictory and confusing this God becomes the more surely will He become theology's central fact.

The injunction of the theologian's God to be compassionate and to love one's neighbour as oneself is the addition of insult to injury. Man is expected to do something God evidently overlooked–in effect to transcend his God. In any case it is the history of theology that the people who have taken its dogmas most seriously have been more concerned with propitiating the Deity than with loving the neighbour. The most logical adherents of the Christian dogma have felt with Torquemada that the best service one can render his erring neighbour is to despatch him to his God before he can do any more damage to his soul's chance of happy return. The fear of God has always been the destruction of the love of humanity.

Science does better. Compelled by the strict terms of its enquiry to confine itself to tangibles, visibles and audibles, it has to leave God–even an interior one in man–out of its research. It has therefore no lofty ideal left but the service of humanity. This service is, however, a trifle vague because, so far as the scientist can see—as scientist—humanity has its origin in birth and its end in death. Before the one and after the other there exists only the vaguest sort of abstraction. So unless the scientist has unscientific interior intimations to bear him up, he must pour all his energy and learning into a flux of forms that have visibility but no meaning. Man is only demonstrably man while he is in the body; therefore, he must argue, body makes man. The beneficiaries of the scientists' devotion have done nothing to deserve it, neither is there any certainty that they can requite it, or even benefit greatly by it. In only a few cases can they transmit it. This is a cold kind of humanism, and I doubt if any scientist with no wider vision than it implies would ever go on with it. So while he is performing a humanistic service, the theory of his effort is to be found elsewhere. He can, just as easily as anyone else, be a man who does the right thing for that wrong reason.

There is a third theory of life, increasingly widespread among us today, immeasurably wider in its sweep than the notions of theology and science, which might conceivably give a motive for humanistic endeavour but which rarely does so. It is that system of thought vaguely described as Hindu philosophy and promulgated in India and the West by exponents of the Advaita Vedanta. Rarely has it been offered in any completeness. What we have is a syncretism drawn from the six Darshanas or philosophical systems of India, better or worse put together.

It starts, as all great philosophies must, with an incognizable First Cause, out of which arises the polarity we recognize as spirit and matter. The Absolute Cause manifests and in the resultant ocean of being myriad centres of consciousness arise, each seeing the other apart from itself and each under the illusion of I and not—I.

These lives begin a long pilgrimage from ignorance through successive stages of self-realization to an ultimate full knowlege of their divinity.

So far there is no division of opinion. This idea of the manifested universe and the flow of souls is common to all Eastern systems and to many Western ones. The modern Vedantin, however, assuming a simple and unbroken rhythm as capable of explaining all phenomena, and as reconciling all contradictions, proceeds to deal with man as having mounted the cosmic stair to the position we now occupy. The Vendantin would say that our present mental consciousness represents our full stature, and that continuing on the wheel of evolution of soul powers and returning life after life to earth, we shall pass presently into a super-human condition and from that on to a higher, so step by step to the innermost. Many of our own order, he would say, have gone on, becoming Mahatmas, Rishis, Arhats, and we must all become so in due course.

This is a great concept, greater by far than any generally accepted theory we have had in the West. It is greater than our theology and greater than our science but as a complete hypothesis it has always been rejected because it does not fit the facts.

The theosophical schools, of which the philosophies are dessicated fragments, refuse it. They say, "No. Unfortunately it is not so simple as all that. There is undoubtedly such an emergence from the Absolute, undoubtedly such a cycle of outpouring and return. Undoubtedly also the evolution or unfolding of the powers of souls is the great law of the Universe. Unfolding consciousness, however, requires also an increasing unfolding of will and the freedom to choose. Whatever permits an individual or an order of individuals to choose permits a wrong choice as well as a right one. If a right choice can result in achievement, a wrong one can result in failure. H.P. Blavatsky speaks of the "necessity of failures even in the ethereal races of Dhyan Chohans."

The theosophist of any school would say, therefore, that man in his present state is not proceeding serenely in his ascent. Somewhere in the past he had made a choice which is now impeding his progress. And even if the theosophist had no more to say about the nature of the choice and the resulting impediments, there are enough indications around us everywhere to show that serious impediments do exist. The theosophist does, however, say more. He says that man—the Ego—is not at the full altitude to which his evolution entitles him, but is considerably below that altitude, and is the partly-conscious possessor of powers more or less in atrophy. There is an order of beings evolving on this earth, a lunar race, but it is far below the stature of man. Man himself is making a bad job of a redemptive act to which the law of the inter-relation of orders of beings has committed him and he is for the most part doing his best to go counter to a law of sacrifice which requires that he raise to the level of mind a creature who without his assistance cannot advance. Because of this failure to lift the animal soul, thereby establishing a rate of progression that will permit him to rise himself, he is in no present process of evolution at all but in one of stagnation. Indeed, in the cases where man is most obstinate in refusing his obligation, and uses the animal organism for selfish and separative magic, he is in a state of active degeneration, with lower levels before him. His remedy against further descent is his memory of the lost wisdom.

Because evolution tends ever to unity, whatever memory we recover will be in terms of a level of unity higher than our present one, a community in which the severances of man from man have formerly disappeared and can be made to disappear again by the exercise of brotherly love.

This is the theosophy of Veda, of Bhagavad Gita and the Upanishads, of the Orphic Mysteries, of Hermes and Plato, of the alchemists, the Rosicrucians, the Sufis, the Kabbalists and of the occultists of the Renaissance in Europe. It is also the theosophy of H.P. Blavatsky and her teachers, so difficult for those who have become indoctrinated with the spurious Hinduism of recent years.

It is also the only "theosophia" which by any conceivable set of conditions can be "remembered" out of our past, as Plato says it must be, or attained by virtue of an earned divinity which all men possess.

These then are the two doctrines that can arise out of the idea of the evolution of the soul. The one is that the soul is proceeding evenly on its way, that it has known nothing higher than it now knows, and that every step is a new one. The other is the same but with the modifying idea of the lapse, of which Kant has said that it is fundamental in religion.

"That the world lieth in wickedness is a complaint as old as history, even as what is still older, poetry . . . All alike nevertheless make the world begin from good: with the Golden Age, with life in Paradise, or one still more happy in communion with heavenly beings. But they represent the happy state as soon vanishing like a dream, and then they fall into badness . . . Later, but much less general, is the opposite, heroic opinion, which has perhaps obtained currency only among philosophers, and in our time chiefly among the instructors of youth, that the world is constantly advancing in precisely the reverse direction, namely from worse to better . . . This opinion, however, is not founded upon experience, if what is meant is moral good or evil, for the history of all times speaks too powerfully against it."

Of the two doctrines, one is a doctrine of ultimate achievement, the other a doctrine of immediate conditions. Each has its place in theosophy but whereas the Vedantin bases his ethic on the ultimate, the theosophist bases his on the immediate.

There is no humanism to be born out of the idea of orderly progression, because none is needed. It is a doctrine of *laisser faire.* If all men are coming out at the same goal—duly and in the course of the cycles—what virtue can there be in fixing one's concern upon the pilgrims. If there is any matter for concern at all it should be the goal.

Humanism can arise only out of the other, the realization that the Ego of man is one of a broken legion, in sore straits in an alien world, and must find his divinity in the restoration of the scattered host.

The line of demarcation between these two positions runs through all human thought and practice. Here are some of the conflicts:

Our Vedantin is the Pollyanna of metaphysics. His scheme is one of glad progress regardless of ethical choice. All suffering is a necessary part of the joyous plan. No matter what a man does, he is doing it for the unfolding of his divine consciousness. The theosophists, on the other hand, have always said that believing this is a glad world is begotten of what one wants to believe. It is not a glad world. On the contrary it is a world of misunderstanding and division, of death and separation and loneliness, of isolation, of tears and sorrow, of cruelty and distorted lusts, of the terror of little children at being born into earth. Gladness is *in spite* of the conditions in which we find ourselves. Gautama Buddha enunciated the doctrine of a sad world out of which we must arise and the Vedantins call him a pessimist.

The Vedantin says there is no urgency. Everything is working out according to immutable plan. All beings must go forward and all must achieve. What are a few scores of years in the sweep of evolution? What is the hurry? But turn to the great theosophists—Gautama, Hermes, Krishna, Jesus. There is the will of man at work in the world, they say, and the will of man is not bound only to the good side of the immutable law. It can be separative as well as unitive; it can do as much evil as it can good. The servitor of mankind who goes to early death, to the faggots and to the rack, who is persecuted in life and slandered in death, is matched by the vampire upon mankind who uses the bondage of the rest to feed his lust. The lovers of mankind find something urgent in man's state. Their world is a field of battle, and they are always too few. Every disciple who comes to them must come as a recruit to an army that never rests. Each enlistment must be an answer to the old question of *The Voice of the Silence;*

"Can there be bliss when all that lives must suffer? Shalt thou be saved and hear the whole world cry?"

The Vedantin argues that reincarnation into this earth is the unalterable law, and then he undertakes to tell how to escape it. The theosophist says that reincarnation is a necessity only until we complete what we came here to do, then we may leave it, unless in compassion we return as teachers to liberate our brothers.

The Vedantin tells us of great time cycles and of a progress that goes step by step with them. In an æon we develop this power, in another æon that; senses come into operation as the cycles unfold. Then if one asks him why anybody should exert any effort at all, why any man should press forward, he will offer some cloudy nonsense about hastening evolution, about speeding up the cycles, as if any man could do that. If he could he would destroy all that is cyclic about them. He would abolish cycles. Theosophists of all schools have, on the contrary, taught "a path to liberation in this life." They say, in effect, "These are not new powers you must steal from the cycles, but old powers you must restore, and you can restore them whenever you will it."

The Vedantin speaks of powers gained anew. When he comes upon a word like "restore" or "regain" he explains it as meaning that all powers are latent in the Absolute and that to gain a power is to draw on a previously existent one. He prefers however to say "attain." The theosophist has always said "attain again." His words are "re-store," "re--new," "re-deem," "re-member," "re-cognize," "re-surrect," "re-ligion," (itself the binding back of something broken), "re-union with the companions of their former toil." The theosophist's figures of speech are of prison-houses of the soul, of bondage, of slavery, of deliverance out of Egypt, of liberation from the wheel of rebirth, of being raised from the dead, from the sepulchre, from the roofed-in cave, from the dark meadow of Ate. They are figures of finding a way out of a labyrinth, of rousing a warrior from sulking in his tent, of rising superior to despondency and going into battle, of rising from lethargy or from drunkenness, of turning from the cities of the plain and going up into the mountains, of forsaking the fleshpots. The theosophist talks of exiles, of wanderers, of prodigal sons who have wasted their substance in a far country, of sons that were dead and are alive again, were lost and are found, of Sophia tempted into the vices of the world, of Narcissus falling in love with his image in the waters of desire, of gods dismembered as Osiris was, of heroes like Odysseus fighting their way home over the raging seas of passions and having to do battle for their old heritage.

The Eastern metaphysician of unbroken rhythms and processes has also—as he must have—a garden-hose theory of illumination. He says our ideals and high aims come from high, kindly beings in the world beyond us. But Hermes and Plato will not have it so. Hermes says, "This race, my son, is never taught, but when it wills it, its memory is restored." Plato makes Socrates say, in the *Meno,* "It is no wonder that she (the soul) should be able to recollect all that she knew before about virtue and other things." And in the *Meno* also he says that the greatest of the things we know, we learned before we were human at all.

The Vedantin has curious ideas about the power of the Ego to go on alone. If you perform austerities until you have shut out the world you can attain to a state in advance of the rest. The great Compassionators agree that within limits you can, but they say of one who tries it that he is a Pratyeka or Ekashringa, which means that he is concerned only with one person—himself. Or they pity him and call him a rhinoceros Buddha—a Buddha of a thick and insensitive skin. There is, they say, by reason of his ancient effort, a previously attained stature he can resume, but if he tries to do it thus without compassion, his nirvana is a condition of negation, of rejection, as long as he can will it, of his bond with the rest of mankind. The great restoration of the high ones cannot be entered alone. It is a communal consciousness.

The Vedantin is amused if you talk of white and black magic. The greatest of the teachers have not been amused. White magic is the return of union: black magic is the inevitable pole of severance from the over-soul and plays far too great a part in the struggle for the redemption of the race to be amusing.

The Vedantin says the soul cannot be destroyed or lost. Such an idea is unthinkable. Divine essence lost? Spirit is indestructible, eternal. And so it is, replies Plotinos, but it is not indivisible. If the Absolute has divided into many, such as you and I also break up into many others. Spirit is indestructible but soul is only an integration and its present integrity is not secure. So we find the old teachers of Yoga suggesting that when a man thinks all he has to do is unite himself with the Oversoul, he is flattering himself. His first task is to unite *himself*—to correct his own tendency to disintegration. He must draw himself out of the multitude of karmic forms into which he has poured his life and by which he is dismembered. When he has re-gathered his own fragments and become the Diamond Soul he may make the restoration of the Unity of which he is himself a fragment.

These are a few of the conflicts, all parts of the greatest battle in human thought. Every lesser conflict stems off from these. What am I to do about my divinity? Shall I go on alone and let the devil take care of the hindmost? This has been the practice of Calvinism and of our Puritan sects. Or shall I find some metaphysical formula that will give me the sweet assurance that the hindmost are softly pillowed in the Great Law and do not need my care? If I can find such a formula I shall have the gratitude of all the lazy, the rich, the top dogs, the feudal-minded, the people who profit by the distress of others. The Brahmin and the Pharisee long ago found such a formula but they pay a heavy price. Some vital current in them stops, their austerities and taboos increase and complicate, their philosophy becomes arid, circular and unserviceable. Filth, squalor and misery grow up around their doors, their world is peopled by pariahs, untouchables, Mlechchas, through whom they must thread their way as they go to prayers. They must spend their lives avoiding the evils they have made.

Or shall I measure my spiritual altitude only by the number of persons for whom I have made myself responsible?

Part III A.

Collectanea by Roy Mitchell

Introduction.

This collectanea has been added to give the background for Roy Mitchell's ideas, to remind the skeptical that this was no hasty conclusion and also to fertilize the student who seeks greater depth in these matters.

Mitchell intuitively knew he had come upon a concept concerning the dualism of man which has long been buried in ancient mysticism. As he followed this thread through his studies on the constitution of man he realized that here was an idea that must again be unfolded. The following collectanea is proof enough of the prodigious labors he undertook to find the fragments which contribute to the truth he sought.

It is quite apparent from these references that Mitchell's starting point came from *The Secret Doctrine* of H. P. Blavatsky. This book is the basic book of the Theosophical Society, which was formed in 1875 by Helena P. Blavatsky, Colonel H. S. Alcott and William Quan Judge in New York City. Though this society is relatively small it has today active groups in many countries of the world. Over the last one hundred years a diversity of views has grown up among its leaders and splinter groups have developed. Nowadays there is a strong tendency for all groups to go back to the original writings of Blavatsky. The word Theosophy is an ancient word meaning "divine knowledge."

Mitchell was a Theosophist who always insisted on the importance of adhering to the original idea sources of Blavatsky. This method was to search for confirming

THE CONSTITUTION OF MAN

Duality	Trinity	Quinary	Septenary				
Western	Western	Medieval	Western	Hindu	Hebrew Kabbala	Greek	Egyptian
God	God	Aether	Spirit	Atma	Tzurah	Pneuma	Khu
		Fire	Spiritual vehicle	Buddhi	Ruach	Pieroma	Khaibit
	Concious mind Ego, I,	Air	Conscious mind Mental vehicle	Manas	Neshameh	Nous	Ba
Animal soul	Animal soul	Water	Passional vehicle Animal soul Shadow	Kama	Nepesh	Phren	Abhati
			Vital essence Breath	Prana	Nur	Pnoe	Shu
		Earth	Astral body	Linga	Tzelem	Psyche	Kha
			Gross body	Sthula	Kush-na-Guf	Soma	Khat

sources which he knew must be tucked away in all religions, traditions, myths and philosophies.

The reader will note contradictions among the references. Mitchell's answer to this was, "Do not become resentful of contradictions–expect them and deal with them with sympathy. Inferences are born of the union of new ideas with what already is there. A new influence fertilizes an old idea lying dormant."

In another small book, *Through Temple Doors*, Mitchell describes the application of his *Exile* ideas to Free Masonry. In this book he assembled a table which delineates the principles in man as a duality, as a trinity, as a fivefold being, and as a sevenfold being. The table reproduced on p. 106 shows the names given by four great religious systems to these principles. It will also be convenient in following the unfamiliar names used in *The Exile* and the collectanea.

As one goes through the collectanea and references in Part III B, some fragments refer to one part of this table and others refer to two or more parts. The table will tie together many of the ideas expressed.

In what follows practically all passages are quotations. The quotation marks have therefore been deleted. Any comments of R.M. or J.L.D. have been indented or bracketed [ ].

The references to the work of others have been set in longer 25 pica lines.

Blavatsky, *Secret Doctrine*.
Vol. II, p. 478.

Adam-Adami is a personation of the dual Adam: of the paradigmatic Adam-Kadmon, the Creator, and of the lower Adam, the terrestrial, who, as the Syrian Kabalists have it, had only Nephesh, the "breath of life", but no Living Soul, until after his Fall.

Blavatsky, *Secret Doctrine*.
Vol. II, p. 98.

Everywhere it is the same. The creating powers produce Man, but fail in their final object. All these logoi strive to endow man with conscious immortal spirit, reflected in the Mind (manas) alone; they fail, and they are all represented as being punished for the failure, if not for the attempt. What is the nature of the punishment? A sentence of imprisonment in the lower or nether region, which is our earth; the lowest in its chain; an "eternity" --- meaning the duration of the life-cycle --- in the darkness of matter, or within animal Man. It has pleased the half ignorant and half designing Church Fathers to disfigure the graphic symbol. They took advantage of the metaphor and allegory found in every old religion to turn them to the benefit of the new one. Thus man was transformed into the darkness of a material hell; his divine consciousness, obtained from his indwelling Principle (the Manasa) or the incarnated Deva, became the glaring flames of the infernal region; and our globe that Hell itself. Pippala, Haoma, the fruit of the Tree of Knowledge, were denounced as the forbidden fruit, and the "Serpent of Wisdom", the Voice of reason and consciousness remained identified for ages with the Fallen Angel, which is the old Dragon, the Devil.

[Vide Part 2. "The Evil Spirit, who or what?) R.M.

Blavatsky, *Secret Doctrine*.
Vol. II, p. 91.

The names of the deities of a certain mystic class change with every Manvantara. Thus the twelve great gods, Jayas, created by Brahma to assist him in the work of creation in the very beginning of the Kalpa, and who, lost in Samadhi, neglected to create --- where-upon they were cursed to be repeatedly born in each Manvantara till the seventh -- are respectively called Ajitas, Tushitas, Satyas, Haris, Vaikunthas, Sadyas, and Adityas; they are Tushitas (in the second Kalpa), and Adityas in this Vaivasvata period (see Vayu Purana), besides other names for each age. But they are identical with the Manasa or Rajasas and these with our incarnating Dhyan Chohans. They are all classes of the Gnana-devas.

Yes, besides those beings, who, like the Yakshas, Gandharvas, Kinaras, etc, etc. taken in their individualities, inhabit the astral plane, there are real Devagnanams, and to these classes of Devas belong the Adityas, the Vairajas, the Kumaras, the Asuras, and all those high celestial beings whom Occult teaching calls Manaswin, the Wise, foremost of all and who would have made all men the self-conscious spiritually intellectual beings they will be, had they not been "cursed" to fall into generation, and to be reborn themselves as mortals for their neglect of duty.

Blavatsky, *Secret Doctrine*.
Vol. II, p. 421. NOTE.

Mankind is obviously divided into god-informed men and lower human creatures. The intellectual difference between the Aryan and other civilized nations and such savages as the South Sea Islanders, is inexplicable on any other grounds. No amount of culture, nor generations of training amid civilization, could raise such human specimens as the Bushmen, the Veddhas of

Ceylon, and some African tribes, to the same intellectual level as the Aryans, the Semites, and the Turanians so called. The "sacred spark" is missing in them and it is they who are the only inferior races on the globe, now happily — owing to the wise adjustment of nature which ever works in that direction — fast dying out. Verily mankind is "of one blood," but not of the same essence. We are the hot-house, artificially quickened plants in nature, having in us a spark, which in them is latent.

The philosophical view of Indian metaphysics places the Root of Evil in the differentiation of the Homogeneous into the Heterogeneous, of the unit into plurality.

Blavatsky, *Secret Doctrine.*
Vol. II, p. 390.

The fallen Angels are made in every ancient system the prototypes of fallen man — allegorically and, those men themselves, — esoterically.

Blavatsky, *Secret Doctrine.*
Vol. II, p. 487.

"But those that came after them, who shooting down like falling stars were enshrined in the shadows — prevailed and to this day": Dhyanis, who by incarnating in those "empty shadows," inaugurated the era of mankind.

Blavatsky, *Secret Doctrine.*
Vol. II, p. 487.

The Asuras who incarnated (call them by any other name), followed in this a law as implacable as any other. They had manifested prior to the Pitris, and as time (in space) proceeds in

Cycles, their turn had come --- hence, the numerous allegories (Vide "Demon est Deus inversus," Part 2., Vol. I.). The name of Asura was first given by the Brahmans indiscriminately to those who opposed their mummeries and sacrifices, as the great Asura called "Asurendra" did.

Blavatsky, *Secret Doctrine*.
Vol. II, p. 487.

. . . the same idea as in our Archaic teachings --- to wit, that the "Fall of the Angels" referred simply to the incarnation of angels "who had broken through the Seven Circles" --- is found in the Zohar.

Blavatsky, *Secret Doctrine*.
Vol. II, p. 420.

The gift of Prometheus thus became a CURSE --- though foreknown and foreseen by the HOST personified in that personage, as his name well shows. It is in this that rests, at one and the same time, its sin and its redemption. For the Host that incarnated in a portion of humanity, though led to it by Karma or Nemesis, preferred free will to passive slavery, intellectual self-conscious pain and even torture --- "while myriad time shall flow" --- to inane, imbecile, instinctual beatitude. Knowing such an incarnation was premature and not in the programme of nature, the heavenly host, "Prometheus", still sacrificed itself to benefit thereby, at least, one portion of mankind. But while saving man from mental darkness, they inflicted upon him the tortures of the self-consciousness of his responsibility --- the result of his free will --- besides every ill to which mortal man and flesh are heir to. This torture Prometheus accepted for himself, since the Host became henceforward blended with the tabernacle prepared for them, which was still unachieved at that period of formation.

Blavatsky, *Secret Doctrine*.
Vol. II, p. 495.

The moon is the deity of the mind (Manas) but only on the lower plane. "Manas is dual --- lunar in the lower, solar in its upper portion," says a commentary. That is to say, it is attracted in its higher aspect towards Buddhi, and in its lower descends into, and listens to the voice of its animal soul full of selfish and sensual desires; and herein is contained the mystery of an adept's as of a profane man's life, as also the post-mortem separation of the divine from the animal man.

Blavatsky, *Secret Doctrine*.
Vol. II, p. 373.

We do not place a bullock or ram over our bullocks or rams, but give them a leader, a shepherd, i.e., a being of a species quite different from their own and of a superior nature. It is just what Saturn did. He loved mankind and placed to rule over it no mortal King or prince but --- "Spirits and genii nature more excellent than that of man."

Blavatsky, *Secret Doctrine*.
Vol. II, p. 373. NOTE.

The *Secret Doctrine* explains and expounds that which Plato says, for it teaches that those "inventors" were gods and demigods (Devas and Rishis) who had become --- some deliberately, some forced to by Karma --- incarnated in man.

Blavatsky, *Secret Doctrine.*
Vol. II, p. 486..

Again, the Tchoon-Tsieoo says allegorically: "one night the stars ceased shining in darkness and deserted it, falling down like rain upon the earth, where they are now hidden." These stars are the Monads.

Blavatsky, *Secrect Doctrine.*
Vol. II, p. 276.

Now the Zohar says that the Ischin, the beautiful B'ne-aleim, were not guilty, but mixed themselves with mortal men because they were sent on earth to do so.

Blavatsky, *Secret Doctrine.*
Vol. II, p. 45.

The whole cycle of the "first War in Heaven", the Tarakamaya, is as full of philosophical as of Cosmogonical and astronomical truths. One can trace therein the biographies of all the planets by the history of their gods and rulers. Usanas (Sukra, or Venus), the bosom friend of Soma and the foe of Brihaspati (Jupiter) the instructor of the gods, whose wife, Tara (or Taraka) had been carried away by the Moon, Soma, --- "of whom he begat Budha" --- took also an active part in this war against "the gods" and forthwith was degraded into a demon (Asura) deity, and so he remains to this day.

Blavatsky, *Secret Doctrine.*
Vol. II, p. 93.

Even in Chaldean exotericism, Beings who refuse to create, i.e. who are said to oppose thereby the Demi-urgos, are also denounced as the Spirits of Darkness. The Suras, who win their intellectual independence, fight the Suras who are devoid thereof, who are shown as passing their lives in profitless ceremonial worship based on blind faith --- a hint now ignored by the orthodox Brahmins --- and forthwith the former become A-Suras. The first and mind-born Sons of the Deity refuse to create progeny, and are cursed by Brahma to be born as men. They are hurled down to Earth, which later on, is transformed, in theological dogma, into the infernal regions.

Blavatsky, *Secret Doctrine*.
Vol. I, p. 445.

Eastern Esotericism has never degraded the One Infinite Deity, the container of all things, to such uses; and this is shown by the absence of Brahma from the Rig Veda and the modest positions occupied therein by Rudra and Vishnu, who became the powerful and great Gods, the "Infinites" of the exoteric creeds, ages later. But even they, "Creators" as the three may be, are not the direct creators and "forefathers of men." The latter are shown occupying a still lower scale, and are called Prajapatis, the Pitris (our lunar ancestors), etc., etc., --- never the "One Infinite God." Esoteric philosophy shows only physical man as created in the image of the Deity; but the latter is but "the minor gods." It is the HIGHER-SELF, the real EGO who alone is divine and GOD.

Blavatsky, *Secret Doctrine*.
Vol. I, p. 267.

Thus, as expressed in the Stanza, the Watchers descended on Earth and reigned over men --- "who are themselves." The reigning kings had finished their cycle on Earth and other worlds, in the preceding Rounds. In the future manvataras they will have risen to higher systems than our planetary world; and it is the Elect of our Humanity, the pioneers on the hard and difficult path of Progress, who will take the place of their predecessors. The next great Manvantara will witness the men of our own life-cycle becoming the instructors and guides of a mankind whose Monads may yet be imprisoned --- semi-conscious --- in the most intellectual of the animal kingdom, while their lower principles will be animating, perhaps, the highest specimens of the Vegetable world.

Blavatsky, *Secret Doctrine*.
Vol. II, p. 78-79.

It thus becomes clear why the Agnishwatta, devoid of the grosser creative fire, hence unable to create physical man, having no double, or astral body, to project, since they were without any form, are shown in exoteric allegories as Yogis, Kumaras (chaste youths), who became "rebels", Asuras, fighting and opposing gods, etc. Yet it is they alone who could complete man, i.e. make of him a self-conscious, almost a divine being --- a god on Earth. The Barhishad, though possessed of creative fire, were devoid of the higher MAHAT-mic element. Being on a level with the lower principles --- those which precede gross objective matter, they could only give birth to the outer man, or rather to the model of the physical, the astral man. Thus, though we see them entrusted with the task by Brahma (the collective Mahat or Universal Divine Mind), the"Mystery of Creation" is repeated on Earth, only in an inverted sense, as in a mirror. It is those who are unable to create the spiritual immortal man, who project the senseless model (the Astral) of the physical Being; and as will be seen, it was those who would not multiply, who sacrificed themselves to the good and salvation of Spiritual Humanity. For, to complete the septenary man, to add to his three lower principles and cement them with the spiritual Monad --- which could never dwell in such a form otherwise than in an absolutely latent state —two connecting principles are needed; Manas and Kama. This required a living Spiritual Fire of the middle Principle from the fifth and third states of Pleroma. But this fire is the possession of the Triangles, not of the (perfect) Cubes, which symbolize the Angelic Beings: the former having from the first creation got hold of it and being said to have appropriated it for themselves, as in the allegory of Prometheus. These are the active, and therefore—in Heaven— no longer "pure" Beings. They have become the independent and free intelligence, shown in every Theogony as fighting for that independence and freedom, and hence --- in the ordinary sense—"rebellious to the divine passive law." These are then those "Flames" (the Agnishwatta) who as shown in Sloka 13, "remain behind" instead of going along with the others to create men on Earth. But the true esoteric meaning is that most of them were destined to incarnate as the Egos of the forthcoming crop of Mankind. The human Ego is neither Atman nor Buddhi, but the higher Manas --- the intellectual fruition and the efflorescence of the intellectual self-conscious Egotism --- in the higher spiritual sense. The ancient works refer to it as Karana Sarira on the plane of Sutrama, which is the golden thread, on which like beads, the various personalities of this higher Ego are strung. If the reader was told, as in the semi-esoteric allegories, that these Beings were returning Nirvanees, from preceding Maha-Manvantaras --- ages of incalculable duration which have rolled away in the Eternity, a still more incalculable time ago --- he would hardly understand the text correctly; while some Vedantin might say: "This is not so; the Nirvanee can never return"; which is true during the Manvantara he belongs to, but is erroneous where Eternity is concerned.

Blavatsky, *Secret Doctrine.*
Vol. II, p. 94.

As to their fashioners of "Ancestors" --- those Angels who in the exoteric legends, obeyed the law --- they must be identical with the Barishad Pitris, or the Pitar-Devata, i.e. those possessed of the physical creative fire. They could only create, or rather clothe, the human Monads with their own astral Selves, but they could not make man in their image and likeness. "Man must not be like one of us," say the creative gods, entrusted with the fabrication of the lower animal --- but higher; (see Con. and Plato's Timaeus). Their creating the semblance of men out of their own divine Essence means, esoterically, that it is they who became the first Race and thus shared its destiny and further evolution. They would not simply because they could not, give to man that sacred spark which burns and expands into the flower of human reason and self-consciousness, for they had not it to give. This was left to that class of Devas who became symbolized in Greece under the name of Prometheus, to those who had nought to do with the physical body, yet everything with the purely spiritual man. (See Part 2 of this volume, "The Fallen Angels"; also "The Gods of Light proceed from the Gods of Darkness.")

Blavatsky, *Secret Doctrine.*
Vol. II, p. 93.

Even in Chaldean exotericism, Beings who refuse to create i.e. who are said to oppose thereby the Demi-urgos, are also denounced as the Spirits of Darkness. The Suras, who win their intellectual independence, fight the Suras who are devoid thereof, who are shown as passing their lives in profitless ceremonial worship based on blind faith---a hint now ignored by the orthodox Brahmins---and forthwith the former become A-Suras. The first and mind-born Sons of the Deity refuse to create progeny, and are cursed by Brahma to be born as men. They are hurled down to Earth, which later on is transformed, in theological dogma, into the infernal regions.

Blavatsky, *Secret Doctrine*.
Vol. II, p. 89.

There are seven classes of Pitris, as shown below, three incorporeal and four corporeal; and two kinds, the Agnishwatta and the Barhishad. And we may add that, as there are two kinds of Pitris, so there is a double and a triple set of Barishad and Agnishwatta. The former, having given birth to their astral doubles, are reborn as Sons of Atri, and are the "Pitris of the Demons", or corporeal beings, on the authority of Manu (III. 196); while the Agnishwatta are reborn as Sons of Marichi (a son of Brahma), and are the Pitris of the Gods (Manu again, Matsya and Padma Puranas and Kulluka in the Laws of the Manavas, III. 195). Moreover the Vayu Purana declares all the seven orders to have originally been the first gods, the Vairajas, whom Brahma "with the eye of Yoga, beheld in the eternal spheres, and who are the gods of gods"; and the Matsya adds that the Gods worshipped them; while the Harivansa (S. I, 935) distinguishes the Virajas as one class of the Pitris only--a statement corroborated in the Secret Teachings, which, however, identify the Virajas with the elder Agnishwattas and the Rajasas, or Abhutarajasas, who are incorporeal without even an astral phantom. Vishnu is said, in most of the MSS to have incarnated in and through them. "In the Rauvata Manvantara, again, Hari, best of gods, was born of Sambhuti, as the Divine Manasas —originating with the deities called Rajasas." Sambhuti was the daughter of Daksha, and wife of Marichi, the father of the Agnishwatta, who along with the Rajasas, are ever associated with Manasas. As remarked by a far more able Sanskritist than Wilson, Mr. Fitzedward Hall, "Manasa is no inappropriate name for a deity associated with the Rajasas. We appear to have in it Manasam—the same as Manas—with the change of termination required to express male personification" (Vishnu Purana Book III. ch. I, p. 17 footnote). All the sons of Viraja are Manasa, says Nilankantha. And Viraja is Brahma, and therefore the incorporeal Pitris are called Virajas and being the sons of Viraja, says Vayu Purana.

Blavatsky, *Secret Doctrine*.
Vol. I, p. 230.

To our spiritual perceptions, however, and to our inner spiritual eye, the Elohim or Dhyanis are no more an abstraction than our soul and spirit are to us. Reject the one and you reject the other--since that which is the surviving Entity in us is partly the direct emanation from, and partly those celestial Entities themselves.

Blavatsky, *Secret Doctrine*.
Vol. II, p. 44. NOTE.

Apollo Karneios is certainly a Greek transformation from the Hindu Krishna Karna. "Karna" means radiant from "carne", "a ray" and Karneios, which was a title of Apollo with the Celts as with the Greeks, meant "Sun born".

Blavatsky, *Secret Doctrine*.
Vol. II, p. 228.

The archaic commentaries explain, as the reader must remember, that, of the host of Dhyanis, whose turn it was to incarnate as the Egos of the immortal, but, on this plane, senseless monads--that some "obeyed" (the law of evolution) immediately when the men of the Third Race became physiologically and physically ready, i.e., when they had separated into sexes. These were those early conscious Beings who, now adding conscious knowledge and will to their inherent Divine purity, created by Kriyasakti the semi-Divine man, who became the seed on earth for future adepts. Those, on the other hand, who, jealous of their intellectual freedom (unfettered as it then was by the bonds of matter), said: "We can choose . . . we have wisdom" (See verse 24), and incarnated far later---these had their first Karmic punishment prepared for them. They got bodies (physiologically) inferior to their astral models, because their chhayas had belonged to progenitors of an inferior degree in the seven classes. As to those "Sons of Wisdom" who had "deferred" their incarnation till the Fourth Race, which was already tainted (physiologically) with sin and impurity, they produced a terrible cause, the Karmic result of which weighs on them to this day. It was produced in themselves, and they became the carriers of that iniquity for aeons to come, because the bodies they had to inform had become defiled through their own procrastination.

Blavatsky, *Secret Doctrine.*
Vol. II, p. 422.

The modern Prometheus has now become Epi-metheus, "he who sees only after the event"; because the universal philanthropy of the former has long ago degenerated into selfishness and self-adoration, Man will re-become the free Titan of old, but not before cyclic evolution has re-established the broken harmony between the two natures---the terrestrial and the divine; after which he becomes impermeable to the lower titanic forces, invulnerable in his personality, and immortal in his individuality, which cannot happen before every animal element is eliminated from his nature. When man understands that "Deus non fecit mortem" (Sap. I. 13.), but that man has created it himself, he will re-become the Prometheus before his Fall.

[See also *A Second Key to Prometheus,* Vol. II, Part II, p.519.]

Blavatsky, *Secret Doctrine.*
Vol. II, p. 525.

Decharme, at any rate, seems to have a correct glimmering of the truth; for he unconsciously corroborates by his remarks all that the Occult sciences teach with regard to the Manas Devas, who have endowed man with the consciousness of his immortal soul; that consciousness which hinders man "from foreseeing death," and makes him know he is immortal.

> [(Note to foregoing) The monad of the animal is as immortal as that of man, yet the brute knows nothing of this; it lives an animal life of sensation just as the first human would have lived, when attaining physical development in the Third Race, had it not been for the Agnishwatta and the Manasa Pitris.]
>
> [See "Manasa" Glossary.] R.M.

Blavatsky, *Secret Doctrine.*
Vol. II, p. 81.

Between man and the animal—whose Monads (or Jivas) are fundamentally identical—there is the impassable abyss of Mentality and Self-consciousness. What is human mind in its higher aspect whence comes it, if it is not a portion of the essence—and, in some rare cases of incarnation, the very essence—of a higher Being: one from a higher and divine plane? Can man—a god in the animal form—be the product of Material Nature by evolution alone, even as is the animal, which differs from man in external shape, but by no means in the materials of its physical fabric, and is informed by the same, though undeveloped, Monad—seeing that the intellectual potentialities of the two differ as the Sun does from the Glow-worm? And what is it that created such difference, unless man is an animal plus a living god within his physical shell? Let us pause and ask ourselves seriously the question, regardless of the vagaries and sophisms of both the materialistic and the psychological modern sciences.

Blavatsky, *Secret Doctrine*.
Vol. II, p. 81.

The mystery attached to the highly spiritual ancestors of the divine man within the earthly man is very great. His dual creation is hinted at in the Puranas, though its esoteric meaning can be approached only by collating together the many varying accounts, and reading them in their symbolical and allegorical character. So it is in the Bible, both in Genesis and even in the Epistles of Paul. For that creator, who is called in the second chapter of Genesis the "Lord God" is in the original the Elohim, or Gods (the Lords), in the plural; and while one of them makes the earthly Adam of dust, the other breathes into him the breath of life, and the third makes of him a living soul (II. 7), all of which readings are implied in the plural number of the Elohim.

Blavatsky, *Secret Doctrine*.
Vol. II, p. 167.

It does not mean that Monads entered forms in which other Monads already were. They were "Essences," "Intelligences," and conscious spirits; entities seeking to become still more conscious by uniting with more developed matter. Their essence was too pure to be distinct from the universal essence; but their "Egos," or Manas (since they are called Manasaputra, born of "Mahat," or Brahma) had to pass through earthly human experiences to become all-wise, and be able to start on the returning ascending cycle.

Blavatsky, *Secret Doctrine*.
Vol. II, p. 285.

The worshippers were giants in stature; but they were giants in knowledge and learning, though it came to them more easily than it does to the men of our modern times. Their Science was innate in them. The Lemure-Atlantean had no need of discovering and fixing in his memory that which his informing PRINCIPLE knew at the moment of its incarnation. Time alone, and the evergrowing obtuseness of matter in which the Principles had clothed themselves, could, the one, weaken the memory of their pre-natal knowledge, the other, blunt and even extinguish every spark of the spiritual and divine in them. Therefore had they, from the first, fallen victims to their animal natures and bred "monsters"–i.e., men of distinct varieties from themselves.

Blavatsky, *Secret Doctrine*.
Vol. II, p. 88.

How precise and true is Plato's expression, how profound and philosophical his remark on the (human) soul or EGO, when he defined it as "a compound of the same and the other." And yet how little this hint has been understood, since the world took it to mean that the soul was the breath of God, of Jehovah. It is "the same and the other," as the great Initiate-Philosopher said; for the EGO (the "Higher Self" when merged with and in the Divine Monad) is Man, and yet the same as the "OTHER," the Angel in him incarnated, as the same with the universal MAHAT. The great classics and philosophers felt this truth, when saying that "there must be something within us which produces our thoughts, Something very subtle; it is a breath; it is fire; it is ether; it is quintessence; it is a slender likeness; it is an intellection; it is a number; it is harmony. . . . . " (Voltaire).

Blavatsky, *Secret Doctrine.*
Vol. II, p. 252.

. . . . . the two higher principles can have no individuality on Earth, cannot be man, unless there is (a) the Mind, the Manas-Ego, to cognize itself, and (b) the terrestrial false personality, or the body of egotistical desires and personal Will, to cement the whole, as if round a pivot (which it is, truly), to the physical form of man. It is the Fifth and the Fourth Principles--Manas and Kama rupa--that contain the dual personality: the real Immortal Ego (if it assimilates itself to the two higher) and the false and transitory personality, the mayavi or astral body, so-called, or the animal-human Soul--. . . . .

Blavatsky, *Secret Doctrine.*
Vol. II, p. 421.

Spiritual evolution being incapable of keeping pace with the physical, once its homogeneity was broken by the admixture, the gift of fires by Prometheus thus became the chief cause, if not the sole origin of Evil! The allegory which shows Kronos cursing Zeus for dethroning him, (in the primitive "golden" age of Saturn, when all men were demi-gods), and for creating a physical race of men weak and helpless in comparison; and then as delivering to his (Zeus') revenge the culprit, who despoiled the gods of their prerogative of creation and who thereby raised man to their level, intellectually and spiritually---is highly philosophical.

Blavatsky, *Secret Doctrine.*
Vol. II, p. 421.

In the case of Prometheus, Zeus represents the Host of the

primeval progenitors, of the PITAR, the "Fathers" who created man senseless and without any mind; while the divine Titan stands for the Spiritual creators, the devas who "fell" into generation. The former are spiritually lower, but physically stronger than the "Prometheans": therefore, the latter are shown conquered. "The lower Host, whose work the Titan spoiled, and thus defeated the plans of Zeus," was on this earth in its own sphere and plane of action; whereas, the superior Host was an exile from Heaven, who had got entangled in the meshes of matter. They (the inferior "Host") were masters of all the Cosmic and lower titanic forces; the higher Titan possessed only the intellectual and spiritual fire.

Blavatsky, *Secret Doctrine.*
Vol. II, p. 422.

The drama of the struggle of Prometheus with the Olympic Tyrant and despot, sensual Zeus, one sees enacted daily within our actual mankind: the lower passions chain the higher aspirations to the rock of matter, to generate in many a case a vulture of sorrow, pain, and repentance. In every case one sees once more--

> "A god . . . in fetters, anguish fraught;
> The foe of Zeus, in hatred held by all . . . . ."

A god, bereft even of that supreme consolation of Prometheus, who suffered in self-sacrifice--

> "For that to men he bare too fond a mind . . . . ."

as the devine Titan is moved by altruism, but the mortal man by Selfishness and Egoism in every instance.

Blavatsky, *Secret Doctrine*.
Vol. II, p. 90.

We could multiply our proofs ad infinitum, but it is useless. The wise will understand our meaning, the unwise are not required to. There are thirty-three crores, or 330 millions, of gods in India. But, as remarked by the learned lecturer on the *Bhagavad Gita*, "they may be all devas, but are by no means all 'gods', in the high spiritual sense one attributes to the term." "This is an unfortunate blunder," he remarks, "generally committed by Europeans. Deva is a kind of spiritual being, and because the same word is used in ordinary parlance to mean god, it by no means follows that we have to worship thirty-three crores of gods." And he adds suggestively: "These beings, as may be naturally inferred have a certain affinity with one of the three component Upadhis (basic principles) into which we have divided man."
(Vide Theosophist, Feb., 1887, et. seq.)

Blavatsky, *Secret Doctrine*.
Vol. II, p. 92.

"The subtle bodies remain without understanding (Manas) until the advent of the Suras (Gods) now called Asuras (not Gods)," says the Commentary.

"Not-Gods", for the Brahmins, perhaps, but the highest Breaths, for the Occultist; since those progenitors (Pitar), the formless and the intellectual, refuse to build man, but endow him with mind; the four corporeal classes creating only his body.

Blavatsky, *Secret Doctrine*.
Vol. II, p. 94.

The supposed "rebels" then, were simply those who, compelled by Karmic law to drink the cup of gall to its last bitter drop, had to incarnate anew, and thus make responsible thinking entities of the astral statues projected by their inferior brethren. Some are said to have refused, because they had not in them the requisite materials—i.e. an astral body—since they were arupa. The refusal of others had reference to their having been Adepts and Yogis of long past preceding Manvantaras; another mystery. But, later on, as Nirmanakayas, they sacrificed themselves for the good and salvation of the Monads which were waiting for their turn, and which otherwise would have had to linger for countless ages in irresponsible, animal-like, though in appearance, human forms. It may be a parable and an allegory within an allegory. Its solution is left to the intuition of the student, if he only reads that which follows with his spiritual eye.

Blavatsky, *Secret Doctrine*.
Vol. II, p. 274.

The "Fallen Angels," so-called, are Humanity itself. The Demon of Pride, Lust, Rebellion, and Hatred has never had any being before the appearance of physical conscious man. It is man who has begotten, nurtured, and allowed the fiend to develop in his heart; he, again, who has contaminated the indwelling god in himself, by linking the pure spirit with the impure demon of matter. And, if the Kabalistic saying, "Demon est Deus inversus" finds its metaphysical and theoretical corroboration in dual manifested nature, its practical application is found in Mankind alone.

Blavatsky, *Secret Doctrine*.
Vol. II, p. 377.

It is the symbolical representation of the great struggle between divine wisdom, nous and its earthly reflection, Psyche, or between Spirit and Soul, in Heaven and on Earth. In Heaven—because the divine MONAD had voluntarily exiled itself therefrom, to descend, for incarnating purposes, to a lower plane and thus transform the animal of clay into an immortal god. For, as Eliphas Levi tells us, "the angels aspire to become Men; for the perfect man, the man-god, is above even angels." On Earth---because no sooner had Spirit descended than it was strangled in the coils of matter.

Blavatsky, *Secret Doctrine*.
Vol. II, p. 167.

We now come to an important point with regard to the double evolution of the human race. The Sons of Wisdom, or the spiritual Dhyanis, had become "intellectual" through their contact with matter, because they had already reached, during previous cycles of incarnation, that degree of intellect which enabled them to become independent and self-conscious entities, on this plane of matter. They were reborn only by reason of Karmic effects. They entered those who were "ready" and became the Arhats, or sages, alluded to above. This needs explanation.

Blavatsky, *Secret Doctrine*.
Vol. II, p. 96.

Nevertheless, as the illusionary distinction exists, it requires a lower order of creative angels to "create" inhabitated globes--especially ours--or to deal with matter on this earthly plane. The philosophical Gnostics were the first to think so, in the historical period, and to invent various systems upon this theory. Therefore in their schemes of creation, one always finds their Creators occupying a place at the very foot of the ladder of spiritual Being. With them, those who created our earth and its mortals were placed on the very limit of mayavic matter, and their followers were taught to think---to the great disgust of the Church Fathers--that for the creation of those wretched races, in a spiritual and a moral sense, which grace our globe, no high divinity could be made responsible, but only angels of a low hierarchy, to which class they relegated the Jewish God, Jehovah.

Blavatsky, *Secret Doctrine*.
Vol. II, p. 232.

There is an eternal cyclic law of re-births, and the series is headed at every new Manvantaric dawn by those who had enjoyed their rest from re-incarnations in previous Kalpas for incalculable Aeons–by the highest and the earliest Nirvanees. It was the turn of those "Gods" to incarnate in the present Manvantara; hence their presence on Earth, and the ensuing allegories; hence, also the perversion of the original meaning. The Gods who had fallen into generation, whose mission it was to complete divine man, are found represented later on as Demons, evil Spirits and fiends, at feud and war with Gods, or the irresponsible agents of the one Eternal law.

Blavatsky, *Secret Doctrine*.
Vol. II, p. 237.

. . . . . the Rosicrucians, who were well acquainted with the secret meaning of the tradition, kept it to themselves, teaching merely that the whole of creation was due to, and the result of, that legendary "War in Heaven" brought on by the rebellion of the angels against creative law, or the Demiurge.

Blavatsky, *Secret Doctrine*.
Vol. II, p. 232.

Nor have the semi-esoteric dogmas of Puranic Hinduism failed to evolve very suggestive symbols and allegories concerning the rebellious and fallen gods. The Puranas teem with them; and we find a direct hint as the truth in the frequent allusions of Parasara (Vishnu Purana), to all those Rudras, Asuras, Kumaras and Munis, having to be born in every age, to re-incarnate in every Manvantara. This (esoterically) is equivalent to saying that the FLAMES born of the Universal Mind (Mahat), owing to the mysterious workings of Karmic Will and an impulse of Evolutionary Law, had, as in Pymander—without any gradual transition—landed on this Earth, having broken through the seven Circles of fire, or the seven intermediate Worlds, in short.

Blavatsky, *Secret Doctrine.*
Vol. II, p. 237.

The Kabala teaches that Pride and Presumption—the two chief prompters of Selfishness and Egotism—are the causes that emptied heaven of one third of its divine denizens—mystically, and of one third of the stars. . . . .

Blavatsky, *Secret Doctrine.*
Vol. II, p. 268.

This war will last till the inner and divine man adjusts his outer and terrestrial self to his own spiritual nature. Till then the dark and fierce passions of the former will be at eternal feud with his master, the Divine Man. But the animal will be tamed one day, because its nature will be changed, and harmony will reign once more between the two as before the "Fall," when even mortal man was created by the Elements and was not born.

Blavatsky, *Secret Doctrine*.
Vol. II, p. 275.

Add to it the claim that a portion of the Mankind in the Third Race—all those Monads of men who had reached the highest point of Merit and Karma in the preceding Manvantara—owed their psychic and rational natures to divine Beings hypostasizing into their fifth principles, and the *Secret Doctrine* must lose caste in the eyes of not only Materialism but even of dogmatic Christianity. For, no sooner will the latter have learned that those angels are identical with their "Fallen" Spirits, than the esoteric tenet will be proclaimed most terribly heretical and pernicious.

Blavatsky, *Secret Doctrine*.
Vol. II, p. 232. NOTE.

We have a passage from a Master's letter which has a direct bearing on these incarnating angels. Says the letter: "Now there are, and there must be, failures in the ethereal races of the many classes of the Dhyan-Chohans, or Devas (progressed entities of a previous planetary period), as well as among men. But still, as the failures are too progressed and spiritualized to be thrown back forcibly from Dhyan-Chohanship into the vortex of a new primordial evolution through the lower Kingdoms, this then happens. Where a new solar system has to be evolved these Dhyan-Chohans are borne in by influx 'ahead' of the Elementals (Entities . . . . . to be developed into humanity at a future time) and remain as a latent or inactive spiritual force, in the aura of a nascent world . . . . . until the stage of human evolution is reached . . . . . Then they become an active force and commingle with the Elementals, to develop little by little the full type of humanity." That is to say, to develop in, and endow man with his Self-conscious mind, or Manas.

Blavatsky, *Secret Doctrine*.
Vol. II, p. 88.

The Progenitors of Man, called in India "Fathers," Pitara or Pitris, are the creators of our bodies and lower principles. They are ourselves, as the first personalities, and we are they. Primeval man would be "the bone of their bone and the flesh of their flesh," if they had body and flesh. As stated, they were "lunar Beings."

The Endowers of man with his conscious, immortal EGO, are the "Solar Angels"–whether so regarded metaphorically or literally. The mysteries of the Conscious EGO or human Soul are great. The esoteric name of these "Solar Angels" is, literally, the "Lords" (Nath) of "Persevering ceaseless devotion" (Pranidhana). Therefore they of the fifth principle (Manas) seem to be connected with, or to have originated the system of the Yogis who make of Pranidhana their fifth observance (see Yoga Shastra, 2., 32.) It has already been explained why the trans-Himalayan Occultists regard them as evidently identical with those who in India are termed Kumaras. Agnishwattas, and the Barhishads.

Blavatsky, *Secret Doctrine*.
Vol. II, p. 77.

The Secret teachings show the divine Progenitors creating men on seven portions of the globe "each on his lot"–i.e., each a different race of men externally and internally, and on different Zones. This polygenistic claim is considered elsewhere (vide Stanza 7). But who are "They" who create, and the "Lords of the Flame", "who do not"? Occultism divides the "Creators" into twelve classes; of which four have reached liberation to the end of the "Great Age," the fifth is ready to reach it, but still remains active on the intellectual planes, which seven are under direct Karmic law. These last act on the man-bearing globes of our chain.

Blavatsky. Glossary.

THUMOS. (Gr). The astral, animal soul, the Kama-Manas; Thumos means passion, desire and confusion and is so used by Homer. The word is probably derived from the Sanskrit Tamas, which has the same meaning.

PERSONALITY. In Occultism—which divides man into seven principles, considering him under the three aspects of the divine, the thinking or the rational, and the animal man—the lower quaternary or the purely astrophysical being; while by Individuality is meant the Higher Triad, considered as a Unity. Thus the Personality embraces all the characteristics and memories of one physical life, while the Individuality is the imperishable Ego which re-incarnates and clothes itself in one personality after another.

MARUT JIVAS. (SK). The monads of Adepts who have attained the final liberation, but prefer to re-incarnate on earth for the sake of Humanity. Not to be confused, however, with the Nirmanakayas, who are far higher.

MARA. (SK). The god of Temptation, the Seducer who tried to turn away Buddha from his Path. He is called the "Destroyer" and "Death" (of the Soul). One of the names of Kama, God of love.

MANASAS. (SK). Those who endowed humanity with manas or intelligence, the immortal EGOS in men.

MANASA DHYANIS. (SK). The highest Pitris in the Puranas; the Agnishwattas, or Solar Ancestors of Man, those who made of Man a rational being, by incarnating in the senseless forms of semi-ethereal flesh of the men of the third race.

Blavatsky. Glossary.

KAMA-MANAS. (SK). "the mind of desire." With the Buddhists it is the sixth of the Chadayatans, or the six organs of knowledge, hence the highest of these, synthesized by the seventh called Klichta, the spiritual perception of that which defiles this (lower) Manas, or the "Human-animal Soul," as the Occultists term it. While the Higher Manas or the Ego is directly related to Vijnana (the 10th of the 12 Nidanas) which is the perfect knowledge of all forms of knowledge, whether relating to objects or subject in the nidanic concatenation of causes and effects, the lower, the Kama Manas is but one of the Indriya or organs (roots) of Sense. Very little can be said of the dual Manas here, as the doctrine that treats of it, is correctly stated only in esoteric works. Its mention can thus be only very superficial.

MANAS. (SK). Lit., "the mind," the mental faculty which makes of man an intelligent and moral being and distinguishes him from mere animal, a synonym of Mahat. Esoterically, however, it means, when unqualified, the Higher Ego, or the sentient, reincarnating Principle in man. When qualified it is called by Theosophists Buddhi-Manas, or the Spiritual Soul in contradistinction to its human reflection—Kama-Manas.

KARMA . . . . . When Buddhism teaches that "Karma is that moral kernel (of any being) which alone survives death and continues in transmigration" or reincarnation, it simply means that there remains nought after each Personality but the causes produced by it, causes which are undying, i.e. which cannot be eliminated from the Universe until replaced by their ligitimate effects, and wiped out by them, so to speak, and such causes—unless compensated during the life of the person who produced them with adequate effects, will follow the reincarnated Ego, and reach it in its subsequent reincarnation until a harmony be-

Blavatsky. Glossary.

tween effects and causes is fully re-established. No "personality" —a mere bundle of material atoms and of instinctual and mental characteristics—can of course continue, as such, in the world of pure Spirit. Only that which is immortal in its very nature and divine in its essence, namely, the Ego, can exist forever. And as it is that Ego which chooses the personality it will inform, after each Devachan, and which receives through these personalities the effects of the Karmic causes produced, it is therefore the Ego, that self which is the "moral kernel" referred to and embodied karma, "which alone survives death."

LARES. (Lat). . . . . The Lares are the manes or ghosts of disembodied people. Apuleius says that the tumulary inscription, To the gods manes who lived, meant that the Soul had been transformed in a Lemure; and adds that though "the human Soul is a demon that our languages may name genius," and "is an immortal god though in a certain sense she is born at the same time as the man in whom she is, yet we may say that she dies in the same way that she is born," which means in plainer language that Lares and Lemures are simply the shells cast off by the EGO the high spiritual and immortal Soul, whose shell, and also its astral reflection, the animal Soul, die, whereas the higher Soul prevails throughout eternity.

KAUMARA (SK). The "Kumara Creation," the virgin youths who sprang from the body of Brahma.

KUMARA. (SK). A virgin boy, or young celibate. The first Kumaras are the seven sons of Brahma, born out of the limbs of the god, in the so-called ninth creation. It is stated that the name was given to them owing to their formal refusal to "procreate their species," and so they "remained Yogis," as the legend says.

Blavatsky. Glossary.

KUMARABUDHI. (SK). An epithet given to the human "Ego."

KARABTANOS. (Gr.) The spirit of blind or animal desire, the symbol of Kama-rupa. The Spirit "without sense or judgement" in the Codex of the Nazarenes. He is the symbol of matter and stands for the father of the seven spirits of concupiscence begotten by him on his mother, the "Spiritus" or Astral Light.

INDIVIDUALITY. One of the names given in Theosophy and Occultism to the Human Higher Ego. We make a distinction, between the immortal and divine Ego, and the mortal human Ego which perishes. The latter, or "personality" (personal Ego), survives the dead body only for a time in the Kama Loka; the Individuality prevails forever.

INNER MAN. An occult term, used to designate the true and immortal Entity in us, not the outward and mortal form of clay that we call our body. The term applies, strictly speaking, only to the Higher Ego, the "astral man" being the appellation of the Double and Kama Rupa or the surviving eidolon.

IMAGE. Occultism permits no other image than that of the living image of divine man (the symbol of Humanity) on earth. The Kabbala teaches that this divine Image, the copy of the sublime and holy upper Image (the Elohim), has now changed into another similitude, owing to the development of men's sinful nature. It is only the upper divine Image (the Ego) which is the same; the lower (personality) has changed, and man, now fearing the wild beasts, has grown to bear on his face the similitude of many of them. (Zohar I. fol. 71a.) In the early period of Egypt there were no images, but later, as Lenormand says: "In the sanctuaries of Egypt they divided the properties of nature and consequently of Divinity (the Elohim, or Egos), into seven abstract qualities, characterized each by an emblem, which are matter, cohesion, fluxion, coagulation, accumulation, station, and division." These were all attributes symbolized in various images.

IMAGINATION. In Occultism this is not to be confused with fancy, as it is one of the plastic powers of the higher Soul, and is the memory of the preceding incarnation, which, however disfigured by the lower Manas, yet rests always on the ground of truth. ("Preceding incarnations must include pre-human ones to fulfil Plato's doctrine.")

IAMBLICHOS. (Gr.) . . . . . the theurgic invocation by which Egyptian Hierophant or Indian Mahatma, of old, could clothe their own or any other person's astral double with the appearance of its Higher EGO, or what Bulwer Lytton terms the "Luminous Self," the Augoeides, and confabulate with IT. This it is which Iamblichos and many others, including the mediaeval Rosicrucians, meant by union with Deity.

[See also Jacob Boehme's vision of God.] R.M.

HUMANITY. Occultly and Kabbalistically, the whole of mankind is symbolized, by Manu in India; by Vajrasattva or Dorjesempa, the head of the Seven Dhyani, in Northern Buddhism; and by Adam Kadmon in the Kabbala. All these represent the totality of mankind whose beginning is in this androgenic protoplast, and whose end is in the Absolute, beyond all these symbols and myths of human origin. Humanity is a great Brotherhood by virtue of the sameness of the material from which it is formed physically and morally. Unless, however, it becomes a Brotherhood also intellectually, it is no better than a superior genus of animals.

Blavatsky. Glossary.

HOANG-TY. (Chin.) "The Great Spirit." His Sons are said to have aquired new wisdom, and imparted what they knew before mortals, by falling—like the rebellious angels—into the "Valley of Pain," which is allegorically our Earth. In other words they are identical with the "Fallen Angels" of exoteric religions, and with the reincarnating Egos, esoterically.

EVOLUTION. The development of higher orders of animals from lower. As said in Isis Unveiled: "modern Science holds but to a one-sided physical evolution, prudently avoiding and ignoring the higher or spiritual evolution, which would force our contempories to confess the superiority of the ancient philosophers and psychologists over themselves. The ancient sages, ascending to the UNKNOWABLE made their starting point from the first manifestation of the unseen, the unavoidable, and, from a strictly logical reasoning, the absolutely necessary creative Being, the Demiurgos of the universe. . . Evolution began with them from pure spirit, which decending lower and lower down, assumed at last a visible and comprehensible form, and became matter. Arrived at this point, they speculated in the Darwinian method, but on a far more large and comprehensive basis."

EGO. (Lat.) "Self," the consciousness in man "I am I"—or the feeling of "I-am-ship." Esoteric philosophy teaches the existence of two Egos in man, the mortal or personal, and the Higher, the Divine and the Impersonal, calling the former "personality" and the latter "Individuality."

EGOITY. From the word "Ego." Egoity means "individuality" never "personality," and is the opposite of egoism or selfishness," the characteristic par excellence of the latter.

DAEMON. (Gr.) In the original Hermetic works and in the

Blavatsky. Glossary.

ancient classics it has a meaning identical with that of "god," "angel," or "genius." The Daemon of Socrates is the incorruptible part of the man, or rather the real inner man which we call Nous or the rational divine Ego. . . . .

BOEHME (Jacob). He was a thorough born Mystic, and evidently of a constitution which is most rare, one of those fine natures whose material envelope impedes in no way the direct, if only occasional, inter-communion between the intellectual and spiritual Ego. It is the Ego which Jacob Boehme, like so many other untrained mystics, mistook for God; "Man must acknowledge," he writes, "that his knowledge is not his own, but from God, who manifests the Ideas of Widsom to the Soul of Man, in what measure he pleases." Had this great Theosophist mastered Eastern Occultism he might have expressed it otherwise. He would have known then that the "god" who spoke through his poor uncultured and untrained brain, was his own divine Ego, the omniscient Deity within himself, and that what that Deity gave out was not "in what measure he pleased," but in the measure of the capacities of the mortal and temporary dwelling IT formed.

BARHISHAD. (SK). A class of "lunar" Pitris or "Ancestors," Fathers, who are believed in popular superstition to have kept in their past incarnations the household sacred flame and made fire-offerings. Esoterically the Pitris who evolved their shadows or "chhayas" to make therewith the first man.
(See *Secret Doctrine*. Vol. II.)

AGNOIA. (Gr.) "Divested of reason," lit., "irrationality," when speaking of the Animal Soul. According to Plutarch, Pythagoras and Plato divided the human soul into two parts (the higher and lower manas)—the rational or noetic and the irrational or agnoia, sometimes written "annoia."

ANOIA. (Gr.) "want of understanding," "folly," Anoia is the name given by Plato and others to the lower Manas when too closely allied with Kama, which is irrational, (agnoia). The Greek word agnoia is evidently a derivation from and cognate to the Sanskrit word ajnana (phonetically agnyana) or ignorance, irrationality, absence of knowledge.

ANTAHKARANA. (SK) or Antaskarana. The term has various meaningss which differ with every school of philosophy and sect. Thus Sankaracharya renders the word as "understanding"; others as "the internal instrument, the Soul, formed by the thinking principle and egoism," whereas the Occultists explain it as the path or bridge between the higher and the Lower Manas, the divine Ego and the personal Soul of man. It serves as a medium of communication between the two, and conveys from the Lower to the Higher Ego all those personal impressions and thoughts of men which can, by their nature, be assimilated and stored by the undying Entity, and be thus made immortal with it, these being the only elements of the evanescent Personality that survive death and time. It thus stands to reason that only that which is noble, spiritual and divine in man can testify in Eternity to his having lived.

ANIMA MUNDI (Lat.). The "Soul of the World," the same as the Alaya of the Northern Buddhists, the divine essence which permeates, animates and informs all, from the smallest atom of matter to man and god. It is in a sense the "seven-skinned mother" of the stanzas in the *Secret Doctrine*, the essence of seven planes of sentience, consciousness and differentiation, moral and physical. In its highest aspect it is Nirvana in its lowest Astral Light. It was feminine with the Gnostics, the early

Blavatsky, Glossary

Christians and the Nazarenes, bisexual with other sects, who considered it only in its four lower planes. Of igneous, ethereal nature in the objective world of form (and then ether), and divine and spiritual in its three higher planes. When it is said that every human soul was born by detaching itself from the Anima Mundi, it means, esoterically, that our higher Egos are of an essence identical with It, which is a radiation of the ever unknown Universal ABSOLUTE.

Blavatsky, *Isis Unveiled*.
Vol. I. pp. XIII-XIV.

Basing all his doctrines upon the presence of the Supreme Mind, Plato taught that the nous, spirit or rational soul of man, being "generated by the Divine Father," possessed a nature kindred or even homogeneous with the Divinity and was capable of beholding the eternal realities. This faculty of contemplating reality in a direct and immediate manner belongs to God alone; and the aspiration of this knowledge constitutes what is really meant by philosophy,—love of wisdom. The love of truth is inherently the love of good, and so, predominating over every desire of the soul, purifying it and assimilating it to the divine, thus governing every act of the individual, it raises man to a participation and communion with Divinity and restores him to the likeness of God. "This flight," says Plato in the Theaetetus, "consists in becoming like God, and this assimilation is the becoming just and holy with wisdom."

The basis of this assimilation is always asserted to be the preexistence of the spirit or nous. In the allegory of the chariot and winged steeds given in the Phaedrus, he represents the physical nature as composite and two-fold, the thumos or epithumetic part, formed from the substances of the world of phenomena, and the thumoeides, the essence of which is linked to the eternal world. The present earth-life is a fall and punishment. The soul dwells in "the grave which we call the body," and in its incorporate state, and previous to the discipline of education (philosophy. M.) the noetic, or spiritual element is "asleep." Life is a dream rather than a reality. Like the captives in the subterranean cave described in the The Republic, the back is turned to the light, we perceive only the shadows of objects, and think them the actual realities. Is not this the idea of Maya, or the illusion of the senses of physical life, which is so marked a feature in Buddhistical philosophy? But these shadows, if we have not given ourselves up absolutely to the sensuous nature, arouse in us reminiscence of that higher world that we once inhabited. "The interior spirit has some dim and shadowy recollections of its ante-natal state of bliss, and some instinctive and prophetic yearnings for its return." It is the province of the discipline of philosophy to disenthral it from the bondage of sense, and raise it into the empyrrean of pure thought, to the vision of eternal truth, goodness and beauty . . . Wherefore the nous, or spirit, of the philosopher (or student of the higher truth) alone is furnished with wings, because he, to the best of his ability, keeps these things in mind, of which the contemplation renders even Deity itself divine. By making the right use of these things remembered from the former life, by perfecting himself constantly in the perfect mysteries, a man becomes truly perfect—an initiate into the divine wisdom.

Mahatma Letters to A. P. Sinnett.
p. 289-90.

It was H. P. B., who, acting under orders of Atrya (one whom you do not know) was the first to explain in the Spiritualist the difference there was between the psyche and nous, nepesh and ruach, Soul and Spirit. She had to bring the whole arsenal of proofs with her, quotations from Paul and Plato, from Plutarch and James etc., before the Spiritualists admitted that the theosophists were right. It was then that she was ordered to write *Isis*—just a year after the Society had been founded. And, as there happened such a war over it, endless polemics and objections to the effect that there could not be in man two souls—we thought it was premature to give the public more than they could possibly assimilate, and before they had digested the "two souls."—And thus the further subdivision of the trinity into seven principles is left unmentioned in *Isis*.

Blavatsky *Letters to A. P. Sinnett*
Note by K. H. p. 7.

Note added by K. H. to a letter by H.P.B. to Sinnett:

"Spirit is strong but flesh is weak, so weak sometimes that it even overpowers the strong spirit 'which knows all truth.' And now, having almost shaken off its control this poor body raves . . . If you are ever to learn any lesson about man's duality and the possibility through occult science of awakening from its dormant state to an independent existence the invisible but real I am, seize the chance. Observe and learn. It is cases like these which puzzle the biologist and physiologist."

Blavatsky. Glossary.

UMBRA. (Lat.) The shadow of an earth-bound spook. The ancient Latin races divided man (in esoteric teachings) into seven principles, as did every old system, and as Theosophists do now. They believed that after death Anima, the pure divine soul, ascending to heaven, a place of bliss; Manes (the Kama Rupa) decended into Hades (Kama Loka); and Umbra (or astral double, the Linga-Sharira) remained on earth hovering about its tomb.

Blavatsky. Glossary.

Therefore they said that nothing but the astral image of the defunct could be seen on earth . . .

TZOOL-MAH. (Kab.) Lit; "shadow." It is stated in the Zohar (I.218 a.I.fol.117 a, col.466.) that during the last seven nights of a man's life, the Neshamah, his spirit, leaves him and the shadow, tzool-mah, acts no longer, his body casting no shadow, and when the tzool-mah disappears entirely, then Ruach and Nephesh —the soul and life—go with it.

Kashf-al-Mahjub.
Tr. R. A. Nicholson.
p. 285.

If any attribute prevents the seeker of God from annihilating himself in unification, he is still veiled by that attribute, and while he is veiled he is not a unitarian, for all except God is unity. This is the interpretation of: There is no God but God.

Quoted Widgery in Comp. St. of Rel. 75.

Sharfud-din-Maneri.
Letters of a Sufi Teacher.
Letter 85.

Alienation from the personality is the first step to acquaintance with God. The one is a necessary conditon for the other. All aspirants find fault with, and impose tasks on, the desire-nature, so that this wall of separation be pulled down, and a way be found to the Divine Sanctuary.

Sharfud-din-Maneri.
Letter 84.

The discipline of the desire-nature is recommended by all creeds and nations, and is known by Sages as a means of developing the supersensuous faculties . . . But thy business lies with discipline only, it is God's to grant supersensuous faculties. Thy labours cannot bear fruit without His grace. Avoid as much as possible the thought of personality and its activities, and never follow the promptings of the desire-nature. It is thy existence that veils thee. Had there been the veil of a single activity, it could be uplifted by another opposite activity. But the whole of thyself being a veil, thou canst not be fit for the Divine Vision, unless and until thou vanish completely. It should not be forgotten in this connection that the discipline of the desire-nature means the transmutation of its qualities, not the destruction of its essential nature—for that is impossible. But its existence need not be regarded as dangerous after it has been subdued by the inner ruler.

Sharfud-din-Maneri.
Letters of a Sufi Teacher.
Letter 81.

Bu Ali saw his desire-nature (Nafs) in the form of a hog. He wished to kill it, but it said to him: "Do not trouble thyself, I belong to the army of God, thou canst not annihilate me."

Mohammed Nuri speaks of his desire-nature coming out of his throat in the form of a minature fox. "I knew it was the desire-nature, so I put it under my feet and began to trample on it. It grew larger and stronger." I said: "Pain and torture destroy all things, but they simply aid your growth!" It said: "This is due to the fact of my constitution being the other way, what is pain for others is pleasure for me."

Abul Abbas saw it in the form of a yellowish dog. When he attempted to turn it out, it came underneath the skirt of his garment, and disappeared.

Abul Qasim saw it in the form of a serpent.

Another Dervesh saw it in the form of a mouse, and asked who it was. It said: "I am the death of the heedless, and the salvation of the Divine Friends. If I were not they would turn proud of their purity and noble deeds.

These stories go to show that the desire-nature is a corporeal being—not a quality—albeit it is endowed with qualities. It should be subdued by ascetic practices, but it cannot completely be destroyed in its essential nature. There need not be any fear from its existence, when it has been subdued by the disciple. . . . This dreary forest cannot be crossed save with the help of a Master of Compassion.

Letters of a Sufi Teacher. Trans. Baijnath Singh.
Adyar 1909. Letter 81.

Sharfud-din-Maneri.
Letters of a Sufi Teacher.
Trans. Baijnath Singh.

Some say the desire-nature, the Nafs, is a substance, placed in the body, similar to the Soul. Others say it is a quality of the body, similar to life. But all take it as the source of evil qualities and acts. These evils are grouped into (a) sins, (b) qualities, e.g. pride, envy, anger. The former pertain more to the outer man, the latter more to the inner man. The former are purified by the ascetic practices, the latter by Taubah, (or Turning). . .

It is said that the desire-nature and the Soul are both mysterious entities in the body, corresponding to demons and angels, hell and heaven in the macrocosm, the one being the centre of evil, the other the centre of god. There is no help against the desire-nature except in ascetic practices.

Man is the epitome of the whole Universe and is composed of the Soul, the desire-nature, and the body. He bears the characteristics of all the worlds. The earth, water, fire and air of this world appear in his body as the four humours: blood, phlegm, melancholy and bile. Other worlds are not less vividly marked in him. The soul leads him to heaven, being its image, the desire-nature leads him to hell, being its image.

Letters of a Sufi Teacher (*Sharfud-din-Maneri*, called *Makhdum-ul-Mulk*.) Trans. Baijnath Singh. Adyar 1909. Letter 81. p. 110 seq.

Sharfud-din-Maneri.
Letters of a Sufi Teacher.
Letter 83.

The desire-nature is the worst foe. It is very difficult to be armed against it, since, firstly, it is an internal foe, and it is almost impossible to guard the house against a thief co-tenant, and, secondly, it is a lovely foe, and a man is blind to the defects of his beloved, whose shortcomings take on the appearance of merits. Such being the case, the desire-nature may ere long hurl a man unaware to the lowest depths of degradation.

If you ponder well, you will find it at the root of all the troubles that beset man in the past or may beset him in the future. This being the foe, one should intelligently strive to overcome it. It is improper to overcome it all at once, as it is a vehicle and instrument of the soul; nor is it proper to let it go wholly unbridled, in view of the probable dangers. So the disciple needs a middle course, and it is this: "You should strengthen it to the extent of enabling it to perform its duties, you should weaken it to the measure of preventing the chance of its leading you astray. Anything besides this rule is objectionable."

It is reported in sacred tradition that in seeing Abdullah Masud, who had by ascetic processes weakened his body, his feet having become incapable of motion, his eyes having sunk in their sockets, Mohammed said: "O Abdullah be warned! Thy desire-nature has claims on thee." So the conclusion is that the desire-nature should be disciplined by knowledge, so that it may neither overcome (nor disobey) them, nor be itself destroyed.

The middle course consists in restraining the desire-nature by temperance. There are three ways of this subduing it: (a) withholding gratification . . . (b) imposing religious observances . . . (c) invoking the divine help for the mastery over it. If you follow this threefold method, the desire-nature will be amenable to discipline.

Yasna. xxx, 4.

And when these twain spirits (Ormuzd and Ahriman) came together in the beginning, they established life and not-life.

Quoted in Widgery's Comp. St. of Rel. 237.

Yasna. 26, 6.

We praise the life (Ahum) knowledge (Daenam) consciousness (Boadhas) soul (Urwanem), and spirit (Frawashem) of the first in religion, the first teachers and hearers (learners) the holy men and holy women who were protectors of purity here (in this world).

A Parsi F.T.S. written in *The Theosophist* (reprinted in *Five Years of Theosophy*, p. 92-97.) analyzes the foregoing as follows:

1.	Ahum, existence, life It includes	1. The physical body. 2. The vital principle. 3. The astral body.
2.	Daenam, knowledge........	4. The astral shape or body of desire.
3.	Boadhas, consciousness	5. The animal or physical intelligence or consciousness, or ego.
4.	Urwanem, soul............	6. The higher or spiritual intelligence or spiritual Ego.
5.	Frawashem, spirit..........	7. The spirit.

Yasna.
Chap. 54. paragraph 1.

Subdivisions of Septenary man according to *Yashna* 54. 1:

1. Tanwas . . . .. i.e. body (the self) that consists of bones—grossest form of matter.

2. Ushtanas . . . . vital heat or force.

3. Keherpas . . . . aerial form, the airy mould, (per Kaleb).

4. Tevishis . . . . will, or where sentient consciousness is formed, also foreknowledge.

5. Boadhas . . . . (in Sanskrit Buddhi) body of physical consciousness, perception by the senses or the animal soul.

6. Urwanem . . . . (Per. Rawan) soul, that which gets its reward or punishment after death.

7. Frawashem or Farohar . . . . spirit, (the guiding energy which is with every man, is absolutely independent and, without mixing with any worldly object, leads man to good. The spark of divinity in every being.)

The above is given in the *Avesta* as follows:

We declare and positively make known this (that) we offer (our) entire property (which is) the body, (the self consisting of) bones (Tanwas) vital heat (Ushtanas), aitial form (Keherpas) knowledge (Tevishis), consciousness (Boadhas) soul (Urwanem) and spirit (Frawashem) to the prosperous, truth-coherent (and) pure Gathas (prayers).

A. Parsi F.T.S. in *Five Years of Theosophy*. 93-95.

Zoroastrian Theology.
Dhalla. M.
p. 144.

(Influencing the man's life, urging him on to the good, is the Fravashi, which accompanies the individual on earth) an infallible monitor who now advises and now admonishes the soul, now applauds its actions, and now raises a voice of warning at a threatening spiritual danger. (In later literature the doctrine is suggested that Fravashi of the righteous man unites with the soul, forming a spiritual unity.)

Quoted by Widgery in Comp. Study of Rel. p. 175. The passages in parentheses are Widgery's, the middle portion is Dhalla's.

BRAHMIN SOURCES

Bhagavad Gita.
trans. Barnett
xii, 13-14.

Hateless towards all born beings, friendly and pitiful, void of the thought of Mine and I, bearing indifferently pain and pleasure, patient, ever content, the Man of the Rule subdued of spirit and steadfast of purpose, who has set his mind and understanding on Me and worships Me, is dear to Me.

Quoted Widgery in Comp. St. of Rel. 349.

Bhagavad Gita.
xii. 7.

I lift them up speedily from the ocean of deathly life wanderings, O son of Pritha, as their mind is laid on Me.

Bhagavad Gita.
xvi. 15.

I am Time that makes worlds to perish away.

Bhagavad Gita.
II.45.

The Vedas have the Three Powers as their object; be thou above the Three Powers, O Arjuna! Be free from duality, ever standing in the real without desire of possessions, full of the soul;

As much use as there is in a well, when the whole land is flooded so much use is there in all the Vedas for a Knower of the Eternal who possesses wisdom.

> [As translated by Charles Johnston, p 47. He encloses the foregoing passages in brackets and believes that they are later additions to the text. The reference is specifically to the "letter" of the Vedas and might easily belong to the original.] R. M.

Bhagavad Gita.
II, 51-2.
Johnston, p. 48.

For the possessors of wisdom, united in soul-vision, giving up the fruit of works, freed from the bondage of rebirth, reach the home where no sorrow dwells.

When thy soul shall pass beyond the forest of delusion, thou shalt no more regard what shall be taught or what has been taught.

Bhagavad Gita, IX, 28-28.
Johnston, p. 116.

He who with love gives Me a leaf, a flower, a fruit, or water, this gift of love I accept from him who is self-conquered.

Whatever thou doest, whatever thou eatest, whatever thou offerest, whatever thou givest, whatever penance thou doest, O son of Kunti, do it as an offering to Me.

Thus shalt thou be set free from the bonds of works, fruits of deeds fair or foul; thy soul united through renunciation and union, liberated, thou shalt come to Me.

I am equal towards all beings; nor is any hated or favored of Me; But they who love Me with dear love, they are in Me and I in them.

Should even a chief of sinners love Me with undivided love, he is to be held a saint for he has decided wisely.

Soon he becomes altogether righteous, entering ever into peace; and know certainly, O son of Kunti, my beloved will not perish.

Bhagavad Gita.
Johnston trans. 171, et seq.
XVI, 1-5

Valour, cleanness of heart, steadfast union with illumination, generous giving, control, sacrifice, study, fervour, righteousness;

Gentleness, truth, freedom from anger, detachment, peace, loyalty, pity for all beings, an unlascivious mind, mildness, modesty, steadfastness,

Fire, patience, firmness, purity, good-will, absence of conceit, these belong to him who is born to the godlike portion, O descendant of Bharata!

Hypocrisy, pride, vanity, anger, meanness, unwisdom, these, O son of Pritha, are his, who is born to the demoniac portion.

The godlike portion makes for liberation, and the demoniac for bondage. But grieve not, son of Pandu! Thou art born to the godlike portion.

Bhagavad Gita.
Johnston, trans.
XVIII, 29-35.

Hear thou the division of understanding and of firmness, threefold according to the powers, declared completely according to their differences, O conqueror of wealth.

The understanding which knows action and abstention, what is to be done, what left undone, what is to be feared and what not, and also bondage and freedom, that, O son of Pritha, is of Substance. (Sattwa.)

The understanding which distinguishes not truly between law and lawlessness, what should and should not be done is of Force (Rajas), O son of Pritha.

The understanding which, enwrapped in darkness, sees the unlawful as lawful, and all things as opposite to their true nature, that, O son of Pritha, is of Darkness, (Tamas).

The firmness whereby one firmly holds the emotional nature, and the actions of the life-powers, unwavering in union, that, O son of Pritha, is the firmness of Substance.

But the firmness, O Arjuna, whereby on desiring reward holds firmly to duty, desire, riches, that, O son of Pritha, is the firmness of Force.

But the firmness through which one of foolish mind will not let go dreams, fears, grief, despondency, arrogance, that, O son of Pritha, is of Darkness.

Johnston p. 193-4.

Bhagavad Gita.
Johnston trans.
XVIII, 36-40.

Hear now from me the three kinds of happiness, O bull of the Bharatas, through following which one finds delight, and makes an end of pain.

That which at the beginning is as poison, but in the outcome is as nectar, that is the happiness of Substance, (Sattwa), springing from clear vision of the Soul.

The happiness which springs from the union of the senses with the objects of desire, in the beginning like nectar, but in the outcome like poison, that is declared to be the happiness of Force, (Rajas).

The happiness which, in the beginning, and to the end, causes blindness to the Soul, springing from a sleep, sloth, negligence, that is declared to be of Darkness. (Tamas).

Johnston p. 194

Bhagavad Gita. VIII, 23-26.
Johnston trans. 107

But at what time going forth, seekers of union return not, or return, that time I shall declare to thee, O bull of the Bharatas.

They who go forth at death in the flame, the light, the day, the moonlit weeks, the summer, they knowers of the Eternal, enter the Eternal.

But the seeker of union who goes forth in the smoke, the night, the moonless weeks, the winter, he entering into the lunar light, returns again.

These are deemed the world's immemorial ways of light and darkness; by the one he goes to return no more, by the other he returns again.

Bhagavad Gita, IX, 20-21.
Johnston, p. 115 and note
in Intro. 111.

The men of the Three Vedas, soma-drinkers, pure from sin, offering sacrifices, seek from Me the way of heaven; they, gaining Lord Indra's paradise, eat divine feasts of the gods in heaven.

They, having enjoyed that wide heavenly world, on the waning of their merit enter the mortal world. Thus, putting their trust in the threefold Vedic law, and full of desires, they gain as their reward their going and return.

Johnston in his introduction to Book IX makes this observation which is worth following up:

"This is the deep line of cleavage, lying at the root of the religions of India, between the Mystery Teaching of the Red Rajanyas or Rajputs, and the ritual worship of the White Brahmans, which at first knew nothing of the Mystery Teaching, nothing of rebirth, nothing of liberation."

Is the White Brahman tradition the Pratyeka Buddha Tradition of the false Asamgha? Is the Red Rajanya school that of Taraka Raja Yoga?

Bhagavad Gita, IX. 11-12.
Johnston, p. 114.

The deluded contemn Me, thus entered into a human form, not knowing My supreme nature, as mighty Lord of beings.

Vain their hopes, vain their works, of little knowledge; they have entered into savage and demoniac natures, full of delusions.

Bhagavad Gita, II, 62-3.
Johnston, p. 49-50.

In the man who broods on things of sense, attachment to them springs up; from attachment is born desire, from desire wrath takes birth.

From wrath comes delusion, from delusion loss of recollection, from loss of recollection comes loss of soul-vision, through loss of soul-vision he perishes.

Bhagavad Gita. III. 39-40.
Johnston, p. 62-63.

Arjuna said:

Then under whose yoke does man here commit sin, unwilling even, O descendant of Vrishni, as though compelled by force?

The Master said:

It is lust, it is wrath, born of the Power of Force, (Rajoguna): the great consumer, the great evil,--know this to be the enemy.

As flame is wrapped by smoke, as a mirror is veiled by rust, as the germ is enwrapped by the womb, so is this developed by that;

Wisdom is enveloped by that eternal enemy of the wise, whose form is Desire, O son of Kunti, an insatiate fire.

The sense-powers, the emotions, the understanding, are its dwelling place; through them Desire deludes the Lord of the body, enveloping wisdom.

Bhagavad Gita. III, 42-43.
Johnston, p. 62-3.

They say the sense-powers are higher than objects; than the sense-powers emotion is higher; than emotion understanding is higher; but higher than understanding is He.

Thus awaking to Him who is above understanding, establishing thy soul on the Soul, slay the enemy, O mighty armed one, whose form is Desire, who is hard to overcome.

Bhagavad Gita. IX. 3.
Johnston, p. 113.

Men without faith in this law, O consumer of the foe, failing to reach Me, turn back again along the way of the circle of death.

Bhagavad Gita.
Johnston trans. p. 171 et seq.
XVI, 6-23

There are two ways of being in this world: the godlike and the demoniac. The godlike has been declared at length; hear now from Me the demoniac, O son of Pritha.

Those of demoniac nature know not right action nor right abstinence, nor purity, nor discipline nor truth are found in them.

This world, they say, is without truth or firm foundation, without a Lord; not ruled by mutual law, driven only by wilfulness.

Resting in this view, self-destroying, of little wisdom, they come forth violent and hostile, for the destruction of the world.

Taking their refuge in desire insatiable, following after hypocrisy, vanity, madness, through delusion grasping after thoughts of evil, they follow unclean lives;

Given to limitless imaginings stopped only by death, they yield themselves up to the enjoyment of their desires, persuaded that there is nothing else;

Bound by a hundred meshes of expectation, filled with lust and wrath, they seek, for the enjoyment of their desires, to heap up wealth unjustly.

"This have I gained today; this desire shall I obtain; this much I have, and this shall I have of further wealth.

"This foe has been slain by me, and I shall slay yet others, I am a lord, I am master of feasts, I have won success and might and happiness;

"I am wealthy and well-born, what other is like unto me? I shall sacrifice, I shall give gifts, I shall exult"; thus say they, deluded by unwisdom.

Wandering in many imaginings, enmeshed by the nets of delusion, fastened to the feasts of their desires, they fall into the impure pit of hell.

Puffed up with self-conceit, vain, following after the pride and intoxication of wealth, their offerings are no true offerings, full of hypocrisy and lawlessness.

Clinging to self-conceit, violence, pride, lust, wrath, hating Me in themselves and in others, and full of cavilling;

Them, full of hate, cruel, basest of men in the world, I cast down quickly in their impurity into demoniac wombs.

Entering demoniac birth, deluded in birth after birth, not finding Me, O son of Kunti, they go the lower way.

Threefold is this door of soul-destroying hell; lust, wrath, and greed are its doors; therefore let him shun these three.

The man who gets free from these three doors of darkness, O son of Kunti, reaches happiness of soul, and henceforth goes the higher way.

He who, scorning the scriptural law, does according to his own lusts, reaches not perfection, nor happiness, nor the higher way.

Bhagavad Gita. XIII. 12-17.
Johnston. 150-1.

What is to be known I shall declare to thee, knowing which thou shalt gain immortality: the beginningless Supreme Eternal, which is neither being nor non-being.

With hands and feet everywhere, with eyes and head and face everywhere, possessed of hearing everywhere in the world, That stands, enveloping all things.

Illuminated by the power that dwells in all the senses, yet free from all sense-powers, detached, all-supporting, not divided into powers, yet enjoying all powers.

Without and within all beings, motionless, yet moving, not to be perceived is That, because of its subtlety, That stands afar, yet close at hand,

Undivided among beings, though standing as if divided, and as the supporter of beings is That to be known, whither they go, and whence they come,

Light of lights also is That called, beyond the darkness, It is wisdom, It is the aim of wisdom, to be gained by wisdom, in the heart of each It is set firm.

Bhagavad Gita, p. 54.
Johnston, Charles.

The Sankhya system, so far as it has come down to us, held that the Spirit of man, Purusha, is chained to Nature, Prakriti, through the forms of Intellect, Buddhi. Regarding Nature through the Intellect, the Spirit of man believes himself to be immersed in Nature, and identifies himself with Nature's triple powers, Substance, Force and Darkness. Thus comes bondage, and intellect is that which ensnares. The Spirit of man must free itself from this snare of false identification; then he will stand alone, eternal, liberated. . . . . Its (Sankhya's) characteristic words are Spirit of (Purusha) Nature (Prakriti), Intellect (Buddhi) and the Three Powers, Substance, (Sattva), Force (Rajas), Darkness (Tamas).

Bhagavad Gita.
XVIII 72-73.
Johnston version.

The Master said:

Say then, O son of Pritha, whether thou hast listened in singleness of heart; say whether the delusion of unwisdom is destroyed, O conqueror of wealth!

Arjuna said:

Gone is my delusion; I have come to right remembrance through Thy grace, O unfallen one! I shall stand with my doubts gone. I shall fulfil thy word!

Johnston trans. 199.

Bhagavata Purana.

(There are ten principal avatars of Vishnu).

Matsa (Fish) rescued Manu, the progenitor of the human race from a great flood.

Kurma (Tortoise) formed a pivot for the churning of the ocean.

Varaha (Boar) rescued the earth from a demon out of the boundless flood.

Narasinha (Man-Lion) slew a demon.

Vamana (Dwarf) rescued earth and heaven from the tyrant Bali, by his three strides.

Parasurama (Rama with the axe.) incarnation for the purpose of destroying the Kshattriyas.

Ram Chandra hero of the Ramayana.

Krishna.

Buddha "By his word as Buddha, Vishnu deludes the heretics."

Kalki (Horse) to come at the end of the Kali Yuga or fourth age.

Upanishads.

There is indeed another different soul, called the elemental soul–he who being overcome by the bright or the dark fruits of action, enters a good or evil womb, so that his course is downward or upward, and wanders around, overcome by the pairs of opposites.

Quoted by Widgery in *The Comparative Study of Religions.* p. 164.

In the footnote he gives the following references:
Either the first is the exact one or all are bearings on the same idea. They should be searched separately.

Taid, Up. ii.
Brih. iv. 3.6.
Kath. xi. 12.
Chand. v. 18. 1.
Maitri. iii. 2. R. M.

ANTHROPOLOGICAL SOURCES

Stefansson, Vilhjalmar.
Red Book, Mar. 1930.

Eskimos believe that children are born with souls as foolish and feeble as the infant looks and is. It seems obvious to them that babies could not get along very well if there were not some way to secure for their use a stronger and abler soul. Moreover the souls of the dead have nowhere else to go and are waiting around graves. The mother's first duty after a child is born is, therefore, to face in the direction of a grave, pronounce a magic spell, and call the soul of the newly dead to become a protecting soul, a guardian angel for the child.

The child's body is now inhabited by two souls, one ignorant, the other very wise. This wise soul does all the thinking. If a child cries for the scissors, it is the wise and experienced soul that wants them. The child must be given the scissors, then, because it is absurd to think that the guardian spirit does not know what is good for the child. Moreover, the guardian soul is easily offended and will leave the child if crossed, whereupon the helpless babe would become the victim of all sorts of troubles, such as being unable to learn to walk and talk.

Widgery.
Comp. Study of Rel. p. 253.

An interesting set of myths seems to refer to an early association of evil with a "primeval watery element" or with a great monster of the ocean and his horde, and to a conflict with this by a savior who eventually became regarded as a bringer of blessings. With these myths is associated another of a golden age in the past, the like of which is in the future to be re-established when the monster is not only conquered but also, as it is not yet, destroyed.

Widgery bases this upon passages in W. O. Cesterley's *Evolution of the Messianic Idea* (no page given).

The Winnebago Tribe.
Paul Radin.
(Johnson Reprints, New York), p. 270

I came from above and I am holy. This is my second life on earth. Many years before my present existence, I lived on this earth. At that time every one seemed to be on the warpath. I also was a warrior, a brave man. Once when I was on the warpath I was killed. It seemed to me, however, as if I had merely stumbled. I rose and went right ahead until I reached my home. At home I found my wife and children, but they would not look at me. Then I spoke to my wife but she seemed to be quite unaware of my presence. "What can the matter be," I thought to myself, "that they pay no attention to me and that they do not even answer when I speak to them." All at once it occurred to me that I might, in reality, be dead. So I immediately started out for the place where I had presumably been killed and surely enough, there I saw my body. Then I knew positively that I had been killed. I tried to return to the place where I had lived as a human being but for four years I was unsuccessful.

At one time I became transformed into a fish. However, the life of the fish is much worse than ours. They are very frequently in lack of food. They are nevertheless very happy beings and have many dances.

At another time I became transformed into a little bird. When the weather is good the life of the birds is very pleasant. But when it is cold they are compelled to undergo many hardships on account of the weather as well as on account of lack of food. When it was very cold I used to go to the camp of some people who were living in the neighborhood and try to steal some meat from their racks. A little boy used to stand near the racks and we were very much afraid of him because he carried something in his hands with which he shot and which made a dreadful noise. Whenever he shot it we would all fly away. What the boy was using was a bow and arrow. At night we slept in a hollow tree. If I entered the tree first and the others came in behind me I would be almost squeezed to death. If, on the other hand, I waited until the last I would sometimes have to stay outside and when the weather was cold I might have frozen to death.

At another time I became a buffalo. The cold weather and the food did not worry me much then, but as buffaloes, we would always have to be on the alert for hunters.

From my buffalo existence I was permitted to go to my higher spirit-home from which I originally came. The one in charge of that spirit-home is my grandfather. I asked for permission to return to this earth again. At first he refused, but then when I had asked him for the fourth time, he consented. He said to me: "Grandson, you had better fast before you go and if any of the spirits take pity upon you (i.e. bless you). You may go and live in peace upon earth." So I fasted for four years and all the spirits above, even to the fourth heaven, approved of my coming. They blessed me. Then I fasted 10 days more and then 20 and then 30. Finally all the spirits blessed me, even those under the earth. When I was ready to come to this earth, the spirits gathered together in a council-lodge and "counseled" about me. All the spirits were present. They told me that I would never fail in anything that I wished to do. Then they decided to make a trial of my powers. They placed an invulnerable spirit-grizzly bear at one end of the lodge and sang the songs that I was to use when I returned to earth. Then I walked around the lodge holding a live coal in the palm of my hand and danced around the fireplace saying wahi—! and striking the palm containing the coal with my other hand. The invulnerable bear fell forward prone upon the ground and a black substance flowed from his mouth. Then they said to me: "You have killed him." Even so great a spirit as this you have been able to kill. Indeed, nothing will ever be able to cross your path." Then they took the "bear" I had killed and cut him into small pieces with a knife, piled these in the center of the lodge, and covered them with some dark material. "Now," they said, "you must again try your powers." I asked them for the articles I would have to use and they gave me a flute and a gourd. Then made myself holy. All those who had blessed me were present. I walked around the object that lay piled up in the center of the lodge and breathed upon it. This I did for the second time and all those within the lodge breathed together with me. Four times I did this and then the spirit-grizzly bear got up and walked away in the shape of a human being. "It is good," they said. "He has restored him to life again. Surely he is holy. After a while they said to me again: "Just as you have done here will you always do below. Whenever you will to, you will be able to kill a person or restore him to life. Most assuredly you have been blessed."

Then they placed a black stone in the shaman's lodge that stood above. There again they made a trial of my powers. There I blew four times on the stone and I blew a hole through it. For that reason, if any person has a pain and lets me blow upon it, I can blow it away. It makes no difference what kind of a pain it is. My breath was made holy by the spirits.

The spirits on the earth and those under the earth also gave me a trial of my powers. They placed an old rotten log before me. I breathed upon it four times, and spat water upon it and it got up in the shape of a human being and walked away.

My ability to spit water upon the people I am treating I received from an eel, from the chief among the eels, one who lives in the center and the deepest part of the ocean. He is absolutely white and he is the one who blessed me. Whenever I spit water it is inexhaustible, because it comes from him, the eel.

Then I came to this earth again. They, the spirits, all gave me advice before I left them. When I came upon this earth I entered a lodge and there I was born, but in reality I was entering my mother's womb. Even in my prenatal existence, I never lost consciousness. Then I grew up and fasted again and again, and all those spirits who had blessed me before sent me their blessing again. I can dictate to all the spirits that exist . . .

EGYPTIAN SOURCES

Hermes Trismegistos.
Lib. VIII, 4, 5, 6.
Everard trans.

4. Suffer not yourselves to be carried with the great stream, but stem the tide, you that can lay hold of the Heavens of Safety and make your full course towards it.

5. Seek one that may lead you by the hand, and conduct you to the door of Truth and Knowledge, where the clear Light that is, is pure from Darkness, where there is not one drunken, but all are sober and in their heart look up to him, whose pleasure it is to be seen.

6. For he cannot be heard with ears, nor seen with eyes, nor expressed in words; but only in mind and heart.

Note: Examine "seen". Is it not 'made manifest'? R. M.

Hermes Trismegistos.
Everard --- Pymander.
Tenth Bk. MIND to HERMES.

126. If therefore thou wilt not equal thyself to God, thou canst not know God.

127. For the like is intelligible by the like.

128. Increase thyself into an immeasureable greatness, leaping beyond every Body; and transcending all Time, become Eternity and thou shalt understand God; If thou believe in thyself that nothing is impossible, but accounteth thyself immortal, and that thou canst understand all things, every Art, every Science and the manner and custom of every living thing.

129. Become higher than all height, lower than all depths, comprehend in thyself the qualities of all the Creatures of the Fire, the Water, the Dry and Moist; and conceive, likewise, that thou canst at once be everywhere in the Sea, in the Earth.

130. Thou shalt not only understand thyself, not yet begotten in the Womb, young, old, to be dead, the things after death, and all these together as also times, places, deeds, qualities, quantities, or else thou canst not yet understand God.

131. But if thou shut up thy Soul in the Body and abuse it, and say, I understand nothing, I am afraid of the Sea, I cannot climb up into Heaven, I know not who I am, I cannot tell what I shall be; what hast thou to do with God; for thou canst understand none of these Fair and Good things; be a lover of the Body, and Evil.

Coll; Herm: Div: Pym: p. 78.

Hermes Trismegistos.
Pymander (Atwood).
Smaragdine Tablet.

True without error, certain and most true;

That which is above is as that which is below, and that which is below is as that which is above, for performing the miracles of the One Thing.

And as all things were from One, by the mediation of One, so all things proceeded from this One Thing by Adaptation.

The Father of it is the Sun, the Mother of it is the Moon, the wind carrieth it in its belly; the nurse thereof is the Earth.

This is the father of all perfection and the consummation of the whole world.

The power of it is integral, if it be turned into Earth.

Thou shalt separate the earth from the fire, the subtle from the gross, gently, with much sagacity.

It ascends from earth to heaven, and descends again to earth; and receives the strength of the Superiors and of the Inferiors.

So thou hast the glory of the whole world; therefore let all obscurity flee before thee.

This is the strong fortitude of all fortitudes overcoming every subtle and penetrating every solid thing. So the world was created. Hence were wonderful adaptations of which this is the manner.

Therefore am I called Thrice Great Hermes, having the three parts of the philosophy of the whole world.

That which I have spoken is consummated concerning the operation of the Sun.

Quoted so in *A Suggestive Inquiry into the Hermetic Mystery.* Belfast, 1920. pp. 498-9. R. M.

Hermes Trismegistos.
Pymander (Everard trans.).
Lib. VII, 54-57.

54. This is Regeneration, O Son, that we should not any longer fix our imaginations upon this Body, subject to the three

dimensions . . . . .

57. The sensible Body of Nature is far from the Essential Generation; for that is subject to Dissolution, but this is not; and that is Mortal but this is Immortal. Dost thou not know that thou art born a God and the Son of the One, as I am?

Hermes Trismegistos.
Pymander (Everard).
Lib. II. 38. 26. 46.

38. And let Him that is endued with Mind, know Himself to be Immortal; and that the cause of Death is the love of the body, and let Him learn all things that are.

26. . . . . . Man above all things that live upon Earth is double; Mortal because of his Body, and Immortal because of the substantial Man; for being Immortal, and having the power of all things, he yet suffers mortal things, and such as are subject to Fate or Destiny.

46. . . . . . there goeth a sad and dismal darkness before its body; of which darkness is the moist Nature, the body consisteth in the sensible World from whence Death is derived . . . . .

Hermes.
Pymander (Everard).
Lib. VIII, 7.8.

7. But first thou must break to pieces and tear through the garment thou wearest; the web of Ignorance, the foundation of all Mischief, the bond of Corruption, the dark coverture, the living death, the sensible Carcass, the Sepulchre carried about

with us; the domestical Thief which in what he loves us, hates us, envies us.

8. Such is the hurtful Apparel, wherewith thou art clothed which draws and pulls thee downward by itself; lest looking up and seeing the beauty of the Truth, and the Good that is reposed therein, thou shouldst hate the wickedness of this garment, and understand the traps and ambushes, which it hath laid for thee.

Hermes Trismegistos.
Everard Pymander.
First Book - 6-12.

6. For never, O Son, shall or can that Soul which while it is in the Body lightens and lifts up itself to know and comprehend that which is Good and True, slide back to the contrary; for it is infinitely enamoured thereof, and forgotteth all Evils; and when it hath learned and known its Father and progenitor it can no more Apostatize or depart from that Good.

7. And let this, O Son, be the end of Religion and Piety; whereunto when thou art once arrived, thou shalt both live well, and die blessedly, whilst thy Soul is not ignorant whether it must return and fly back again.

8. For this only, O Son, is the way to the Truth, which our Progenitors travelled in; and by which, making their Journey, they at length attained to the Good. It is a Venerable way, and plain, but hard and difficult for the Soul to go that is in the Body.

9. For first it must war against its own self, and after much Strife and Dissension it must be overcome of one part; for the

Contention is of one against two, whilst it flies away and they strive to hold and detain it.

10. But the victory of both is not like; for the one hasteth to that which is Good, but the other is a neighbor to the things that are Evil, and that which is Good desireth to be set at Liberty; but the things that are Evil love Bondage and Slavery.

11. And if the two parts be overcome, they become quiet, and are content to accept of it as their Ruler; but if the one be overcome of the two, it is by them led and carried to be punished by its being and continuance here.

12. This is, O Son, the Guide in the way that leads thither; for thou must first forsake the Body before thy end, and get the Victory in this Contention and Strifeful life, and when thou hast overcome, return.

Coll. Herm. Div. Pym. 15-6.

Hermes Trismegistos.
Everard Pymander.
Seventh Book - Secret
Sermon, 3-10.

3. TAT. . . . . Now then fulfil my defects, and as thou saidst instruct me of Regeneration, either by word of mouth or secretly; for I know not, O Trismegistos, of what Substance, of what Womb or what Seed a Man is thus born.

4. HERMES. O Son, this Wisdom is to be understood in silence, and the Seed is the true Good.

5. TAT. Who soweth it, O Father? For I am utterly ignorant

and doubtful.

6. HERMES. The Will of God, O Son.

7. TAT. And what manner of Man is he that is thus born? For in this point I am clean deprived of the Essence that understandeth in me.

8. HERMES. The Son of God will be another, God made the universe, that in everything consisteth of all powers.

9. TAT. Thou tellest me a riddle, Father, and dost not speak as a Father to his Son.

10. HERMES. Son, things of this kind are not taught, but are by God, when he pleaseth, brought to remembrance.

Hermes Trismegistos.
Everard Pymander.
Book 2 - 2.

48. PYMAND. That which the Word of God said, say I; Because the Father of all things consists of Life and Light, whereof Man is made.

49. TRISM. Thou sayest very well.

50. PYMAND. God and the Father is Light and Life, of which Man is made. If therefore thou learn and believe thyself to be of the Life and Light, thou shalt again pass into Life.

Coll. Herm. Div. Pym. pp. 24-27.

Egyptian Book of Breaths.
Renouf, Rel. of Anc. Egypt.
pp. 207-8.

(Title is) *The Book of the Breaths of Life*, made by Isis for her brother Osiris, for giving new life to his soul and body, and renewing all his limbs, that he may reach the horizon with his Father the Sun, that his soul may rise to heaven in the disc of the Moon, that his body may shine in the stars of the constellation Orion, on the bosom of Nut.

Quoted by Widgery, *Comp. St. of Rel.* p. 49.

Examine original to see if more likely reading "may rise to heaven from the disc of the Moon" is not justified.

CHALDEAN SOURCES

Chaldean Oracles.

It is not proper to understand the Intelligible with vehemence, but if you incline your mind, you will apprehend it; not too earnestly, but bringing a pure and inquiring eye. You will not understand it as when understanding some particular thing, but with the flower of the mind. Things divine are not attainable by mortals who understand sensual things, but only the light armed arrive at the summit. (As quoted and simplified by Emerson.)

Quoted by Harrison in *Teachers of Emerson*, p. 212.

Chaldean Oracles.
Cory's Anc. Frag.
No. 13.

The Father out-perfected all, and gave them over to His second Mind, whom ye, all nations of mankind, sing of as the first.

Chaldean Oracles.
Cory's Anc. Frag. No. 17.

The Mind of the Father, vehicled in rare Drawers-of-straight-lines, flashing inflexibly in furrows of implacable Fire.

G. R. S. Mead's *Chaldean Oracles* V. I, p. 64.
NOTE: Mead says straight lines are characteristic of Mind. R. M.

Chaldean Oracles.
Cory's Anc. Frag. No. 149.

Turn not thy face Naturewards; for her Name is identical with Fate.

G. R. S. Mead's *Chaldean Oracles* V. II, p. 40.
NOTE: Iamblichos says the whole
being of fate is in Nature. R. M.

Chaldean Oracles.
Cory's Anc. Frag. No. 18.

Having mingled the Spark of soul with two in unanimity -- with Mind and Breath Divine -- to them He added, as a third, pure Love, the august Master binding all.

These things the Father thought, and made mortal to be ensouled.

The Father of men and gods placed Mind in Soul and Soul in inert Body.

The Soul, being shining Fire, by reason of the Father's Power, both keeps immune from Death, and body is of Life and hath the fullnesses (pleromata) of many wombs.

Mead's *Chaldean Oracles* pp. 30-32.

Chaldean Oracles.

For the Mind of the Father hath sown symbols through the world – (the Mind) that understands things understandable, and that thinks forth ineffable beauties.

Mead's *Chaldean Oracles*. II. 43.

Psellos' variant.
The Mind of the Father hath sown symbols in the souls.

Chaldean Oracles.
Cory's Anc. Fragments
No. 163, 167, 61, 62, 166.

Yes, there is That which is the End-of-understanding, the that which thou must understand with the flower of mind.

For should'st thou turn thy mind inwards on It, and understand it as understanding "something", thou shalt not understand it.

For that there is a power of (the mind's) prime that shineth forth in all directions, flashing with intellectual rays (lit. sectors).

Yet, in good sooth, thou should'st not (strive) with vehemence (to) understand that End-of-understanding, nor even with the wide-extended flame of wide-extended mind that measures all things – except that End-of-understanding (only).

Indeed there is no need of strain in understanding This; but thou should'st have the vision of thy soul in purity, turned from aught else, so as to make thy mind, empty (of all things else), attentive to that End, in order that thou mayest learn that End-of-understanding; for it subsists beyond the mind.

Mead's *Chaldean Oracles*, pp. 23-24.

Mead has evidently inserted the words and phrases in parentheses. He says the End-of-understanding is generally rendered the Intelligible. But to noeton he says signifies the Self-creative Mind, that is the Mind that creates its own understanding.

The Father, says Mead is equated by Proclus with Essence (ousia) or Subsistence (hyparxis); the Motherhood with Life (zoe) or Power (dynamis) and the Sonship with Operation or Actuality, (energeia). R. M.

Chaldean Oracles.
Mead.

Many are those who leaping mount upon the shining worlds; among them are three excellencies (or heights).

The whirls (iynges) created by the Father's thought are themselves, too, intelligent, being moved by will impossible to understand.

Quoted by Mead in *Chaldean Oracles* II, 14-15. He equates the Iynges with the Sons of Will and Yoga in the Stanzas of Dyzan. They are called in the Oracles "swifts." Cf. therein, the swift runners, Plat Kratylos.

Chaldean Oracles
Cory 164.
Mead *Chald. Orac.* II 44.

But the Mind of the Father doth not receive her will, until she hath departed from Oblivion, and uttereth the word, by putting in its place (Oblivion's) the Memory of the Fatherhood's pure token.

Psellos commenting on this says, "Each, therefore, diving into the ineffable depths of his own nature, findeth the symbol of the All-Father.

Chaldean Oracles.
Cory. A.A. 83.

The soul of men shall press God closely to Itself, with naught subject to death in it; (but now) it is all drunk for it doth glory in the Harmony (the Sublunary or Fate Spheres) beneath whose sway the mortal frame exists.

Mead's *Chal. Orac.* I, 31.
Cory's Anc. Frag. 2nd edn.

Chaldean Oracles.
Cory 172.
Mead *Chal. Or.* II 44.

Seek out the channel of the Soul-stream -- whence and from what order is it that the soul in slavery to body (did descend, and) to what order thou again shalt arise, at-one-ing work with the holy word.

Armed at all points, clad in the bloom of Sounding Light, arming both mind and soul with three-barbed Might, he must set in his heart the Triad's every symbol, and not move scatteredly along the empyrean ways, (or channels) but (move) collectively.

Yea, verily, full-armed without and armed within like a goddess.

Urging himself to the centre of Sounding Light. [Mead translating "kentron" as "goad" offers the variant translation. Urging himself on with the goad of Sounding Light.]

The mortal once endowed with Mind must on his soul put bridle, in order that it may not plunge into the ill-starred Earth but win to freedom.

Dowsed in the frenzies of the Earth and the necessities of Nature.

For if the mortal draw nigh to the Fire, he shall have Light from God.

Chaldean Oracles.

But they lie in God, drawing vigorous (i.e. unities, images of the one), descending from the father, and from these descending, the soul plucks of empyrean fruits, the soul-nourishing flower.

Quoted by Harrison in *Teachers of Emerson*, p. 94.
The torches which H. calls images are perhaps better to be understood as momentary enlightenments than as images, Of. Lords of the Flame.

ORPHIC SOURCES

Ta Phusis.
Empedokles.

There is an oracle of Necessity, a decree of the gods from old, everlasting, with broad oath fast sealed, that, whensoever one of the daimons, whose portion is length of days, has sinfully stained his hands with blood, or followed strife and sworn a false oath, he must wander thrice ten thousand seasons away from the Blessed, being born throughout the time in all manner of mortal forms, passing from one to another of the painful paths of life.

For the power of the Air drives him seaward, and the Sea spews him out on the dry land, Earth hurls him into the rays of the blazing Sun, and the Sun into the eddies of Air. One from another receives him and he is loathed of all.

Of these now am I also one, an exile from (the) god and a wanderer, having put my trust in raging Strife (Eros).

Quoted in F. M. Cornford's *From Religion to Philosophy*, p. 228.

C. H. Moore in his translation of the foregoing (as quoted by Widgery in Comp. Study of Rel. 192) . . . "joining in the strife swears falsely, they become the spirits who have long life as their portion, who are doomed to wander thrice ten thousand . . .
. . . being born in the course of time into all forms of mortal creatures . . .
. . . land bares to the rays of the bright sun . . .
. . . and the sun throws them in whirls of ether . . . ."

These variations offer useful suggestions and should be verified from the text.
Religious thought of the Greeks, Cambridge, U.S.A. 1916.

Makrobios
Orphic Heptad
Planetary Correspondences.

Saturn	Rational Contemplative	logikon theoretikon	reason intellect	ratiocinatio intelligentia
Jupiter	Energic	praktikon	power of organization	vim agendi
Mars	passional courageous	thumikon	passion	animositas
Sun	sensational imaginative	aisthetikon phantastikon	power of feeling & believing	sentiendi opinandique naturam
Venus	desiderative	epithumetikon	desire	desiderii motum
Mercury	interpretive	hermeneutikon	power of interpreting & expressing sensation.	pronunciandi et interpret-andi quae sentiat
Moon	conceptive & generative	phutikon	power of sowing & developing bodies on entering the lunar globe.	

The passage of the soul through the planets is sometimes called the Ladder of Mithras (Scala Mithraica) or the Seven-gated Stairs (klimax heptapulos).

Makrobios.
Somnium. I, xxi, 63.

The soul having fallen from the sphere of fixed stars and the Milky Way into the planetary spheres, develops during its passage through them a peculiar phase of motion in each, which it will acquire as a permanent possession by due exercise.

Quoted by G. R. S. Mead, *Orpheus*, 274. Then follows Makrobios' table of planetary correspondences to the Orphic Heptad. (See Orphic Heptad.)

Macrobius.
Somnium. I, xxi, 67.

By Father Liber (Dionysos) the Orphics seem to understand the Hylic Mind which is born from the Impartible (Mind) and is separated into individual minds. And so, in their Sacred Rites, (Dionysos) is represented to have been torn into separate members, and the pieces buried, and then he is resurrected intact.

Quoted Mead *Orpheus* 184.
[Note: Mead interprets Hylic Mind as Mundane Soul or human Soul, and calls the individual minds (see above) personalities.]

On the Theology of Plato.
Marsilius Ficinus.

The professors of the Orphic theology consider a two-fold power in souls, and in the celestial orbs; the one consisting in knowledge, the other in vivifying and governing that orb with which that power is connected. Thus in the orb of the earth, they call the gnostic power Pluto, but the other Proserpine. In water they denominate the former power Ocean, and the latter Tethys. In air, that thundering Jove and this Juno. In fire, that Phanes, and this Aurora. In the soul of the lunar sphere they call the gnostic power Liknitan Bacchus, the other Thalia. In the sphere of Mercury, that Bacchus Silenus, this Euterpe. In the orb of Venus, that Lysius Bacchus, this Erato. In the orb of Mars, that Bassareus Bacchus, this Clio. In the sphere of the sun, that Trietericus Bacchus, this Melpomene. In the sphere of Jupiter, that Sebazius, this Terpsichore. In the orb of Saturn, that Amphietus, this Polymnia. In the eighth sphere, that Perici Pericionus, this Urania. But in the soul of the world they call the gnostic power Bacchus Erobromius, but the animating power Calliope.

From all which the Orphic theologists infer that the particular epithets of Bacchus are compared with those of the Muses, for the purpose of informing us that the powers of the Muses are, as it were, intoxicated with the nectar of divine knowledge; and in order that we may consider the nine Muses and nine Bacchuses revolving round one Apollo, that is, about the splendour of one invisible Sun. The greater part of this passage is preserved by Gyraldus in his *Syntagma de Musis* and by Natales Comes in his *Mythology*, but without mentioning the original author. As in each of the celestial spheres, therefore, the soul of the ruling deity is of the female, and the intellect is of the male characteristic, it is by no means wonderful that the Moon is called in this hymn "female and male."

Quoted in Mead's *Orpheus*, pp. 139-40.
Quoted in Thos. Taylor's *Myst.Hymns of Orpheus*, pp. 26-7.

Taylor says Ficinus got his information from some MS Commentary of Proclus or some other and later Platonist but does not reveal the source of it.

Enn. i. 83, 89.
Ficinus, L. IX.

Because men were generated from the Titans, who had been nourished with the body of Dionysos, he (Orpheus) therefore calls them Dionysiacal, as though some of their members were from the Titans, so that the human body is partly of a Dionysiacal, and partly of a mundane nature.

Quoted by Mead in *Orpheus*, p. 182.

What God is According to Plato.
Dissertation I.
Maximus Tyrius.

"This is indeed the enigma of the Syracusian poet (Epicharmus)."

"Tis mind alone that sees and hears."

"How, therefore, does intellect see, and how does it hear? If with an erect and robust soul it surveys that incorruptible light, and is not involved in darkness, nor depressed to earth, but closing the ears, and turning from the sight, and the other senses, converts itself to itself. If forgetting terrene lamentations and sighs, pleasure and glory, honour and dishonour, it commits the guidance of itself to true reason and robust love, reason pointing out the road, and presiding love, by persuasion and bland allurements alleviating the labours of the journey. But to intellect approaching thither and departing from things below, whatever presents itself is clear, and perfectly splendid and is a prelude to the nature of divinity, and in its progression, indeed, it hears the nature of God, but having arrived thither, it sees him. The end however of this journey is not Heaven, nor the bodies it contains (though these indeed are beautiful and divine as being the accurate and genuine progeny of divinity, and harmonizing with that which is most beautiful), but it is requisite to pass even beyond these, till we arrive at the Supercelestial Place, and Plane of Truth and the serenity which is there:

'Nor clouds nor rain nor winter there are found
But a white splendour spreads its radiance round.'

(*Odyssey* iv 566; vi 43 seq.)

"Where no corporeal passion disturbs the miserable soul, and hurls her from contemplation by its uproar and tumult."

Quoted by Mead in *Orpheus* p. 109.

GREEK AND ROMAN SOURCES

Hippolytus.
Peratae Gnostics.
Mead's Summary in FFF.
p. 185-6.

The Myth of the Going Forth was common to a number of schools, but Hippolytus ascribes it to an otherwise unknown school called the Perate, supposed to mean Transcendalists, or those who by means of the Gnosis had "passed beyond" or "crossed over." Thus then they explained the Exodus myth. Egypt is the body; all those who identify themselves with the body are the ignorant, the Egyptians. To "come forth" out of Egypt is to leave the body; and to pass through the Red Sea is to cross over the ocean of generation, the animal and sensual nature, which is hidden within the blood. Yet even then they are not safe; crossing the Red Sea they enter the Desert, the intermediate state of the doubting lower mind. There they are attacked by the "gods of destruction," which Moses called the "serpents of the desert," and which plague those who seek to escape from the "the gods of destruction," To them Moses, the teacher, shows the true serpent crucified on the cross of matter, and by its means they escape from the Desert and enter the Promised Land, the realm of the spiritual mind, where there is the Heavenly Jordan, the World-soul. When the Waters of the Jordan flow downwards, then is the generation of men; but when they flow upwards then is the generation of the gods. Jesus was one who had caused the Waters of the Jordan to flow upwards.

Iliad.
Homer.

What could I do? It is the god who accomplishes all. Eldest daughter of Zeus, Ate, who blindeth all, a power of bane; delicate are her feet for not upon earth she goeth, but walketh over the heads of men and women and entangleth this one and that.

Quoted by Widgery in *Comp. St. of Rel.* 139. James Adam in *Vitality of Platonism and Other Essays*, pp. 198, 200-1.

Philosophumena.
Hippolytus.
Vol. 6.

Mead in Orpheus, (p. 293.) says the Phrygians in their Mysteries called the souls imprisoned in the body and "dead." The writer of the Naasenian School of Gnosticism quoted by Hippolitus (*Philosophumens*, Vol. 6.) tells us:

"The Phrygians also called it the 'dead', inasmuch as it is in the tomb and sepulchre, buried in the body. This he says, is what is written' 'Ye are whited sepulchres, filled within with the bones of the dead' (cf. Matthew xxiii, 27)–for the 'living man' is not in you. And again: 'The "dead" shall leap forth from the tomb' (cf. Matthew xxvii, 52, 53; xi, 5; Luke vii, 22). That is to say, from their earthly bodies regenerated spiritual men, not fleshly. For this (he says) is the resurrection which takes place through the Gate of the Heavens, and they who pass not through it all remain dead."

Hymn to Demeter.
Homer.
Vol. II, pp. 47-53.

Then for nine days Queenly Deo wandered over the earth with flaming torches in her hands, so grieved that she never tasted ambrosia and the sweet draught of nectar, nor sprinkled her body with water. But when the tenth enlightening dawn had come, Hekate, with a torch in her hands, met her, and spoke to her and told her news.

Trans. Evelyn-White, Loeb Lib.
Hesiod and Homeric Hymns, p. 293.

De Vita Phthag.
Olympiodorus.
Quoted T. Taylor.
p. 245 (new edn).

It is well observed too here, by Olympiodorus that Plato calls the cathartic and theoretic virtues, those which are in reality true virtues. He also separates them in another way, viz. that the political are not telestic, i.e. do not pertain to mystic ceremonies, but that the cathartic and theoretic are telestic. Hence, Olympiodorus adds, the cathartic virtues are denominated from the purification which is used in the mysteries; but the theoretic from perceiving things divine. On this account he accords with the Orphic verses, that

The soul that uninitiated dies,
Plung'd in the blackest mire in Hades lies.

For initiation is the divinely-inspired energy of the virtues. Olympiodorus also further observes that by the thyrsus-bearers Plato means those that energize according to the political virtues, but by the Bacchuses those that exercise the cathartic virtues. For we are bound in matter as Titans, through the greater partibility* of our nature, but we rise from the dark mire as Bacchuses. Hence we become more prophetic at the time of death: and Bacchus is the inspective guardian of death, because he is likewise of every thing pertaining to the Bacchic sacred rites.

*Partibility–divisibility.

Symposium.
Plato.

(Love) is a great daimon . . . and being in the middle space between gods and men it fills up the whole.

Quoted by Harrison in his *Teachers of Emerson.* 147.

Phaidros.
Plato.

And this is the reason for the great anxiety to behold the field of truth, where it is, the proper pasture for the best part of the soul happens to be in the meadow there, and it is the nature of the wing by which the soul is born aloft, to be nourished by it, and this is a law of Adrasteia, that whatever soul, in accompanying a deity, has beheld any of the true essences, it shall be free from harm until the next revolution, and if it can always accomplish this, it shall always be free from harm.

Quoted in Harrison's *Teacher of Emerson.* pp. 136-137.
Note: This passage should be amplified from *Phaidros* and the text examined for several debatable words. Plato has been explaining how the soul, which is immortal, lived in the eternal world before it appeared on earth. R. M.

Phaidros.
Plato.

Every soul of man has from its very nature beheld real existence, or it would not have entered into the human form. The soul which has never seen the Truth cannot enter into the human form*; for it is necessary that a man should understand according to a generic form which, proceeding from many perceptions, is by reasoning combined into one. And this is the reminiscence of those things which our soul formerly saw when journeying with the gods, despising the things which we now say are, and looking up to that which really is.

> *Note: Read—"cannot create a human form out of the animal one into which it descends." The Atma rupa by which the animal body is connected, is a memory body, a memory of divinity the soul has formerly known. Look up exact Greek. R. M.

Meno.
Plato.

Seeing then that the soul is immortal and has been born many times, and has beheld all things both in this world and in the nether realms, she has acquired knowledge of all and everything; so that it is no wonder that she should be able to recollect all that she knew before about virtue and other things. For as all nature is akin and the soul has learned all things, there is no reason why we should not, by remembering one single thing—an act which men call learning—discover everything else, if we have courage and faint not in the search, since, it would seem, research and learning are wholly recollection.

> Loeb Classic Translation. Lamb.
> Look up "nether realms" and see if it means the kingdom below man through which man passed in earlier world periods. R. M.

Plato.
?.

This actual present priest, who initiates you or me, is himself already an image of God, but above him there are greater and wiser priests, above them others, and above them all there is one eternal, divine mediator, who being in perfection both man and god, can alone fully reveal the god to man, lead man's soul up the heavenly path beyond change and fate and the Houses of the Seven Rulers to its ultimate peace.

Quoted by Widgery (*Comp. Study of Rel.*)
Gilbert Murray's *Four Stages of Greek Rel.*
p. 47. 141-2. Now Five Stages.

Dirges.
Pindar.

For from whomsoever Persephone shall accept requital for ancient wrong, the soul of these she restores in the ninth year to the upper sun again; from them arise glorious kings and men of splendid might and surpassing wisdom, and for all remaining time they are called holy heroes among mankind.

Quoted by Plato in the *Meno.*

De Officiic.
Cicero.
Book I. xliii. (Loeb 157).

My view therefore is that those duties are closer to nature which depend upon the social instinct (communitas is Cicero's word) than those which depend upon knowledge (cognito); and this view can be confirmed by the following argument:

(1) Suppose that a wise man should be vouchsafed such a life that, with an abundance of everything pouring in upon him, he might in perfect peace ponder over and study everything that is worth knowing, still, if the solitude were so complete

that if he could never see a human being, he would die. And then the foremost of all virtues is wisdom–what the Greeks call *sophia*; for by prudence, which they call *phronesis*, we understand something else, namely, the practical knowledge of things to be sought for and of things to be avoided.

(2) Again, that wisdom which I have given the foremost place is the knowledge of things human and divine, which is concerned also with the bonds of union between gods and men and the relations of man to man. If wisdom is the most important of the virtues, as it certainly is, it necessarily follows that the duty which is connected with the social obligation (communitas) is the most important duty.

(3) And again service is better than mere theoretical knowledge, for the study and knowledge of the universe would somehow be lame and defective, were no practical results to follow. Such results, moreover, are best seen in the safeguarding of human interests. It is essential then to human society (Societatem) (generis humani), and it should therefore be ranked above speculative knowledge.

Hortensio.
Cicero.
Frag. p. 60.

The ancients, whether they were seers, or interpreters of the divine mind in the tradition of the sacred initiations, seem to have known the truth, when they affirmed that we were born into the body to pay the penalty for the sins committed in a former life (*vita superiore*).

Quoted in Mead's *Orpheus*. The translation of *vita superiore* as former life is an index of Mead's carefulness! It means what it says, superior life, i.e. a life superior to the one we are now suffering. Leverett gives two values of superior, one meaning higher and one used of time meaning former or earlier. It may mean either but the context plainly shows that Cicero is contrasting a condition of birth with a condition that does not involve birth. For what otherwise was the first birth on earth the punishment? R. M.

Evolution of Theology.
Caird. Vol. II, p. 206.
Plato and Philo.

. . . A further consideration of Philo's psychology shows that the main difference of it from that of Plato is just that in the former the dualistic tendency is more fully developed. Plato's idea of the body as the tomb or prison of the soul, his idea of the moral life as an effort to dissociate the soul from the passions which it acquires by its commerce with the body, his idea that practical life involves a disturbance of the soul's peace and a darkening of its inner light, and that its only pure exercise is to be found in the contemplation of absolute, ideal reality—all these Platonic conceptions are literally accepted by Philo. He even gives some countenance to . . . conception that the very entrance of the soul into mortal life involves a certain tainting of its purity. Man, for Philo, is distinctly a compound of dross and deity," and the proper object of his life-effort is declared to be the liberation of his intelligence from its baser companion, the attainment of that apathy* or freedom from passions, in which alone the spirit can energize freely according to the inmost tendency of its own being.

*Apathy in its strict Greek sense, *a-pathos.*

Empedocles..
Greek.

Fools, who think aught can begin to be which formerly was not, or that aught which is can perish and utterly decay! Another truth I now unfold: No natural birth is there of mortal thing nor is death's destruction final. Nothing is there but a mingling, and then a separation of the mingled, which are called a birth and death by ignorant mortals.

See also Walt Whitman: "I too have knitted the old knot of contrariety." *Crossing Brooklyn Ferry. 6.* R.M.

NEOPLATONIST SOURCES

Enneades.
Plotinos.

(From Plato, Plotinos inherited the manner of conceiving spiritual notions from the figure of light. The part that the figure plays in his explanation of the mystical experiences of the soul is an important one. Thus he speaks of the mystical trance when the soul enjoys the presence of the One.)

Then also it is requisite to believe that we have seen it, when the soul receives a sudden light. For this light is from him, and is him. And then it is proper to think that he is present, when like another god entering into the house of someone who invokes him, he fills it with splendour. And thus the soul would be without light and without the possession of this god. But when illuminated, it has that which it sought for. This likeness is the true end to the soul, to come into contact with his light, and to behold him through it, not by the light of another thing, but to perceive that very thing itself through which it sees. For that through which it is illuminated, is the very thing which it is necessary to behold.

Quoted by John S. Harrison in his *Teachers of Emerson*, pp. 89-90. The first paragraph, in brackets, is Harrison's comment.

Enneades.
Plotinos.

Becoming wholly absorbed in deity, she is one, conjoining, as it were, centre for centre. For here concurring, they are one, but they are then two when they are separate . . . . Since, therefore (in this conjunction with deity), there were not two things, but the perceiver was one with the thing perceived, as not being (properly speaking) vision, but union, whoever become one by mingling with deity, and afterwards recollects this union, will have with himself an image of it.

Quoted by Harrison in *Teachers of Emerson*, p. 92.
The words in parentheses are Harrison's elucidations and scarcely necessary. R. M.

Enneades.
Plotinos.

Perhaps, however, neither must it be said that he sees, but that he is the thing seen, if it is necessary to call these two things, i.e. the perceiver and the thing perceived. But both are one, though it is bold to assert this.

Quoted by Harrison in *Teachers of Emerson*, p. 93.
Cf. Boehme's so called vision of God and H. P. Blavatsky's remarks on it in the Glossary in which she says it was his own divine self he saw. R. M.

Enneades.
Plotinos.

But it is said of matter that it ought to be void of all qualities, in order that it may receive the impressions of all things, thus also, and in a much greater degree, is it necessary that the soul should become formless, in order that there may be no impediment to its being filled and illuminated by the first principles of things.

And how, therefore, can this be accomplished? By an ablation of all things.

Quoted by Harrison in *Teachers of Emerson*, p. 98.

Enneades.
Plotinos.

To purify the Soul (signifies) to detach it from the body and to elevate it to the spiritual world. The Soul is to strip off all its lower nature, as well as to cleanse itself from external stains, what remains when this is done will be the "image of Spirit."

Retire into the Self and examine thyself. If thou dost not yet find beauty there, do like the sculptor who chisels, planes, polishes, till he has adorned his statue with all the attributes of beauty. So do thou chisel away from thy Soul what is superfluous, straighten that which is crooked, purify and enlighten what is dark, and do not cease working at thy statue, until virtue shines before thine eyes with its divine splendour, and thou seest temperance seated in thy bosom with its holy purity! This purification is mainly a matter of constant self-discipline, and especially of the thoughts.

The foregoing passage is from that excessively badly edited book of Widgery's *Comp. Study of Rel.* and there is nothing to show who said what. Widgery refers to B.A.G. Fuller's *Problem of Evil in Plotinos.*

Select Works (Bohn).
Intra. p. lxxx. note.
Plotinos.

They (the divine souls of men) likewise see all things, not those with which generation, but those with which essence is present. And they perceive themselves in others. For all things there are diaphanous, and nothing is dark and resisting, but everything is apparent to everyone internally and throughout. For light everywhere meets with light, since everything contains all things in itself, and again sees all things in another. So that all things are everywhere, and all is all. Each thing likewise is everything.

Quoted by Harrison in *Teachers of Emerson*, p. 82.

Select Works (Bohn) 343.
Plotinos.

For it (the soul) abiding on high. And the world is animated after such a manner, that it cannot with so much propriety be said to have a soul of its own, as to have a soul presiding over it, being subdued by and not subduing it, and being possessed and not possessing. For it lies in soul which sustains it, and no part is destitute of soul, being moistened with life, like a net in water.

Quoted by John S. Harrison in *Teachers of Emerson*, p. 84.

Enneades.
Vol. III, p. 14.
Plotinos.

. . . And its end being only in relation to itself, it makes good its own defects and attains self-sufficiency by the unity which it gives to all the elements of its consciousness,–having communion with itself alone and directing all its thoughts to itself. Such consciousness then is the perception of a manifold content, as indeed is indicated by its name (–*conscientia*), and the thinking which is presupposed in it, when thus turns upon itself, *ipso facto*, finds its unity broken, for if it even only says: "I am being," it speaks as one who makes a discovery, and that with good reason, for being is manifold. Thus when in the very act of apprehending its own simple nature, it declares, "I am being," it fails to grasp either being or itself . . . . It appears, therefore that if there is something that possesses absolute simplicity, it cannot think itself.

"How then are we to speak of it? We speak, indeed about it, but itself we do not express, nor have we any knowledge or even thought of it. How, then, can we speak of it all, when we do not grasp it was itself? The answer is that, though it escapes our knowledge, it does not entirely escape us. We have possession of it in such a way that we can speak of it, but not in such a way that we can express it, for we can say what it is not, but not what it is. Hence we speak of it in terms borrowed from things that are posterior to it, but we are not shut out from the possession of it, even if we have no words for it. We are like men inspired and possessed, who know only that they have in themselves something greater than themselves–something they know not what–and who, therefore, have some possession of that which has moved them. So it is with relation to the absolute One. When we use pure intelligence, we recognize that it is the mind within the mind, the source of being and of all things that are of the same order with itself, but we see at the same time that the One is not identified with any of them but is greater than all we call being, greater and better than reason and intelligence and sense, though it is that which gives them whatsoever reality they have."

Quoted in Caird *Ev. Theol. Gr. Phil.* II. 218-9.

Enneades.
Plotinos.

This spectacle is a thing difficult to explain by words. For how can anyone narrate that as something different from himself which when he sees he does not behold as different, but as one with himself? This, therefore, is manifested by the mandate of the mysteries, which orders that they shall not be divulged to those who are uninitiated. For as that which is divine cannot be unfolded to the multitude, this mandate forbids the attempt to elucidate it to anyone but him who is fortunately able to perceive it.

Quoted by John S. Harrison in *Teachers of Emerson*, p. 101.

Enneades.
Plotinos.

There, however, everybody is pure, and each inhabitant is, as it were, an eye. Nothing likewise is there concealed, or fictitious, but before one can speak to another, the latter knows what the former intended to say.

Quoted by Harrison in *Teachers of Emerson*, p. 105.

Enneades.
Plotinos.

Since matter is neither soul nor intellect, nor life, nor form, nor reason, nor bound, for it is infinite, nor power, for what can it affect, but falls off from all these, neither can it rightly receive the appellation of being. But it may deservedly be called non-being . . . . It likewise seems to be full and be all things, and yet has nothing. But the things which enter into and depart from matter, are imitations and images of beings, flowing about a formless resemblance; and on account of its formless nature are seen within it. They also appear, indeed, to effect something in it, but effect nothing, for they are vain and debile, and have no resistance, they pervade without dividing it, like images in water, or as if someone should send, as it were, forms in to what is called vacuum. *(Select Works*. 142-44*)*

So that if someone should say that matter is evil, he will assert what is true, if they say it is impassive to impassive to the god, which is the same thing as to say that it is entirely impassive. (*Select Works.* Bohn, p. 153.)

Quoted by John S. Harrison in *Teachers of Emerson.* p. 113.

Enneades.
Plotinos.

Now, however, men perceiving that the soul of the greater part of the human race is defiled with vice, they do not reason about it either as a divine or an immortal thing. But it is necessary, in considering the nature of everything, to direct our attention to the purity of it, since whatever is added, is always an impediment to the knowledge of that to which it is added. Consider the soul, therefore, by taking away (that which is extraneous), or rather, let him who takes this away survey himself, and he will believe himself to be immortal, when he beholds himself in the intelligible world, and situated in a pure abode. For he will perceive intellect seeing not anything sensible, nor any of these mortal objects, but an eternal power contemplating that which is eternal, everything in the intelligible world and itself also being then luminous, in consequence of being enlightened by the truth proceeding from the good, which illuminates all intelligibles with reality. By such a soul as this, therefore, it may be properly said:

Farewell, a god immortal now am I.

Having ascended to divinity, and earnestly striving to become similar to him. (Selected Works. p. 243.)

Quoted by Harrison in *Teachers of Emerson.* p. 136.

Auxiliaries to the Perception of Intelligibles.
Porphyry.
Myst. Hymns of Orpheus. p. 162.
Thomas Taylor.

That which Nature binds, nature also dissolves, and that which the soul binds, the soul likewise dissolves. Nature, indeed, bound the body to the soul, but the soul binds herself to the body. Nature therefore liberates the body from the soul, but the soul liberates herself from the body . . . . Hence there is a twofold death, indeed, universally known, in which the body is the one liberated from the soul, but the other peculiar to philosophers,* in which the soul is liberated from the body. Nor does the one entirely follow the other.

Thomas Taylor explaining the foregoing says:

Though the body, by the death which is universally known, may be loosened from the soul, yet while material passions and affections reside in the soul, the soul will continually verge to another body, and as long as this inclination continues remain connected with the body.

Quoted by Mead in *Orpheus.* p. 304.
*Mead interprets "Initiates."

De Ant. Nymph.
p. 259.
Porphyry.

. . . the blood is the food and nourishment of the spirit . . . that is the subtle body called the animal spirit . . . and this spirit is the vehicle of the soul (presumable psyche).

Quoted by Mead *Orpheus*. p. 280.

[The original Greek of this would be interesting. Mead does not give any of the words for spirit, animal spirit or soul—which he should.] R. M.

Theosophy and Psychological Religion.
Proklos.
Max Muller.

As the Mystae in the holiest of their initiations meet first with a multiform and manifold race of gods, but when entered into the sanctuary and surrounded by holy ceremonies receive at once divine illumination in their bosom and like lightly armed warriors take quick possession of the Divine, the same thing happens at the intuition of the One and All.

If the soul looks to what is behind, it sees the shadows and illusions only of what is. If it turns into its own essence and discovers its own relations, it sees itself only; but, if penetrating more deeply into the knowledge of itself, it discovers the spirit in itself and in all orders of things.

And if it reaches into its inmost recess, as it were into the Adyton (sanctuary) of the soul, it can see the race of gods and the unities of all things even with closed eyes.

Thomas Taylor.
Note to FS. & TT. Plato.
III. 343. note 1.

They (the daimos) stand as it were, over our heads, discourse with each other, and in the meantime speculate our affairs, disapprove our evil deeds, and comment such as are good.

Quoted by Harrison in *Teachers of Emerson*, p. 151.

On the E. at Delphi.
Plutarch. Sect. 11.

The fifth element some call Heaven, some Light, and some Aether.

De Mysteriis.
p. 322.
Iamblichos.

I say, therefore, that the more divine and intelligible man, who was formerly united to the gods by the vision of them, afterwards entered into another soul, which co-adapted to the human form, and through this became fettered with the bonds of necessity and fate.

Quoted by Harrison in *Teachers of Emerson*, p. 248.

De Mysteriis.
pp. 271-273.
Iamblichos.

The third and most perfect species of prayer is the seal of ineffable union with the divinities, in whom is established all the power and authority of prayer; and thus causes the soul to repose in the gods, as in a never-failing port. . . . It also gradually and silently draws upwards the manners of our soul, by divesting them of everything foreign to a divine nature, and clothes us with the perfection of the gods. Besides this it produces an indissoluble communion and friendship with divinity, nourishes a divine love, and inflames the divine part of the soul. Whatever is of an opposing and contrary nature in the soul, it expiates and purifies, expels whatever is prone to generation, and retains anything of the dregs of mortality in its ethereal and splendid spirit, perfects a good hope and faith concerning the reception of divine light, and, in one word, renders those by whom it is employed the familiars and domestics of the gods.

Quoted by Harrison in *Teachers of Emerson*, pp. 282-83.

De Vita Pythag. p. 170.
Iamblichos.

They (the Pythagoreans) perpetually exhorted each other, not to divulse the god within them. Hence all the endeavour of their friendship, both in deeds and words, was directed to a certain divine mixture, to a union with divinity, and to a communion with intellect and a divine soul.

Quoted by Harrison in *Teachers of Emerson*, p. 159.

De Mysteriis. p. 322.
Iamblichos.

There is one daimon who is guardian and governor of everything that is in us.

De Mysteriis.
Iamblichos.

We are comprehended in it, or rather we are filled by it, and we possess that very thing which we are (or by which our essence is characterized) in knowing the gods.

Quoted from Wilder edition p. 24 in Harrison's *Teachers of Emerson*, p. 93.

De Mysteriis. p. 164.
Iamblichos.

For, since it is not possible to speak rightly about the gods without the gods, much less can any one perform works which are of an equal dignity with divinity and obtain the foreknowledge of everything without the gods. For the human race is imbecile, and of small estimation, sees but little and possesses a connascent nothingness, and the only remedy of its inherent terror, perturbation and unstable mutation, is its participation, as much as possible, of a certain portion of divine light.

Quoted by Harrison in *Teachers of Emerson*, p. 286.

Synesius.

These (evil) daimons, who are the progeny of matter wish to make souls their own, and the manner in which they attract them is as follows: It is not possible in the earth that there should be someone who has not a portion of the irrational soul . . . Evil daimons, through this, as through that which is allied to them, invade and betray the animal. –Thus daimons inflame desire, thus they inflame anger, and all such evils as are the sisters of these, associating with souls through the parts that are adapted to themselves, which naturally perceive the presence of the daimons, and are excited and corroborated by them, rising against intellect, till they either vanquish the whole soul, or despair of its caption.

Quoted by Harrison in *Teachers of Emerson*, p. 153.

Proklos.

(Sokrates) according to the energy of his daimon, received

the light proceeding from thence, neither in his dianoetic part alone, nor in his doxastic powers, but also in his spirit, the illumination of the daimon suddenly diffusing itself through the whole of his life, and now moving sense itself.

Quoted by Harrison in *Teachers of Emerson*, p. 149.

Theol. Plat. Proclus.
p. 7. Introd.
Trans. T. Taylor.

True reason asserts that the human soul may be lodged in brutes, yet in such a manner, as that it may obtain its own proper life, and that the degraded soul may, as it were, be carried above it and be bound to the baser nature by a propensity and similitude of affection. And that this is the mode of insinuation we have proved by a multitude of arguments in our Commentaries on the Phaedrus.

Quoted by Mead in *Orpheus*, p. 303.

Proklos.

From the beginning, therefore, and at first, the soul was united to the gods, and its unity to their one. But afterwards the soul, departing from this divine union, descended into intellect and no longer possessed real being unitedly and in one, but apprehended and surveyed them by simple projections, and as it were, contacts of its intellect. In the next place, departing from intellect and descending into reason and dianoia, it no longer apprehended real beings by simple intuitions, but syllogistically and transitively, proceeding from one thing to another, propositions to conclusions. Afterwards, abandoning true reasoning, and the dissolving peculiarity, it descended into generation, and became filled with much irrationality and perturbation.

Quoted by Harrison in *Teachers of Emerson*, p. 285.
H. gives it as occurring in the translation (Taylor's) of *De Mysteriis* as a note on p. 355. R.M.

On the Theology of Plato.
II. 456. 464.
Proklus.

In short, we must say, that the rational and intellectual soul in whatever way it may energize, is beyond body and sense, and therefore it is necessary that it should have an essence separable from both these. This, however, though of itself now evident, I will again manifest from hence, that when it energizes according to nature, it is superior to the influence of Fate, but that when it falls into sense, and becomes irrational and corporeal, it follows the natures that are beneath it, and living with them as with intoxicated neighbours, is held in subjection by a cause that has dominion over things that are different from the rational essence. II. 456.

The highest form of intellectual action is obtained by exciting the profundity of the soul, which is no longer intellectual, and adapting it to union with *the one*. (II. 464.) R. M.

Quoted by Harrison in *Teachers of Emerson*, p. 133.

De Vita Pythag. p. 3.
Note to Iamblichus.
Thomas Taylor.

According to ancient theology between those perpetual attendants of a divine nature, called essential heroes, who are impassive and pure, and the bulk of human souls who descend to earth with passivity and impurity, it is necessary there should be an order of human souls who descend with impassivity and purity. For as there is no vacuum either in incorporeal or corporeal natures it is necessary that the last link of a superior order should coalesce with the summit of one proximately inferior. These souls were called by the ancients terrestrial heroes, on account of their high degree of proximity and alliance to such as are essentially heroes. Hercules, Theseus, Pythagoras, Plato, e.t.c. were souls of this kind who descended into mortality, both to benefit other souls and in compliance with that necessity by which all natures inferior to the perpetual attendants of the Gods are at times obliged to descend.

Note to passage on the divine birth of Pythagoras.

Compare statement about the fifth round men in the *Mahatma Letters*. R. M.

Eleus & Bacch. Myst.
Thomas Taylor.
Wilder edn. p. 8. et. seq.

The ancients by Hades signified nothing more than the profound union of the soul with the present body, and consequently that till the soul separated herself by philosophy from such a ruinous conjunction, she subsisted in Hades even in the present life; her punishment hereafter being nothing more than a continuation of her state upon earth, and a transmigration, as it were, from sleep to sleep, and from dream to dream, and this, too, was occultly signified by the shows of the lesser mysteries.

Quoted in Mead's *Orpheus*, p. 294.

De Mysteriis.
Note to Iamb.
Thomas Taylor.

According to the Egyptians everyone received his proper daimon at the hour of his birth. (p. 320).

Eleusinian and Bacchic Mysteries.
Trans. T. Taylor.
p. 46.

But notwithstanding this important truth was obscurely hinted by the Lesser Mysteries, we must not suppose it was generally known even to the initiated persons themselves; for as individuals of almost all descriptions were admitted to these rites, it would have been ridiculous prostitution to disclose to the multitude a theory so abstracted and sublime. It was sufficient to instruct these in a doctrine of a future state of rewards and punishments, and in the means of returning to the principles from which they originally fell; for this last piece of information was, according to Plato in the Phaedo, the ultimate design of the Mysteries. Hence the reason why it was obvious to none but the Pythagorean and Platonic philosophers, who derived their theology from Orpheus himself,* the original founder of the sacred institutions; and why we meet with no information in this particular in any writer prior to Plotinos; as he was the first who, having penetrated the profound interior wisdom of antiquity, delivered it to posterity without the concealments of mystic symbols and fabulous narratives.

**Herodotus* ii, 51, 81. "What Orpheus delivered in hidden allegories, Pythagoras learned when he was initiated into the Orphic Mysteries: and Plato next received a knowledge of them from the Orphic and Pythagorean writings."

Emerson.
Comp. Wks. II. 3.

There is one mind common to all individual men. Every man is an inlet to the same and to all of the same. He that is once admitted to the right of reason is made a freeman of the whole estate. What Plato has thought, he may think: What a saint has felt, he may feel; what at any time has befallen any man, he can understand. Who has access to this universal mind is a part to all that is or can be done, for this is the only and sovereign agent.

Emerson.

This energy does not descend into individual life or any other condition than entire possession. It comes to the lowly and simple; it comes to whomsoever will put off what is foreign and proud.

Quoted in Harrison's *Teachers of Emerson*, p. 98.
Note: See Plotinos "But it is said of matter" etc.

Emerson.

The ancients believed that a genius or demon took possession at birth of each mortal, to guide him, that these genii were sometimes seen as a flame of fire partly immersed in the bodies which they governed; on an evil man, resting on his head; in a good man, mixed with his substance. They thought the same genius, at the death of his ward, entered a new-born child, and they pretended to guess the pilot by the sailing of the ship.

Quoted by Harrison in *Teachers of Emerson*, pp. 147-8.

Love.
Emerson.

. . . that high philosophy of Beauty which the ancient philosophers delighted in; for they said that the soul of man, embodied here on earth, went roaming up and down in quest of that other world of its own out of which it came into this, but was soon stupified by the light of the natural sun, and unable to see any other objects than those of this world which are but shadows of real things. Therefore the Deity sends the glory of youth before the soul, that it may avail itself of beautiful bodies as aids to its recollections of the celestial good and fair; and a man beholding such a person in the female sex, runs to her and finds the highest joy in contemplating the form, movement and intelligence of this person, because it suggests to him the presence of that which is indeed within the beauty, and the cause of the beauty.

Quoted by Harrison in *Teachers of Emerson*, p. 164.

Emerson. (contd)

There is one Mind common to all individual men. Every man is an inlet to the same and to all of the same . . . . Who hath access to this universal Mind, is a party to all that is or can be done, for this is the only and sovereign agent . . . . Of the works of this Mind, history is the record. . . .

Quoted by Johnson in his *Bhagavad Gita*, p. 109.

Emerson.

The Supreme Critic on the errors of the past and the present, and the only prophet of that which must be, is that great nature in which we rest, as the earth lies in the soft arms of the atmosphere; that Unity, that Oversoul, within which every man's particular being is contained and made one with all others; that common heart, of which all sincere conversation is the worship . . . .

Quoted by Charles Johnston in his translation of *Bhagavad Gita*, p. 109.

Plato. III. 343. Note l.
Thomas Taylor.
Note to FS. & TT.

They (the daimos) stand as it were, over our heads, discourse with each other, and in the meantime speculate our affairs, disapprove our evil deeds, and comment such as are good.

Quoted by Harrison in *Teachers of Emerson*. p. 151.

Enneades.
Plotinos.

But soul, by the power of essence, has dominion over bodies, in such a way, that they are granted and subsist, just as she leads them since they are unable from the first to oppose her will.

Quoted by Harrison in *Teachers of Emerson*. p. 141.

Enneades.
Plotinos.

For the nature of *the one* being generative of all things, is not any one of them. Neither, therefore, is it a certain thing, nor quality, nor a quantity, nor intellect, nor soul, nor that which is moved nor again that which stands still. Nor is it in place, or in time, but is by itself uniform, or rather without form, being prior to all form, to motion and to permanency. (*Select Works.* p. 478.)

Enneades.
Plotinos.

. . . he will be ignorant of the manner in which he sees it (*the one*), but the vision filling the eyes with light, will prevent him from seeing anything else, since the light itself will be the object of his vision.

Quoted by Harrison in *Teachers of Emerson.* p. 162.

Enneades.
Plotinos.

That which is called nature is the offspring of a higher soul, which hath a more powerful life in it.

Quoted by Cudworth in *True Intell.* Sys. I. 256.

Contra Celsum. VII, 46.
Origen.

The disciples of Jesus fix their gaze on the domain of becoming (genesis) in order to use it as a step for rising to the contemplation of the domain of Ideas.

Quoted by De Fay in *Origen and His Work*, p. 155. There is some ambiguity in his reference. The passage may occur in *In Joh*, I. 6. or thereabouts. R. M.

Enneades.
Plotinos.

The assertions, therefore, are by no means discordant with each other, which declare that souls are sown in generation, and that they descend for the sake of causing the perfection of the universe; likewise that they are condemned to suffer punishment, and are confined in a cave.

Quoted by Harrison in *Teachers of Emerson*, p. 241.

Enneades.
Plotinos.

. . . what has made the soul forget its divine Father? How is it that being of a divine nature and born of God, it has come to be ignorant of itself as well as of him? The beginning of evil was its audacious revolt, its fall into the region of becoming and difference, its desire to be something for itself. When it has once tasted of the pleasures of self-will, it makes large use of its power of determining itself as it pleases, and thus is carried so far away from the principle of itself and its being that it loses all consciousness of its original. Such souls are like children torn away from their parents and brought up in a foreign country, till they have forgotten what they themselves are, and who are their parents. Thus seeing neither God nor themselves, they are degraded by ignorance of their kinship. They have learned, indeed, to honor everything rather than themselves, to spend all wonder and reverence and affection upon external things, and to break, so far as they can, all the ties that bound them to the divine. Their ignorance of God is bound up with their admiration of such things, and with their contempt for themselves. For he who pursues and admires that which is alien to himself, *ipso facto* confesses his own inferiority; and believing himself to be lower than the things of this world, he regards himself as the most degraded and transitory of all the creatures that come into being and pass away, and the thoughts of the nature and power of God, is entirely banished from his mind.

Quoted in Caird Vol II. pp. 293-4.

MEDIEVAL SOURCES

Paracelsus.
De Virtute Imaginative.

Imagination is like the sun. The sun has a light which is not tangible, but which, nevertheless, can set a house on fire; thus the imagination is like a sun in man acting in that place to which its light is directed.

Man is mind; he is what he thinks. If he thinks fire, he is on fire; if he thinks war, then he will cause war; it all depends merely on that the whole of his imagination become an entire sun, i.e., that he wholly imagines that which he wills.

Quoted by Hartmann in his *Life of Paracelsus*.

Paracelsus.
Philosophia Occulta.
summarized by Hartmann.

Theosophy is the wisdom of God in man, and therefore cannot be appropriated by any person. It cannot become manifested in man as long as there exists in him the delusion of 'self' because that 'self' is a limited thing, which cannot grasp the infinate (?) indivisible reality. For this reason love, that is to say, the abandonment of 'self' is the beginning of wisdom. This doctrine is generally misunderstood. It does not teach merely that I should desire nothing for myself; but it teaches that there should be no conception of I in my mind that loves or desires anything. Only when that illusion of self has disappeared from my heart and mind, and my consciousness risen to that state in which there will be no I, then will not I be the doer of works, but the spirit of wisdom will perform its wonders through my instrumentality.

Life of Paracelsus. p. 286-87.

Paracelsus.
Philosophia Occulta.
Liber I. Prologue.

Above all we must pay attention to the fact that there are two kinds of spirit in man, (the one originating in nature, the other coming from heaven). Man ought to be a human being according to the spirit of (divine) life, and not according to terrestial spirit of the Limbus. It is a truth that (the heavenly) man is an image of God, having in him a divine spirit (life). In all other respects he is an animal, having as such an animal spirit. These two are opposed to each other, but one of the two is bound to succumb. Man is destined to be a human being, he must live within the spirit of (immortal) life and do away with the animal spirit.

Quoted in Hartmann's *Occult Science in Medicine*, p. 20. Note: The passages in brackets are confusing. The first long one is evidently in the text, the others are probably not very successful efforts on Hartmann's part to elucidate the passage. R. M.

Paracelsus.
De Lunaticis.

Man has two spirits, a divine and a terrestrial spirit. The former is from the breath of God; the latter from the elements of the air and the fire. He ought to live according to the life of the divine spirit, and not according to that of the animal.

Quoted in Hartmann's *Life of Paracelsus*, p. 82.

Paracelsus.
De Invent Art (?)

Men do not know themselves, and therefore they do not

understand the things of their inner world. Each man has the essence of God and all the wisdom and power of the world in himself; he possesses one kind of knowledge as much as another, and he who does not find that which is within him cannot truly say that he does not truly possess it, but only that he was not capable of successfully seeking for it.

> Quoted by Hartmann in his *Life of Paracelsus*, p. 132. H. does not say from which of the books of Paracelsus it is taken but the passage preceding it is from *De Inventione Artium* and the one following is from *Lib. Philos.*

Paracelsus.
De Generat. Hom.

There are two kinds of intelligence, that of the carnal man and that of the spirit; the former argues, the latter knows Animals also have reasoning qualities; but their understanding is not from the light of the spirit.

> Quoted by Hartmann in his *Life of Paracelsus*, p. 134. In the last line "light" Hartmann interpolates the word "direct" in parentheses. If spirit means the Atma in Buddhi or the oversoul, the "direct" is unnecessary.

Paracelsus.
Philosophia Sagax.

There is a light in the spirit of man illuminating everything, and by which he may even perceive supernatural things. Those who seek in the light of external Nature know the things of Nature; those who seek knowledge in the light of men know the things above Nature, which belong to the kingdom of God. Man is an animal, a spirit and an angel, for he has all three qualities. As long as he remains in Nature he serves Nature; if he moves in the spirit, he serves the spirit; if he lives in the angel he serves as an angel. The first quality belongs to the body, the two others to the soul, and they are its jewels. The body of man remains on the earth, but man, having a soul and the two additional qualities, is enabled to rise above Nature, and to know that which does not belong to Nature. He has the power to learn all that belongs to Heaven and Hell, to know God and His kingdom, the angels and spirits, and the origin of evil. If a man is to go to a certain place, it will be useful for him to know all about that place before he goes there; he will then after his arrival be enabled to move about freely and to go wherever he pleases. The quality of each thing created by God, whether it be visible or invisible to the senses, may be perceived and known. If man knows the essence of things, their attributes, their attractions, and the elements of which they consist, he will be a master of Nature, of the elements, and of all the spirits.

> Quoted by Hartmann in his *Life of Paracelsus,* p. 133. In Line 10 after "serves the spirit" he inserts (in him) which loses the point of the oversoul running through the extract.

Paracelsus,
Philosophia Sagax.

Each child receives at the time of its birth a familiar spirit or genius, and such spirits sometimes instruct their pupils even while the latter are in their earliest youth. They often teach them to do very extraordinary things. There is an incalculable number of such genii in the universe and we may learn through them all the mysteries of the Chaos in consequence of their connection with the Mysterium Magnum. Such familiar spirits are called Flagae.

Paracelsus.
Philosophis Sagax.

Man is a twofold being, having a divine and an animal nature. If he feels, and thinks, and acts as divine beings should act, he is the true man; if he feels and acts like an animal, he is then an animal, and the equal of those animals whose mental characteristics are manifested in him. An exalted imagination caused by a desire for the good raises him up; a low imagination caused by a desire for that which is low and vulgar drags him down and degrades him.

Quoted by Hartmann in his *Life of Paracelsus*, p. 140.

Paracelsus.
De Peste.

The wisdom which man ought to have does not come from the earth, nor from the astral spirit, but from the fifth essence -- the Spirit of Wisdom, Therefore man is superior to the stars and constellation provided he lives in the power of that superior wisdom. Such a person, being the master over heaven and earth, by means of his freewill, is called a Magus, and therefore Magic is not sorcery, but supreme wisdom.

Quoted by Hartmann in his *Life of Paracelsus*, p. 130.
Note: In a note Hartmann says the will is only free when it is free from the delusion of self and its desires.

Paracelsus.
Mort. Invis.

Nature is the universal teacher. Whatever we cannot learn from the external appearance of Nature we can learn from her spirit. Both are one. Everything is taught by Nature to her disciple, if he asks for information in an appropriate manner. Nature is a light, and by looking at Nature in her own light we will understand her. Visible Nature can be seen in her visible light; invisible Nature will become visible if we acquire the power to perceive her in her inner light.

The hidden things are there like a pillar of rock before a blind person. He can see it if he is able to open his eyes. The moon shines, but does not show things in their true colours; but if the sun arises, then will the true colours be seen. Thus the external light in Nature is like the moon, beyond which shines the internal light, and in this light that which has been invisible will appear visibly and comprehensively.

Quoted by Hartmann in his *Life of Paracelsus*, p. 132-33.

Paracelsus.
Vera Influentia Rerum.

All things are vehicles of virtues, everything in Nature is a house wherein dwell certain powers and virtues such as God has infused throughout Nature and which inhabit all things in the same sense as the soul is in man; but the soul is a creature originating of God and returns again to God. Natural man is a son of Nature, and ought to know Nature, his mother; but the soul being a son of God, ought to know the Father, the Creator of all.

Quoted by Hartmann in his *Life of Paracelsus*, p. 276.

Paracelsus.
De Lepid. Philosoph.

But this physical body, which is believed to be of so little importance by those who love to dream about the mysteries of the spirit, is the most secret and valuable thing. It is the true "stone which the builders rejected" but which must become the cornerstone of the temple. It is the stone which is considered worthless by those who seek for a God above the clouds and reject Him when He enters their house. This physical body is not merely an instrument for divine power, but it is also the soil from which that which is immortal in man receives its strength. A seed requires the power of the sunshine to enable it to take from the earth the elements necessary for its growth, and in the same sense the spiritual body of man receiving its nutriment from the spirit could not unfold and develop if it were not for the presence of the physical body of man with its elementary and elemental forces; for the physical body is comparable to the wood from which is produced the fire which gives light; there would be no light if there were nothing to burn.

Passage from Hartmann's *Life of Paracelsus* in comment (and summary) on the *De Lapide Philosophorum*, p. 79.

Paracelsus.
De Lunaticis.

Men have two spirits -- an animal spirit and a human spirit -- in them. A man who lives in his animal spirit is like an animal during life, and will be an animal after death; but a man who lives in his human spirit will remain human. Animals have consciousness and reason, but they have no spiritual intelligence. It is the presence of the latter that raises man above the animal, and its absence that makes an animal of what once appeared to be a man. A man in whom the animal reason alone is active is a lunatic, and his character resembles that of some animal. One man acts like a wolf, another like a dog, another like a hog, a snake or a fox, etc. It is their animal principle that makes them act as they do and their animal principle will perish like the animals themselves. But the human reason is not of an animal nature, but comes from God, and being a part of God, it is necessarily immortal.

> Quoted by Franz Hartmann in the *Life of Paracelsus*. In a note on the first sentence Hartmann says, "The human spirit has a twofold aspect, a human and a divine one." See pp. 297-298.

Paracelsus.
De Peste.

The truth does not grow from your speculation and phantasy; but he who understands his own nature in the light of Nature possesses true knowledge. It is not sufficient that we should have a theory of the truth, but we should know the truth in ourselves.

> Quoted by Hartmann in his *Life of Paracelsus*, p. 134.

KABBALA SOURCES

*Etz Chayin.**
Rabbi Chayin Vital.
Kabbala.

The Seven Kings of Edom (mentioned in the Bible symbolically) have emanated from the divine essence before that emanation of which the present universe is a manifestation. They have been, in consequence of their failure, shattered into spiritual fragments. When the new emanation occurred the purer fragments were taken up and became the essence of the angelic hosts, cherubim, seraphim, etc. Others have formed human souls for future incarnation, still others have formed different other entities.

The lowest of all were caught in the whirl of the evil side, and formed the Satanic hosts. And it is the task of the sons of men to elevate those divine sparks which have been lost and immersed in the evil regions, and save them from perdition.

Adam, the first-born, was spiritually the essence of all humanity; he was the prototype of Adam Kadmon; he was the chosen messenger to redeem the divine sparks that were, by their own default, caught in the whirlpool of the Satanic hosts, from their pernicious chains, but he failed too.

After his fall, the divinity in him was contaminated by relentless evil. He lost his power of redemption. Only by a pure and righteous life, and by his death, the grand and spiritual in him separates and emerges from the evil, and a partial redemption is effected.

*Dr. Eisinger translates *Etz Chayin*, "Tree of Life."

Sepher Ha Gilgulim.
Trans. B. Eisinger.
Kabbala.

By the fall of Adam the confusion occurred; the good (spiritual) was dragged down into the evil (gross material), and ever since all the latter-born souls, proceeding from the first-born man, are, as a natural consequence, condemned to bear the brunt of travail to rescue the exiled divine essence from the dark regions. Whatever one accomplishes in life by self-purification and holy conduct is of some value, but the greatest part of his task he achieves by his agony of death, which each one has to go through with no escape.

Most every human soul has to go through various incarnations, suffer many deaths, to restore the divine essence within him and outside of him to the original source of spiritual purity.

The pure, the righteous, and the holy ones, do not have to be reincarnated again and again, but they do so voluntarily to hasten the process and to pave the way for universal salvation.

Sepher Ha Gilgulim.
Trans. B. Eisinger.
Kabbala.

If a great soul is caught on the evil side, its possibility of escape is very narrow. But the inner spiritual force, the divine self, succeeds in the end in overcoming the evil forces, and not only saves itself from destruction, but also draws along with itself some of the drowned divine sparks.

Sepher Ha Gilgulim.
Trans. B. Eisinger.
Kabbala.

When all the divine sparks shall have been freed from their exile, the Messiah will appear in all his glory, the Universe will be renewed, earth and heaven will renew themselves in insuperable brightness, beauty and glory.

Sepher Ha Gilgulim.
Trans. B. Eisinger.
Kabbala.

It was the human being who caused the exile of the divine essence into the dark regions by his disloyalty, disobedience and folly, and it is his task to help in the rescue.

Sepher Ha Gilgulim.
Trans. B. Eisinger.
Kabbala.

In addition to the regular metempsychosis there is also an irregular one, and this occurs when a departed soul enters a living man, so that they may in unison accomplish greater results in rescuing the exiled than they could individually.

Sepher Ha Gilgulim.
Trans. B. Eisinger.
Kabbala.

When the divine essence finds it necessary to enter the exile, and this occurs in every generation, it clothes itself in the ten sephiroth of the evil side, thereby acquiring the ability to enter the manifested universe, and saving a great number of the divine sparks (of the shattered seven Kings of Edom).

> Compare sephiroth with ladder of ten stars. Isabella Maars gives us part of ideagraph, "the superior man."
> Does evil side refer to the descending one?
> "The Exile" means "state of exile." The translation should read "enter into exile." R. M.

Evolution of the Messianic Idea.
Oesterley.

Tehom, the primeval watery monster, is the enemy of gods and men . . . . Tehom comes to be known under a variety of names, viz., the Serpent, the Leviathan, the Dragon and Rahab, and moreover Tehom is identified with the sea . . . . In the great primeval conflict between Tehom and the champion of the gods, the former is indeed overcome but not finally annihilated . . . . In all probability two other Old Testament stories are to be regarded as "extensions" of the Tehom myth: thus in the story of the Fall, the Serpent who is identified with Tehom appears as the embodiment of the principle of evil; and in the story of the Flood, Tehom Rabbah once more appears as the enemy of God.

In the Jahwe myth, the earlier conceptions concerning a semidivine hero who overcame the Dragon and brought blessings to his people are transferred to Jahwe. The underlying idea (of the Paradise myth) is that long ago gods and men lived happily together, there was sufficiency of food, there was ease and comfort and universal peace reigned—the very animals were at peace with one another. A divine personality, who had, however, some human characteristics, ruled over men in justice and equity. There was a specified locality which was the scene of this happy era, the return of which at some future time was looked for.

Widgery (*Comp. St. of Rel..* pp. 253-54) quotes this from Oesterley's *Evolution of the Messianic Idea* , but omits to give the page. R. M.

Genesis.
Old Testament.

When thou tillest the ground, it shall not henceforth yield to thee her strength; a fugitive and a vagabond shalt thou be in the earth.

If thou doest not well sin lieth at the door.

Psalms.
lxxxviii.12.

Wilt thou show wonders to the dead? Shall the dead rise and praise thee? Shall thy loving kindness be declared in the grave? or thy faithfulness in destruction? Shall thy wonders be known in the dark? and thy righteousness in the land of forgetfulness?

Examine context to see if earth life of the soul is meant, especially in the last line. What do the Kabbalists say? R. M.

Old Testament.
Job. viii, 9.

Our days upon earth are a shadow.

Old Testament.
Psalm lxxxii.

God standeth in the congregation of El,
He judgeth among the gods,
How long will ye judge unjustly,
And accept the persons of the wicked? . . . .
I have said, Ye are gods;
And all of you are children of the Most High,
But ye shall die like men,
And fall like one of the princes.

This is the passage to which Jesus has reference in *John*, X, 34-37. R. M.

Sepher Ha Zohar. ii, 70 B.
Kabbala.

The whole universe was incomplete and did not receive its finishing stroke till man was formed, who is the acme of creation and the microcosm, uniting in himself the totality of beings. The Heavenly Adam who emanated from the highest primordial obscurity, created the earthly Adam.

MISCELLANEOUS SOURCES

Mahatma Letters to A. P. Sinnett.
p. 87.

Now there are—there must be—"failures" in the etherial races of the many classes of Dyan Chohans or Devas, as well as among men? But still as these failures are too far progressed and spiritualized to be thrown back forcibly from their Dyan Chohanship into the vortex of a new primordial evolution through the lower kingdoms—this then happens.

When a new solar system is to be evolved these Dyan Chohans are (remember the Hindu allegory of the fallen Devas hurled by Siva into Hudarah who are allowed by Para Brahm to consider it as an intermediate state where they may prepare themselves by a series of rebirths in that sphere for a higher state—a new regeneration) borne in by the influx "ahead" of the elementals and remains as a latent or inactive spiritual force in the aura of the nascent world of a new system until the stage of human evolution is reached.

Then Karma has reached them and they will have to accept to the last drop in the bitter cup of retribution. Then they become an active force and commingle with the Elementals, or progressed entities of the pure animal kingdom to develope little by little the full type of humanity.

In this commingling they lose their high intelligence and spirituality of Devaship to regain them in the end of the seventh ring in the seventh round.

The Paragraphing is mine. R. M.
Text carries cap B on word "borne."
"Remains" should be remain.

Through the Gates of Gold.
Written down by Mabel Collins.
p. 117. ff.

In man, taken individually or as a whole, there clearly exists a double constitution. I am speaking roughly now, being well aware that the various schools of philosophy cut him up and subdivide him according to their several theories.

What I mean is this; that two great tides of emotion sweep through his nature, two great forces guide his life—the one makes him an animal and the other makes him a god. No brute of the earth is so brutal as the man who subjects his godly power to his animal power. This is a matter of course, because the whole force of the double nature is then used in one direction. The animal pure and simple obeys his instincts only, and desires no more than to gratify his love of pleasure, he pays but little regard to the existence of other beings except in so far as they offer him pleasure or pain. He knows nothing of the abstract love of cruelty or of any of these vicious tendencies of the human being which have in themselves their own gratifications.

Thus the man who becomes a beast has a million times the grasp of life over the natural beast, and that which is in the pure animal sufficiently innocent, uninterrupted by an arbitrary moral standard, becomes in him vice because it is gratified on principle. Moreover he turns all the divine powers of his being into this channel, and degrades his soul by making it the slave of his senses. The god, deformed and disguised, waits on the animal and feeds it.

Consider then whether it is not possible to change the situation. The man himself is king of the country in which this strange spectacle is seen. He allows the beast to usurp the place of the god because for the moment the beast pleases his capricious fancy the most. This cannot last always, why let it last any longer? So long as the animal rules there will be the keenest suffering in consequence of change of the vibration between pleasure and pain, of the desire for prolonged and pleasant physical life. And the god in his capacity of servant adds a thousandfold to all this, by making physical life so much more filled with keenness of pleasure—rare, voluptuous, aesthetic pleasure—and by intensity of pain so passionate that one knows not where it ends and where pleasure commences. So long as the god serves, so long the life of the animal will be enriched and increasingly valuable. But let the king resolve to change the face of his court and forcibly evict the animal from the chair of state, restoring the god to the place of divinity.

Ah, the profound peace that falls upon the place! All is indeed changed. No longer is there the fever of personal longings or desires, no longer is there any rebellion or distress, no longer any hunger for pleasure or dread of pain. It is like a great calm decending on a stormy ocean, it is like the soft rain of summer falling on parched ground, it is like the deep pool found amidst the weary, thirsty labyrinth of the unfriendly forest.

But there is much more than this. Not only is man more than an animal because there is the god in him, but he is more than a god because there is the animal in him.

Once force the animal into his rightful place, that of the inferior, and you find yourself in possession of a great force hitherto unsuspected and unknown. The god as servant adds a thousand-fold to the pleasures of the animal, the animal as servant adds a thousand-fold to the powers of the god. And it is upon the union, the right relation of these two forces in himself, that man stands as a strong king, and is capable to raise his hand and lift the bar of the Golden Gate. When these forces are unfitly related, then the king is but a crowned voluptuary, without power, and whose dignity does but mock him; for the animals, undivine, at least know peace and are not torn by vice and despair.

That is the whole secret. That is what makes man strong, powerful, able to grasp heaven and earth in his hands. Do not fancy it is easily done. Do not be deluded into the idea that the religious or the virtuous man does it. Not so! They do no more than fix a standard, a routine, a law by which they hold the animal in check. The god is compelled to serve him in a certain way, and does so, pleasing him with the beliefs and cherished fantasies of the religious, with the lofty sense of personal pride which makes the joy of the virtuous.

These special and canonized vices are things too low and base to be possible to the pure animal, whose only inspirer is Nature herself, always fresh as the dawn. The god in man, degraded, is a thing unspeakable in its power of production.

The animal in man, elevated, is a thing unimaginable in its great powers of service and of strength.

You forget, you who let your animal-self live on, merely checked and held within certain bounds, that it is a great force, an integral portion of the animal life of the world you live in. With it you can sway men, and influence the very world itself, more or less perceptibly according to your strength. The god, given his right place, will so inspire and guide this extraordinary creature, so educate and develop it, so force it into action and recognition of its kind, that it will make you tremble when you recognize the power that has awakened within you. The animal in yourself will then be a king among the animals of the world.

This is the secret of the old-world magicians, who made Nature serve them and work miracles every day for their convenience. This is the secret of the coming race which Lord Lytton foreshadowed for us.

But this power can only be attained by giving the god sovereignty. Make your animal ruler over yourself and he will never rule others.

Suggestive Inquiry Into The Hermetic Mystery.
Mary Atwood
p. 528.

For if a man does not enter in to understand himself and the evil under which he lies enchanted in this life, he cannot understand the ancient doctrine concerning the fall or regeneration, or presume to deliver matter from the original curse, or be instrumental in the restoration.

Awakening of Faith in the Mahayana.
Acvagosha.
Trans. Suzuki, 60, of. 97.

The soul as birth-and-death (samsara) comes forth (as the law of causation) from the Tathagata's womb (Tathagatagarbha). But the immortal (suchness) and the mortal (birth-and-death) coincide with each other. Though they are not identical, they are not a duality.

Quoted: Widgery, *Comparative Study of Religions.* p. 172.

Anaxagoras of Clazomene.

All things were in chaos until reason came to arrange them.

Quoted Caird, *Ev. Theol. in Greek Phil.* II, 33.

Anaximander.

Things perish into those things out of which they have their birth, according to that which is ordained; for they give reparation to one another and pay the penalty of their injustice according to the disposition of time.

Jacob Boehme.
Quoted from Craven's
Michael Maier, p. 93.

By death and contrition of the agent in the patient, and vice versa, the old life is finally crucified, and out of that crucifixion, by reunion of the principles under another law, the new life is elected, which life is a very real and pure quintessence—the mercury so much sought after, even the Elixir of Life, which needs only the corroborative virtue of the Divine Light, which it draws in order to become the living gold of the philosophers, transmuting and multiplicative, the concrete form of that which in the dead metal we esteem.

True Intellectual System of the Universe.
III, 71.
Cudworth.

. . . there can be but one only original mind, or no more than one understanding Being self-existent; all other minds whatsoever partaking of one original mind; and being, as it were, stamped with the impression or signature of one and the same seal. From whence it cometh to pass, that all minds, in the several places and ages of the world, have ideas or notions of things exactly alike, and truths indivisibly the same. Truths are not multiplied by the diversity of minds that apprehend them; because they are all but ectypal participations of one and the same original or archetypal mind and truth. As the same face may be reflected in several glasses; and the image of the same sun may be in a thousand eyes at once beholding it; and one and the same voice may be in a thousand ears listening to it; so when innumerable created minds have the same ideas of things, and understand the same truths, it is but one and the same eternal light that is reflected in them all, (that light which enlighteneth every man that cometh into the world), or the same voice of that one everlasting Word, that is never silent, re-echoed by them.

Quoted in Harrison's *Teachers of Emerson.* p. 81.
See Emerson's passage drawn from this—
"There is one mind, etc."

True Intellectual System.
I. 237-8.
Cudworth.

Nature is not the Deity itself, but a thing very remote from it, and far below it, so neither is it the divine art, as it is in itself pure and abstract, but concrete and embodied only; for the divine art considered in itself is nothing but Knowledge, understanding, or wisdom in the mind of God. (I 237-8.)

Nature is not master of that consummate art and wisdom, according to which it acts, but only a servant to it, and a drudging executioner of the dictates of it. (I. 239.)

Quoted in Harrison's *Teachers of Emerson*. p. 190.

Dio. Chrysosom.
(Or. xxx. 550.)

"I will tell you something which is neither pleasant nor agreeable. We men are of the blood of the Titans;* and since they are hostile to the Gods,** we also are not friends with the latter, but are ever being punished by them, and ever on the watch for punishment to fall on our heads."

Quoted by Mead, *Orpheus*. p. 183.
*In parentheses Mead gives "Asuras."
**In parentheses Mead gives "Devas."

Vit. Isodori.
Phot. ccxlii, 526.
Damascius.

(Speaking of the dismemberment of Osiris and his resurrection) "this should be a mingling with God, an all-perfect at-one-ment, a return upwards of our souls to the divine.

Quoted by Mead in *Orpheus*. p. 186.

Tao Teh King.
Lao Tsze.
Parker Trans. II, 47.

One may know the world without ever crossing the threshold; one may discern the Providence of Heaven (divine oversoul) without ever looking out of the window. In fact the farther abroad you go the less you may know. For which reason the highest form of man knows without walking forth; gives names without seeing; and accomplishes without seeming to do anything.

Parker's *Studies in Chinese Religion*. p. 120.

Manichean Fragment from
Turfan.

When we had come to know the true God and the pure law we knew the Two Roots and the law of the Three Times. The Bright Root we knew to be the Paradise of God, the Dark Root we knew to be the Empire of Hell. We knew what had been in existence before there was an Earth-God. We knew who had created Heaven and Earth and by what means the argon Earth-God will again be reduced to naught, and how, thereby, Light and Darkness will again be parted; we know what will happen after these events. Believing in and placing our reliance upon Azrua, the God, upon the Sun and Moon God, upon the powerful God and upon the Burkhans, we became Auditores.

–Prayer of a layman or hearer.
See other extract for origin.

Manichean Fragment from
Turfan.

Khormuzta, the God, (and) the Five God came descending with the purity of all the gods, in order to engage in battle against the demon; he battled against the Smnudom, inclining to evil deeds, and against the five kinds of demonry. God and the demons, light and darkness at that time intermingled. God Khormuzta's youth, the Five God, our souls, engaging in combat with sin and demonry became ensnared and intertangled.

(Forgiveness is asked for) the Born and Created who forgot and forfeited the eternal heaven of the Gods, and became separated from the Light Gods. Thereafter, my God, if, because the Smnu, intending evil deeds, has led our understandings and our thoughts astray . . . to demoniacal actions, and if, because thereby we have become unwise and void of understanding, we should have sinned and erred against the foundation and root of all bright spirits, against pure Azrua, the Lord . . . .

Passage from a prayer and confession discovered by Drs. Stein and Grunwedel at Turfan on the borders of China. Published Berlin 1904 in the Vigur dialect of old Turkish and in German translation by Dr. F.W.K. Muller.

See article in *Royal Asiatic Soc's Journal*, April 1911, by A.V. LeCoq.

See article *The Religion of Mani*, Guest Vol. III. 1911-12 by F.C. Conyleers from which above is quoted.

Nagarjuna (?).
Trans. Beal in *Catena* etc.
p. 374.

For if the heart, the inner self, be the same as the universal self, such a close connection, rather identity, necessitates the idea of a most intimate communion of interest.

Quoted by Widgery in *Comp. St. of Rel.* p. 75.

Samyutta Nikaya.
i, 4, 4.
Warren Trans.

Through birth and rebirth's endless round,
Seeking in vain I hastened on,
To find who framed this edifice,
What misery! I've discovered thee!
This fabric thou shalt ne'er rebuild!
Thy rafters are all broken now,
And pointed roof demolished lies,
This mind has demolition reached,
And seen the last of all desire.

Widgery who quotes this version of the Liberation speech gives two sources for the original. One is *Samyutta Nikaya* i, 4, 4. The other is *Therigatha*, 14; 67; H. C. Warren, Buddhism in Translation, p. 83. He refers also to the introduction to *Jataka,* i, 76. This muddle of references occurs at p. 227 of his book *Comp. Study of Rel.*

Empedocles.
Greek.

Fools, who think aught can begin to be which formerly was not, or that aught which is can perish and utterly decay! Another truth I now unfold: No natural birth is there of mortal thing nor is death's destruction final. Nothing is there but a mingling, and then a separation of the mingled, which are called a birth and death by ignorant mortals.

[See also Walt Whitman: "I too have knitted the old knot of contrariety." *Crossing Brooklyn Ferry.*] R.M.

New Testament.
James, Epistle. Ch. 3.

"The wisdom that is from above is first pure, then peaceable, gentle, and easy to be entreated . . . full of mercy and good fruits, without partiality and without hypocrisy. And the fruit of righteousness is sown in peace of them that make peace.

"But if ye have bitter envying and strife in your hearts, glory not and lie not against truth. This wisdom descendeth not from above, but is earthly, psychical, devilish."

Quoted by Widgery in Com. St. of Rel. p.75.

Crock of Gold. p.50.
James Stephens.

But she listened, not with her ears, but with her blood. The fingers of her soul stretched out to clasp a stranger's hand, and her disquietude was quickened through with an eagerness which was neither physical nor mental, for neither her body nor her mind was definitely interested. Some dim region between them grew alarmed, and watched and waited and did not sleep or grow weary at all.

Bridge of San Luis Rey.
Wilder, Thornton.
p. 165;

We came from a world where we have known incredible

standards of excellence, and we dimly remember beauties which we have not seized again, and we go back to that world. Uncle Pio and Camila Perichole were tormenting themselves in an effort to establish in Peru the standards of the theatres in some Heaven whither Calderon had preceded them. The public for which masterpieces are intended is not on this earth.

Ode on Immortality.
Wordsworth.

Our birth is but a sleep and a forgetting;
The Soul that riseth with us, our life's Star,
Hath had elsewhere its setting,
And rises* from afar.

*Cometh. R. M.

Part III B.

A Further Collection of References and Comments

By John L. Davenport

These references were found over many years. Such references may be found by anyone who is on the alert for them after gaining an understanding of Mr. Mitchell's writings. His ideas are inherent in each of us. They may be observed in everyday life by watching the eternal contention that goes on between I (the ego) and the lower entity (animal soul). Their arguments never cease. It is often seen in cartoons which poke fun at human foibles. For instance everyone understands the cartoon of Al Johns which is clearly an argument between the man (as redeemer) and another strong entity within him (see p. 248).

Mention has been made that decisions on the conduct of man's life must be made daily. The contentious animal soul argues continually with the conscious mind (ego) for his particular likes, dislikes, comforts and pleasure. He will put obstacles in the way and argue against anything that looks like hard work particularly if it has no emotional phase.

Sometimes these arguments are so confusing it is dificult to know who is talking to whom. The secret of our well-being is to be able to discriminate between the two, the choice of direction is then clear for the ego.

> Thou shalt separate the earth from the fire, the subtle from the gross, gently, with much sagacity.
>
> *Hermes Trismegistos.*

The worst situation comes about when the lower soul

"I think we'd better have another little talk."

THE SATURDAY EVENING POST
Courtesy of Al Johns

has been slowly, even stealthily, winning dominance as for instance in the consumption of food, alcohol or drugs. The bitter conflicts that take place can destroy the person's health, progress and achievements.

Discrimination may be achieved if the attributes of the two sides are analyzed in accordance with the accompanying table. Then take the path of the redeeming soul with deliberation.

Attributes of the Higher Soul	Attributes of the Lower Animal Soul
Love and brotherhood	Five senses
Conscious mind	Seat of emotions
Subliminal (psych.)	Subconscious mind (psych.)
Rationality	Unconscious mind (psych.)
Peace of mind	Shadow (psych. Jung)
Noble ideals	Passion
Inspiration	Irrationality
Conscience	Desires
Loyalty	Likes and dislikes
Sense of duty	Hate
Humanism	Anger
Humility	Murder
Truth	Meanness
Intellect	Lying
Frankness	Jealousy
Cosmic consciousness	Covetness
Devotion	Slander
Altruism	Boasting
Quest of beauty	Arrogance
Self-sacrifice	Fears
Generosity	Insecurity
Long suffering	Doubts
Kindness	Vitality

Goodness
Faith
Hope
Charity
Temperance
Reverence
Sympathy
Compassion
Forgiveness
Speak well of others
Sublime
Redeemer
Sincerity
Intuition
Communicates through language

Etheric double
Astral (psych.)
Personality
Water (symbol)
Temptation
Thwarter of higher aspirations
Complaints
Center is heart
Suspicious
Laziness
Greed
Grief
Despondency
Brutality
Depression
Melancholy
Sullen
Personal comfort
Insincerity
Selfishness
Pleasure
Sex abuse
Communicates through images

The ego (conscious mind) being part of the higher soul is the active redeemer of the animal soul. It stands as the bridge between the spirit and the animal soul bringing down the powers of the spirit to purify and still the emotional desires of the animal soul.

The ego has the power of making imaginative forms which can be used in the work of purification or made available to the animal soul who will use it to magnify its own fears, passions and powers.

CHINESE SOURCES

Hist. of Relig. Beliefs and Philos.
Opinions in China (1927), pp. 120, 680ff;
L. Wieger, *Textes Philosophiques* (1930), p. 346ff.;
D.H. Smith, 'Chinese Concepts of the Soul',
Numen, vol. 2 (1958)
A Dictionary of Comparative Religion
General Editor , S.G.F. Brandon, (1970)

HUN and P'O. According to Chinese theory, the nature of man is essentially dualistic. He possesses two soul elements, one partaking of nature of *Yang* and the other of *Yin*. These two soul-elements went by different names, the most common being *hun* and *p'o*. The *hun* is *yang*, pure and intelligent; the *p'o* is *yin*, turbid and earthy. At birth they combine; at death they separate. According to some late Taoist accounts, there were 3 *hun* and 7 *p'o*.

The *p'o* is the animal spirit which appertains to form, gives perception to the senses, and is ruling element in man's emotive nature. Wieger is probably right in connecting it with sperm, so that it becomes a constituent of human nature at conception. At death it still clings to the corpse, becomes a ghost and returns with the corpse to earth, gradually to dissipate its vital force.

The *hun* enters the child with the first breath at birth, and is the first to depart at death, ascending like vapor to become a a spirit. To die is therefore 'to sever or cut off the *hun*'. To lose one's wits is to 'lose the *hun*'. To call back the soul and thus to be resuscitated, is to 'call back the *hun*'.

The developed doctrine is set forth in the *Shu Chu Tzu*, a Taoist work of the 13th century. There it states that 'the human personality is said to have two souls, the *hun* and the *p'o*. . . . . . The true man nourishes the *hun* whilst the majority of mankind nourish the *p'o*. . . . . At birth the *p'o* is first produced and then the *hun*. At death the *hun* first departs, and afterwards the *p'o* is dissipated. . . . . In a living man the *hun* and *p'o* live together in a harmonious relationship like husband and wife. At death they separate, the *hun* to rise, the *p'o* to descend, and they no longer have any regard for each other. . . . . If a former *hun* can receive a new *p'o* it can return to life. The *p'o* of a dead man, if it can receive the vital force, can also return to life. When the bones decay, the *p'o* is also destroyed. There are cases in which a *p'o* has not been dissipated for a hundred years. No *hun* can exist for more than five generations.'

D.H.S.

The Religious System of China (1875), vol. 4, pp.5ff.
J.J.M. de Groot; D.H. Smith, '*Chinese Concepts of the Soul*',
in *Numen,* vol. 5 (1958).
A Dictionary of Comparative Religion
General Editor, S.G.F. Brandon, (1970)

KUEI (KWEI). Chinese term used for disembodied spirits, demons, spirits of the dead, ghosts or goblins. The character, being a pictogram depicting a being of fearsome aspect, is one of oldest in the language, being frequently used on the Oracle Bones. It is a 'primitive' or 'radical', whilst other characters used to designate the soul, the spirit of the vital breath *(shen, ch'i, hun, p'o, ling*, etc.) are all composite in form, which suggests that they were invented later. From very early times Chinese literature refers to spiritual beings as *kuei shen* corresponding to the *p'o* and the *hun,* the vital elements or soul constituents of a living man. The *kuei* were thought of as living on for awhile after death with the corpse in the earth, receiving sustenance from sacrifices made to the ancestor spirit. Improper burial, neglect of sacrifices, or death through unpropitious circumstances might lead to *kuei* as maleficient ghosts or demons to haunt the living. These *kuei* became the subject of innumerable tales in Chinese folklore.

D.H.S.

[At the entrances to the temples of the Far East there are usually two huge ugly evil monsters. The inquiring tourist is told that they are there to frighten away the evil spirits. Evil frighten evil?
The real answer is a symbolic one. The person approaching the temple seeking enlightenment must first conquer and purify his lower self (the evil one) before gaining admittance.]

GREEK SOURCES

Hierocles–Greek Philospher.
From General Introduction
of Thomas Taylor's
Translations of The Works of Plato.
Vol. I, p. 3.

Philosophy is the purification and perfection of human life. It is the purification, indeed, from material irrationality, and the mortal body; but the perfection, in consequence of being the resumption of our proper felicity, and a reascent to the divine likeness. To effect these two is the province of *Virtue* and *Truth*; the former exterminating the immoderation of the passions; and the latter introducing the divine form to those who are naturally adapted to its reception.

The Key To Theosophy.
The Septenary Nature of Man.
H. P. Blavatsky.
p. 89.

. . . he who is acquainted with the archaic doctrine finds the seven in Plato's various combinations of Soul and Spirit. He regarded man as constituted of two parts–one eternal, formed of the same essence as the Absoluteness; the other mortal and corruptible, deriving its constituent parts from the minor "created" Gods. Man is composed, he shows, of 1) a mortal body; 2) an immortal principle; and 3) a "separate mortal kind of Soul." It is that which we respectively call the physical man, the Spiritual Soul or Spirit (*nous*), and the animal soul (*psuche*). . . .Now, so plain is it that Plato, and even Pythagoras, while speaking but of three "principles," give them seven separate functions in their various combinations, that if we contrast our teachings this will become quite plain. Let us take a cursory view of these seven aspects by drawing a table. [See also table on p. 276.]

Sanskrit Terms	Exoteric Meaning	Explanatory
(a) Rupa, or Sthula Sharira.	(a) Physical body.	(a) Is the vehicle of all the other "principles" during life.
(b) Prana.	(b) Life, or vital principle.	(b) Necessary only to *a, c, d,* and the functions of the lower Manas, which embrace all those limited to the (*physical*) brain.
(c) Linga Sharira.	(c) Astral body.	(c) The *Double*, the phantom body.
(d) Kama Rupa	(d) The seat of animal desires and passions.	(d) This is the center of the animal man, where lies the line of demarcation which separates the mortal man from the immortal entity.
(e) Manas—a dual principle in its functions.	(e) Mind, intelligence; the higher human mind, whose light, or radiation, links the Monad for the lifetime, to the mortal man.	(e) The future state and the Karmic destiny of man depend on whether Manas gravitates more downward to Kama Rupa, the seat of the animal passions, or upward to Buddhi, the Spiritual *Ego*. In the latter case, the higher consciousness of the individual Spiritual aspirations of *mind* (Manas), assimilating Buddhi, is absorbed by it and forms the *Ego*, which goes into Devachanic bliss.
(f) Buddhi.	(f) The Spiritual Soul.	(f) The vehicle of pure universal spirit.
(g) Atma.	(g) Spirit.	(g) One with the Absolute, as its radiation.

The Works of Plato.
General Introduction.
Thomas Taylor, 1804.
Vol. I, pp. xvii, xviii, xix.

And indeed the soul which moves the body, must be considered as a more proper self-moved essence. This, however, is twofold, the one rational, the other irrational. For that there is a rational soul is evident: or has not everyone a cosensation of himself, more clear or more obscure, when converted to himself in the attentions to and investigations of himself, and in the vital and gnostic animadversions of himself? For the essence which is capable of this, and which can collect universals by reasoning, will very justly be rational. The irrational soul also, though it does not appear to investigate these things, and to reason with itself, yet at the same time it moves bodies from place to place, being itself previously moved from itself; for at different times it exerts a different impulse.

. . . For if the irrational soul is a certain essence, it will have peculiar energies of its own, not imparted from something else, but proceeding from itself.

. . . Nor does irrational appetite desire itself, but aspires after a certain object of desire, such as honour, or pleasure, or riches . . . and the irrational soul which verges to the separable; for it appears in a certain respect to subsist by itself separate from a subject;

. . . On this account, to some of the antients, it [irrational soul] appeared to be a certain soul, but to others, nature.

Ibid. Vol. I, p. xxix.

From this divine self-perfect and self-producing multitude, a series of self-perfect natures viz. of beings, lines, intellects, and souls proceeds, according to Plato, in the last link of which series he also classes the human soul; proximately suspended from the daemoniacal order: for this order, as he clearly asserts in *The Banquet*, stands in the middle rank between the divine and human, fills up the vacant space, and links together all intelligent nature.

Ibid.
Vol. I, p. lvix.

In consequence of this middle subsistance, the mundane soul, from which all partial souls are derived, it is said by Plato, in *The Timaeus* to be a medium between that which is indivisible and that which is divisible about bodies, i.e. the mundane soul is a medium between the mundane intellect and the whole of that corporeal life which the world participates.

> [Note: The important thing here is that Plato like R. M. has the idea of an ego between the divine and the human animal.]

Ibid.
Vol. I, p. lvix.

He (man) has likewise an ethereal vehicle analagous to the heavens, and a terrestrial body composed from the four elements, and with which it is coordinate.

Ibid.
Vol. I, p. lxi.

After this follows the irrational nature [soul] the summit of which is the fantasy which perceives everything accompanied with figure [space] and interval [time]; on this account may be called *a figured intelligence* . . . . Under this subsist anger and desire, the former resembling a raging lion and the latter a many-headed beast; and the whole is bounded by sense.

Further still, in order that the union of the soul with this gross terrestrial body may be effected in a becoming manner, two vehicles, according to Plato, are necessary as media, one which is ethereal, and the other aerial; and of these, the ethereal is *simple and immaterial* but the aerial, *simple and material*; and this dense earthly body is *composite and material.*

Ibid.
Vol. I, p. lxiii.

It remains therefore, that every soul must perform periods, both of ascensions from generation, and of descensions into generation; and that this will never fail, through an infinite time.

From all this it follows that the soul, which is an inhabitant of earth, is in a fallen condition, an apostate from deity, an exile from the orb of light.

[Comment: These statements refer to the continuous departure and return to earth of the exiled soul.]

Ibid.
Vol. I, p. lxvii.

From this account of the human [or rational] soul that most important Platonic dogma [truth] necessarily follows. That our soul essentially contains all knowledge, and that whatever knowledge she acquires in the present life, is in reality nothing more than a recovery of what she once possessed. This recovery is very properly called by Plato reminiscence, not as being attended with actual recollection in the present life, but as being an actual repossession of what the soul had lost through her oblivious union with the body.

Ibid.
Vol. I, p. lii.

But as the divine Plato says, it is the province of our soul to collect things into one by a reasoning process, and to possess a reminiscence of those transcendant spectacles, which we once beheld when governing the universe in conjunction with deity.

> [Comment: This gives an inkling as to how far we had advanced before being required to redeem the animal soul.]

Ibid.
Vol. I, p. xlix.

The divine Pythagoras, and all those who have legitimately received his doctrines, among whom Plato holds the most distinguished rank, asserted that there are many orders of beings, viz. intelligible, intellectual, dianoetic, physical, or in short, vital and corporeal essences.

MS. Commentary of Proclus on
The First Alcibiades.
Trans. by T. Taylor in
Vol. I of *The Works of Plato.*

Nor are natures subordinate to the human and which are called irrational, adapted to learn any dianoetic discipline, or to discover anything by themselves. But the human soul containing in itself all reasons, and preassuming all sciences, is indeed darkened from generation, respecting the theory of what it possesses, and requires discipline and invention; and through discipline it may excite its intellections, and through invention may discover itself, and the plenitude of reasons it contains. And there are the gifts of the gods, benefiting it in its fallen condition and recalling it to an intellectual life.

Ibid.
Vol. I, p. 481.

For his (Plato's) design, as we have said, was to unfold our nature, and the whole essence according to which each of us is defined; and to unveil the Delphic mandate Know Thyself through demonstrative methods. But the preface itself converts the young man to himself, and represents him as exploring his own pre-subsisting conceptions; and at the same time that it converts him to himself, leads him to a survey, as from a watch tower, of Socratic Science.

Proclus Notes on *The First Alcibiades.*
From T. Taylor's *The Works of Plato.*
Vol. I, p. 492.

The descent of the soul into body separates it from divine souls, from whom it is filled with intelligence, power, and purity, and conjoins it with generation, and nature, and material things, from which it is filled with oblivion, wandering, and ignorance. For, in its descent, multiform lives and various vestments grow upon it, which draw it down into a mortal composition, and darken its vision of real being. It is requisite therefore that the soul which is about to be led properly from hence to that ever-vigilant nature, should amputate those second and third powers which are suspended from its essence, in the same manner as weeds, stones and shells, from the marine Glaucus; should restrain its externally proceeding impulses, and recollect true beings and a divine essence, from which it descended, and to which it is fit that the whole of our life should hasten. But the parts or powers which are in want of perfection in us, are: the irrational life, which is naturally adapted to be adorned and disciplined through manners; the proaeretic* part, which requires to be withdrawn from irrational appetites, and a connection with them; and besides these our gnostic power, which requires a reminiscence of true beings.

**Proaeresis* is a deliberative tendency to things within the reach of our ability to effect.

The Republic of Plato.
Book IX, p. 435-6.
The Works of Plato.
Thomas Taylor's trans.

And do you not think that to be intemperate, has of old been discommended on such accounts as these, because that in such a one that terrible, great and multiform beast was indulged more than was meet? And are not arrogance and moroseness blamed, when the lion and the serpentine disposition increases and stretches beyond measure. . . . Shall we say it is on any other account than this, that when a man has the form of that which is best in his soul naturally weak, so as not to be able to govern the creatures within himself, but to minister to them, he is able only to learn what flatters them? . . . Do we not say that he [the animal] must be servant of one who is best, and who has within him the divine governor?

Ibid.
Book IX, p. 417.

Socrates:

But what we want to be known is this, that there is in every one a certain species of desire which is terrible, savage and irregular, even in some who entirely seem to us to be moderate.

[See also Robert Louis Stevenson's *Books Which Have Influenced Me*. See p. 3 in Section I, Whither.]

Thomas Taylor the Platonist.
Concerning the Cave of the Nymphs. p. 319.
Princeton University Press. 1969.

Two urns by Jove's high throne have ever stood,
The source of evil one, and one of good.

[Comment: See also p. 269.]

Footnote by Proclus in *The Republic of Plato.*
T. Taylor's trans., p. 438.

The following admirable account of poetry, from the Explanation of the more difficult questions in the Republic, by Proclus, will I doubt not be highly acceptable to the reader, as it both contains a most accurate and scientific division of poetry, and perfectly reconciles the prince of philosophers with the first of poets. T. T.

"There are three lives in the soul, of which the best and most perfect is that according to which it is conjoined with the Gods, and lives a life most allied, and through the highest similitude united to them; no longer subsisting from itself but from them, running under its own intellect, exciting the ineffable impression of *the one* which it contains, and connecting like with like, its own light with that of the Gods, and that which is most uniform in its own essence and life, with *the one* which is above all essence and life. That which is second to this in dignity and power, has a middle arrangement in the middle of the soul, according to which indeed it is converted to itself, descending from a divinely inspired life; and placing intellect and science as the principles of its energy, it evolves the multitude of its reasons, surveys the all-various mutations of forms, collects into sameness, intellect, and that which is the object of intellect, and expresses in images an intellectual and intelligible essence. The third life of the soul is that which accords with its inferior powers, and energizes together with them, employing phantasies and irrational senses, and being entirely filled with things of a subordinate nature."

Porphyry's *De Antro Nympharum*
From the Commentaries of Proclus.
Trans. by Thomas Taylor. (London 1788-1789)

After the same manner the Persians, mystically signifying the descent of the soul into an inferior nature and its ascent into the intelligible world, initiate the priest or mystic in a place which they denominate a cave.

The Platonic Philosopher's Creed.
Miscellanies in Prose and Verse.
Thomas Taylor. 1805.

I also believe that man is a microcosm, comprehending in himself *partially* every thing which the world contains divinely and *totally*. That hence he is endued with an intellect subsisting in energy, and a rational soul proceeding from the same causes as those from which the intellect and soul of the universe proceed. And that he has likewise an ethereal vehicle analogous to the heavens, and a terrestrial body composed from the four elements, and with which also it is co-ordinate.

I believe that the rational part of man, in which his essence consists, is of a self-motive nature, and that it subsists between intellect, which is immovable both in essence and energy, and nature, which both moves and is moved.

I believe that the human as well as every mundane soul uses periods and restitutions of its proper life. For in consequence of being measured by time, it energizes transitively, and possesses a proper motion. But every thing which is moved perpetually, and participates of time, revolves periodically, and proceeds from the same to the same.

I also believe that the human soul ranks among the number of those souls that *sometimes* follows the mundane divinities, in consequence of subsisting immediately after daemons and heroes the perpetual attendants of the gods, it possesses a power of descending infinitely into the sublunary region, and of ascending from thence to real being. That in consequence of this, the soul while an inhabitant of earth is in a fallen condition, an apostate from deity, and exile from the orb of light. That she can only be restored while on earth the divine likeness, and be able after death to reascend to the intelligible world, by the exercise of the *cathartic* and *theoretic* virtues; the former purifying her from the defilements of a mortal nature, and the latter elevating her to the vision of true being. And that such a soul returns after death to her kindred star from which she fell, and enjoys a blessed life.

I believe that the human soul essentially contains all knowledge, and that whatever knowledge she acquires in the present life is nothing more than a recovery of what she once possessed; and which discipline evocates from its dormant retreats.

I also believe that the soul is punished in a future for the crimes she has committed in the present life; but that this punishment is proportioned to the crimes, and is not perpetual; divinity punishing, not from anger or revenge, but in order to purify the guilty soul, and restore her to the proper perfection of her nature.

I also believe that the human soul on its departure from the present life will, if not properly purified, pass into other terrene bodies; and that if it passes into a human body, it becomes the soul of that body; but if into the body of a brute, it does not become the soul of the brute, but is externally connected with the brutal soul in the same manner as presiding daemons are connected in their beneficent operations with mankind; for the rational part never becomes the soul of the irrational nature.

Lastly, I believe that souls that live according to virtue shall in other respects be happy; and when separated from the irrational nature, and purified from all body, shall be conjoined with the gods, and govern the whole world, together with the deities by whom it was produced.

The Timaeus.
The Works of Plato—trans. by Thomas Taylor.
The Timaeus and Critias, Bollingen Series III.
Princeton University Press. 1944.

True (real) being . . . is apprehended by intelligence and in conjunction with reason. p. 107-108. A Proclus note . . . .

But the latter (the generated body) is perceived by opinion in conjunction with *irrational sense*; since it subsists in a state of generation and corruption, and never truly is. p. 108 . . . .

Hence, Divinity placed water and air in the middle of fire and earth and fabricated them as much as possible in the same ratio to each other; so that fire might be to air as air to water; and that as air is to water so water might be to earth. p. 116-117. . . .

The mortal natures, therefore, may subsist and that the universe may be truly all, convert yourselves, according to your nature, to the fabrication of animals, imitating the power which I (the demiurgus) employed in your generation. And whatever among these is of such a nature as to deserve the same appellation with immortals, which obtain sovereignty in these, and willingly pursues justice and reverences you—of this I myself will deliver the seed and the beginning; it is your business to accomplish the rest; to weave together the mortal and immortal nature; by this means fabricating and generating animals, causing them to increase by supplying them with aliment, and receiving them back again when dissolved by corruption. p. 146.

Ibid.
Footnote. p. 156-157.

Plato, says Proclus, immediately conjoining the soul to the body, omits all the problems pertaining to the descent of the soul, such as the prophet, the allotments, the lives, the elections, the daemon, the residence in the plain of oblivion, the sleeping, the oblivious potion, the thunders, and all such particulars as the fable in the Republic discusses. But neither does he here deliver such things as pertain to the soul after its departure from the body, such as the terrors, the rivers, Tartarus, those savage and fiery daemons. the thorns, the bellowing and mouth, the triple road, and the judges, concerning which the fable in the Republic, in the Gorgias, and in the Phaedo, instructs us. What, then, you will say, is the cause of this omission? We reply, Because Plato preserves that which is adapted to the design of the dialogue. For here he admits whatever is physical in the theory respecting the soul, and its association with the body.

It is requisite, however, to inquire why souls fall into bodies. And we may reply, with Proclus, Because they wish to imitate the providential energies of the Gods, and on this account proceed into generation, and leave the contemplation of true being: for, as Divine perfection is twofold, one kind being intellectual, and the other providential, and one kind consisting in an abiding energy, and the other in motion, hence souls imitate the prolific, intellectual, and immutable energy of the Gods by contemplation, but their providential and motive characteristic through a life conversant with generation. As the intelligence, too, of the human soul is partial, so likewise is her providence; but, being partial, it associates with a partial body. But still further, the descent of the soul contributes to the perfection of the universe; for it is necessary that there should not only be immortal and intellectual animals, such as are the perpetual attendants of the Gods, nor yet mortal and irrational animals only, such as are the last progeny of the demiurgus of the universe, but likewise such as subsist between these, and which are by no means immortal,* but are capable of participating reason and intellect. And in many parts of the universe there are many animals of this kind; for man is not the only rational and mortal animal, but there are other such-like species, some of which are more daemoniacal, and others approximate nearer to our essence. But the descents of a partial soul contribute to the perfect composition of all animals, which are at the same time mortal and rational.

Should it be again asked, Why, therefore, are partial souls descending into generation filled with such material perturbation, and such numerous evils? we reply, that this takes place through

*For the whole composite which we call man is not immortal, but only the rational soul.

the inclination arising from their free will; through their vehement familiarity with body; through their sympathy with the image of soul, or that divisible life which is distributed about body; through their abundant mutation from an intelligible to a sensible nature, and from a quiet energy to one entirely conversant with motion; and through a disordered condition of being, naturally arising from the composition of dissimilar natures, viz. of the immortal and mortal, of the intellectual and that which is deprived of intellect, of the indivisible and that which is endued with interval. For all these become the cause to the soul of this mighty tumult and labour in the realms of generation; since we pursue a flying mockery which is ever in motion. And the soul, indeed, by verging to a material life, kindles a light in her dark tenement the body, but she herself becomes situated in obscurity; and by giving life to the body, she destroys herself and her own intellect, in as great a degree as these are capable of receiving destruction. For thus the mortal nature participates of intellect, but the intellectual part of death, and the whole becomes a prodigy, as Plato beautifully observes in his Laws, composed of the mortal and immortal, of the intellectual, and that which is deprived of intellect. For this physical law, which binds the soul to the body, is the death of the immortal life, but is the cause of vivification to the mortal body.

Ibid.
p. 194-195.

The demiurgus in the first place adorned all these, afterwards established the world from their conjunction, and rendered it one animal, containing in itself all mortal and immortal animals. And of divine natures, indeed, he himself became the author; but he delivered to his offspring the junior Gods the fabrication of mortal natures. Hence, these imitating their father's power, and receiving the immortal principle of the soul, fashioned posterior to this the mortal body, assigned the whole body as a vehicle to the soul, and fabricated in it another mortal species of soul, possessing dire and necessary passions through its union with the body. The first indeed of these passions is pleasure, which is the greatest allurement to evil; but the next is pain, which is the exile of good. After these follow boldness and fear, those mad advisers; anger, hard to be appeased; hope, which is easily deceived; together with irrational sense, and love, the general invader of all things. In consequence, therefore, of mingling these together, the junior Gods necessarily composed the mortal race. And religiously fearing lest the divine nature should be defiled through this rout of molestations more than extreme necessity required, they lodged the mortal part, separate from the divine, in a different receptacle of the body; fabricating the head and breast, and placing the neck between as an isthmus and boundary, that the two extremes might be separate from each other.

In the breast, therefore, and that which is called the thorax, they seated the mortal genus of the soul. And as one part of it is naturally better, but another naturally worse, they fabricated the cavity of the thorax; distributing this receptacle in the woman different from that of the man, and placing in the middle of these the midriff or diaphragm. That part of the soul, therefore, which participates of fortitude and anger, and is fond of contention, they seated nearer the head, between the midriff and the neck; that becoming obedient to reason, and uniting with it in amicable conjunction, it might together with reason forcibly repress the race of desires, whenever they should be found unwilling to obey the mandates of reason, issuing her orders from her lofty place of abode. But they established the heart, *which is both the fountain of the veins, and of the blood, which is vehemently impelled through all the members of the body in a* CIRCULAR PROGRESSION, in an habitation corresponding to that of a satellite; that when the irascible part becomes inflamed, reason at the same time announcing that some unjust action has taken place externally, or has been performed by some one of the inward desires, then every thing sensitive in the body may swiftly through all the narrow pores perceive the threatenings and exhortations, may be in every respect obedient, and may thus permit that which is the best in all these to maintain the sovereign command.

Thomas Taylor the Platonist.
Concerning the Cave of the Nymphs, p. 319.
Bollingen Series LXXXVIII.
Princeton University Press. 1969.

But Plato, in his Gorgias, by vases understands souls, some of which are beneficent and others malignant, and again some are rational and others irrational. But souls are denominated vases because they are capacious of certain energies and habits, after the manner of vessels.

Ibid.
p. 324-325.

Nine prosp'rous days, we ply'd the lab'ring oar;
The tenth presents our welcome native shore:
The hills display the beacon's friendly light,
And rising mountains gain upon our sight.
Then first my eyes by watchful toils opprest,
Comply'd to take the balmy gifts of rest;
Then first my hands did from the rudder part,
(So much the love of home possess'd my heart.)

Lib. x. l. 28, &c.

[Comment: It is said by many that the journey-wanderings of Ulysses is symbolic of the struggles of men through incarnations to return to their rightful place from exile on the earth.]

Phaedo
Dialogues of Plato
Edited by J. D. Kaplan
Pocket Books, Inc.

[In speaking of suicide Socrates has this to say]

I admit the appearance of inconsistency in what I am saying, but there may not be any real inconsistency after all. There is a doctrine whispered in secret that man is a prisoner who has no right to open the door and run away: There is a great mystery which I do not quite understand. Yet I too believe that the gods are our guardians, and that we men are a possession of theirs. . . . Then, if we look at the matter thus, there may be a reason in saying that a man should wait, and not take his own life until God summons him as he is now summoning me.

Ibid.
p. 80.

And when real philosophers consider all these things, will they not be led to make a reflection which they will express in words something like the following? "Have we not found," they will say, "a path of thought which seems to bring us and our argument to the conclusion, that while we are in the body, and while the soul is infected with the evils of the body, our desire will not be satisfied, and our desire is of the truth? For the body is a source of endless trouble to us by reason of the mere requirement of food; and is liable also to diseases which overtake and impede us in the search after true being; it fills us full of loves, and lusts, and fears, and fancies of all kinds, and endless foolery, and in fact, as men say, takes away from us the power of thinking at all. Whence come wars, and fightings, and factions? Wars are occasioned by the love of money, and money has to be acquired for the sake and service of the body; and by reason of all these impediments we have no time to give to philosophy; and, last and worst of all, even if we are at leisure and betake ourselves to some speculation, the body is always breaking in upon us, causing turmoil and confusion in our enquiries, and so amazing us that we are prevented from seeing the truth. It has been proved to us by experience that if we would have pure knowledge of anything we must be quit of the body—the soul in herself must behold things in themselves: and then we shall attain the wisdom which we desire, and of which we say that we are lovers; not while we live, but after death; for if while in company with the body, the soul cannot have pure knowledge, one of two things follows—either knowledge is not to be attained at all, or, if at all, after death. For then, and not till then, the soul will be parted from the body and exist in herself alone. In this present life, I reckon that we make the nearest approach to knowledge when we have the least possible intercourse or communion with the body, and are not surfeited with the bodily nature, but keep ourselves pure until the hour when God himself is pleased to release us. And thus having got rid of the foolishness of the body we shall be pure and hold converse with the pure, and know of ourselves the clear light everywhere, which is no other than the light of truth."

Ibid.
p. 99.

Still I suspect that you and Simmias would be glad to probe the argument further. Like children, you are haunted with a fear that when the soul leaves the body, the wind may really blow her away and scatter her; especially if a man should happen to die in a great storm and not when the sky is calm.

Cebes answered with a smile: Then, Socrates, you must argue us out of our fears—and yet, strictly speaking, they are not our fears, but there is a child within us to whom death is a sort of hobgoblin: him too we must persuade not to be afraid when he is alone in the dark.

Socrates said: Let the voice of the charmer be applied daily until you have charmed away the fear.

[Comment: In the foregoing, this may be the first reference in literature to a psychologist because Cebes is obviously referring to Jung's "shadow".]

Ibid.
p. 102.

—were we not saying that the soul too is then dragged by the body into the region of the changeable, and wanders and is confused; the world spins round her, and she is like a drunkard, when she touches change?

Very true.

But when returning into herself she reflects, then she passes into the other world, the region of purity, and eternity, and immortality, and unchangeableness, which are her kindred, and with them she ever lives, when she is by herself and is not let or hindered; then she ceases from her erring ways, and being in communion with the unchanging is unchanging. And this state of the soul is called wisdom?

Ibid.
p. 103.

Then reflect, Cebes: of all which has been said is not this the conclusion?—that the soul is in the very likeness of the divine, and immortal, and intellectual, and uniform, and indissoluble, and unchangeable; and that the body is the very likeness of the human, and mortal, and unintellectual, and multiform, and dissoluble, and changeable. Can this, my dear Cebes, be denied?

Ibid.
p. 108–110.

I will tell you, he said. The lovers of knowledge are conscious that the soul was simply fastened and glued to the body—until philosophy received her, she could only view real existence through the bars of a prison, not in and through herself; she was wallowing in the mire of every sort of ignorance, and by reason of lust had become the principal accomplice in her own captivity. This was her original state; and then, as I was saying, and as the lovers of knowledge are well aware, philosophy, seeing how terrible was her confinement, of which she was herself the cause, received and gently comforted her and sought to release her, pointing out that the eye and the ear and the other senses are full of deception, and persuading her to retire from them, and abstain from all the necessary use of them, and be gathered up and collected into herself, bidding her trust in herself and her own pure apprehension of pure existence, and to mistrust whatever comes to her through other channels and is subject to variation; for such things are visible and tangible, but what she sees in her own nature is intelligible and invisible. And the soul of the true philosopher thinks that she ought not to resist this deliverance, and therefore abstains from pleasures and desires and pains and fears, as far as she is able; reflecting that when a man has great joys or sorrows or fears or desires, he suffers from them, not merely the sort of evil which might be anticipated—as, for example, the loss of his health or property which he has sacrificed to his lusts—but an evil greater far, which is the greatest and worst of all evils, and one of which he never thinks.

What is it, Socrates? said Cebes.

The evil is that when the feeling of pleasure or pain is most intense, every soul of man imagines the objects of this intense feeling to be then plainest and truest: but this is not so, they are really the things of sight.

Very true.

And is not this the state in which the soul is most enthralled by the body?

How so?

Why, because each pleasure and pain is a sort of nail which nails and rivets the soul to the body, until she becomes like the body, and believes that to be true which the body affirms to be true; and from agreeing with the body and having the same delights she is obliged to have the same habits and haunts, and is not likely ever to be pure at her departure to the world below, but is always infected by the body; and so she sinks into another body and there germinates and grows, and has therefore no part in the communion of the divine and pure and simple.

Most true, Socrates, answered Cebes.

And this, Cebes, is the reason why the true lovers of knowledge are temperate and brave; and not for the reason which the world gives.

Certainly not.

Certainly not! The soul of a philosopher will reason in quite another way; she will not ask philosophy to release her in order that when released she may deliver herself up again to the thraldom of pleasures and pains, doing a work only to be outdone again, weaving instead of unweaving her Penelope's web. But she will calm passion, and follow reason, and dwell in the contemplation of her, beholding the true and divine (which is not matter of opinion), and thence deriving nourishment. Thus she seeks to live while she lives, and after death she hopes to go to her own kindred and to that which is like her, and to be freed from human ills. Never fear, Simmias and Cebes, that a soul which has been thus nurtured and has had these pursuits, will at her departure from the body be scattered and blown away by the winds and be nowhere and nothing.

Ibid.
p. 125.

And yet do we not now discover the soul to be doing the exact opposite–leading the elements of which she is believed to be composed; almost always opposing and coercing them in all sorts of ways throughout life, sometimes more violently with the pains of medicine and gymnastic; then again more gently; now threatening, now admonishing the desires, passions, fears, as if talking to a thing which is not herself, as Homer in the Odyssey represents Odysseus doing in the words–

"He beat his breast, and thus reproached his heart:
Endure, my heart: far worse hast thou endured!"

Ibid.
p. 155.

A man of sense ought not to say, nor will I be very confident, that the description which I have given of the soul and her mansions is exactly true. But I do say that, inasmuch as the soul is shown to be immortal, he may venture to think, not improperly or unworthily, that something of the kind is true. The venture is a glorious one, and he ought to comfort himself with words like these which is the reason why I lengthen out the tale. Wherefore, I say, let a man be of good cheer about his soul, who having cast away the pleasures and ornaments of the body as alien to him and working harm rather than good, has sought after the pleasures of knowledge; and has arrayed the soul, not in some foreign attire, but in her own proper jewels, temperance, and justice, and courage, and nobility, and truth–in these adorned she is ready to go on her journey to the world below, when her hour comes.

Parmenides.
Dialogues of Plato.
T. Taylor Translation, Vol. III.

[In the sevenfold constitution of man (see p. 106) it will be noted that the highest summit of the Eastern religions is Atma. It is unknowable, the nameless, the highest of the high, not even understood by the soul or the lesser gods and it permeates all things.
It is to this subject Parmenides the Greek turns his attention. He calls it *the one*. Its characteristics are discussed in this dialogue at great length and they are akin to Atma.]

The one has no parts; it is incorporeal; it is not a whole; it does not have a beginning, a middle or an end and is therefore infinite. It is without figure or form; it is nowhere; it cannot stand nor be moved; it is not the same either with another or with itself; it cannot be different either with another or with itself; it is not similar or dissimilar to itself or to another; it will be neither equal nor unequal to itself or to another; it is not equal or unequal to itself or to another. It does not participate in time hence it cannot be older or younger than anything and it does not participate in being or essence. No name belongs to it, nor discourse nor any science nor opinion and it cannot be known nor conceived nor perceived by any being.

The Works of Plato.
General Introduction.
Thomas Taylor.
Vol. I.

[Comment: The following is a summary of the first part of the introduction of 125 pages. Taylor first describes the philosophy of Plato in terms of God and man, on the basis of what moves or is moved and what part is indigent (in need of) and what part unindigent, he sets forth a hierarchy defined as follows. Compare this with the Hindu names placed to right. See p. 106.]

Philosophy of Plato	Eastern Religions Counterparts
1) The Highest God Superessential God The First Cause Principle of Principles Has no being *The One* (used in *Parmenides* and also later by Plotinus.) *The One* is in every respect prior to being Not named, cannot be known Perfectly ineffable Unindigent	Atman

*2) Soul Rational soul Can collect universals (truths) by reasoning Indigent Can be an essence	Buddhi
3) Intellect Mind Indigent Cannot reason	Manas [ego] [conscious mind]
4) Irrational soul Nature Indigent of Rational soul Cannot reason with itself It must have a separate subsistance Cannot discover anything by itself (p. 487, *First Alcibiades*)	Kama [animal soul]
5) Body	Sthula

*Between the Highest God and The Soul are a hierachy of lesser gods with many missions. They were deified by illumination from *The One*.

MISCELLANEOUS SOURCES

The Bhagavad Gita
Peter Pauper Press, Mount Vernon, N.Y.

Therefore, O mightiest of the Bharata race, subdue the sinner, and so loose yourself from this sinful one, destroyer of wisdom and soul awareness.

The man of the Rule whose joy is within, whose pleasure is within, and whose light is within, becomes Brahma and wins to extinction in Brahma.

The saintly man who is subdued in sense, mind and understanding, who has made liberation his supreme goal and is ever void of desire, fear, and wrath, is in truth liberated.

O great-armed one, the Moods of Goodness, Fieryness, and Darkness, which arise from Nature, fetter the body's changeless dweller inside the body.

Thoughts. Chap. 10, 1
Blaise Pascal [1623-1662]

What a chimera, then is man! What a novelty, what a monster, what a chaos, what a subject of contradiction, what a prodigy! A judge of all things, feeble worm of the earth, depositary of the truth, cloaca of uncertainty and error, the glory and shame of the universe!

Faust—Goethe.

Two souls, alas, are dwelling in my breast,
And either would be severed from its brother;
The one holds fast with joyous earthy lust
Onto the world of man with organs clinging;
The other soars impassioned from the dust,
To realms of lofty forebears winging.

Horace. 65-8 B.C.

Conquer your own nature: for if you do not teach it to obey you, it will compel you to obey it.

[Of key importance to an understanding of Roy Mitchell's thesis is the long journey of the soul as it returns again and again to earth to accomplish its task of purification and redemption of the animal soul.

The idea of reincarnation is almost an axiom in Eastern religions. Its acceptance in the Western world has been slow due to the teachings of Christianity but it has been gaining ground as increasing numbers of Western thinkers have come to the conclusion that it is the only rational basis for the facts they see about them.

The outstanding book of Joseph Head and S. L. Cranston has made a valuable contribution in this field. They have searched out organizations and individuals in history who have become convinced of the reality of reincarnation.

Certain selections have been taken from their book which go beyond the field of reincarnation to the subject of the "Exile".]

Reincarnation in World Thought, p. 75.
Joseph Head and S. L. Cranston. 1967.
Synesius (c. 370–430).
Church Father and Neoplatonist.
The Virgin of the World.

Souls do not, then, return confusedly [to the after death states], nor by chance, into one and the same place, but each is despatched into the condition which belongs to her. And this is determined by that which the soul experiences while yet she is in the tenement of the body, loaded with a burden contrary to her nature . . . . The law of equity presides over the changes which take place above, even as upon earth also it moulds and constructs the vessels in which the souls are immured. (Part III.)

Ibid.
Treatise on Dreams, p. 107.
Synesius (c. 370–430).

Philosophy speaks of souls being prepared by a course of transmigrations. . . . When first it comes down to earth, it [the soul] embarks on this animal spirit as on a boat, and through it is brought into contact with matter. The soul's object is to take this spirit back with her; for if she were to abandon it and leave it behind on earth . . . the manner of her return would bring disgrace on her. . . . The soul which did not quickly return to the heavenly region from which it was sent down to earth had to go through many lives of wandering.

Ibid.
Reincarnation in World Thought, p. 121.
Joseph Head and S.L. Cranston. 1967.

Karma and Reincarnation imply individual responsibility; each man his own saviour and redeemer; each enjoys or suffers in exact proportion to thoughts and deeds in this or a former incarnation.

Ibid. p. 119.
Massacre at Montésqur;
A History of the Albigenses Crusade.
Zoe Oldenbourg.

"The Cathars, generally speaking, acknowledged the doctrine of metempsychosis as held by the Hindus, with the same precise calculations governing posthumous retribution for the individual. A man who had led a just life would be reincarnated in a body better suited for his further spiritual development; whereas the criminal was liable, after his death, to be reborn in a body full of flaws and hereditary vices. . . ."

Ibid. p. 122.
The Philosophical Principles of Natural and Revealed Religion.
Chevalier Ramsay (1686–1743).

The holy oracles always represent paradise as our native country and our present life as an exile. How can we be said to have been banished from a place in which we never were?

Ibid. p. 97.

St. John in Revelation 3:12 states: "Him that overcometh will I make a pillar in the temple of my God, *and he shall go no more out.*" (Italics added.) Evidently he had gone out into incarnation before, otherwise the words "no more" could have no place or meaning. It may have been the old idea of the exile of the soul and the need for it to be purified by long wandering before it could be admitted as a "pillar in the temple of God."

Ibid. p. 315.
Walden.
Henry Thoreau.

I am conscious of the presence and criticism of a part of me which, as it were, is not a part of me, but spectator, sharing no experience, but taking note of it and that is no more I than it is you.

[Comment: Note how close this is to Whitman's *A Noiseless Patient Spider.* See p. 333.]

Ibid. p. 320.
In the Twilight.
James Russell Lowell (1819–1891).

Sometimes a breath floats by me,
An odor from Dreamland sent,

That makes the ghost seem nigh me
Of a splendor that came and went,
Of a life lived somewhere, I know not
In what diviner sphere. . . .
A something too vague, could I name it,
For others to know,
As if I had lived it or dreamed it,
As if I had acted or schemed it
Long ago!

Ibid. p. 324.
Empedocles on Etna. (Act II).
Matthew Arnold (1822–1888).

And then we shall unwillingly return
Back to this meadow of calamity,
This uncongenial place, this human life;
And in our individual human state
Go through the sad probation all again,
To see if we will poise our life at last,
To see if we will now at last be true
To our own only true, deep-buried selves,
Being one with which we are one with the whole world;
Or whether we will once more fall away
Into some bondage of the flesh or mind,
Some slough of sense, or some fantastic maze
Forged by the imperious lonely thinking-power.

Ibid. p. 159.
A Buddhist's Catechism.
Henry Steel Olcott (1832–1907).

On this point [of reincarnation] the Western world is for the most part as far from understanding the Oriental conception as it is in mistaking Nirvana for "annihilation." . . . Much of the

Western misconception is due to ignorance of the difference between [a man's] individuality and his personality at any given period. These two are only temporarily coincident and conjoined . . . . In each birth the personality differs from that of a previous or next succeeding birth . . . . But though personalities ever shift, the one line of life along which they are strung, like beads, runs unbroken; it is ever that *particular line*, never any other. It is therefore, individual, an individual vital undulation, which began in Nirvana . . . and leads through many cyclic changes back to Nirvana.

[Comment: When Olcott refers here to the individuality he undoubtedly means the soul and when he refers to the personality he means the animal soul. This is Oriental terminology.]

Louis Lambert
Honore De Balzac
Publisher: Thomas Y. Crowell & Company. N. Y.
Vol. III-IV, p. 175. 1900.

In each of us there are two distinct beings. According to Swedenborg, the angel is an individual in whom the inner being conquers the external being. If a man desires to earn his call to be an angel, as soon as his mind reveals to him his twofold existence, he must strive to foster the delicate angelic essence that exists within him. If, for lack of a lucid appreciation of his destiny, he allows bodily action to predominate, instead of confirming his intellectual being, all his powers will be absorbed in the use of his external senses, and the angel will slowly perish by the materialization of both natures. In the contrary case, if he nourishes his inner being with the aliment needful to it, the soul triumphs over matter and strives to get free.

When they separate by the act of what we call death, the angel, strong enough then to cast off its wrappings, survives and begins its real life. The infinite variety which differentiates individual men can only be explained by this twofold existence, which, again, is proved and made intelligible by that variety.

The Exiles
Ibid. p. 282

[In a mystical story written by Balzac, two exiles, Dante and Godefroid de Mahant were brought together in a lodging house under the shadow of Notre-Dame. One was an exile from his homeland Italy but the other, a particularly sensitive youth, recognized that he was an exile from heaven. The following was retrieved from the story.]

"But you, poor child," he went on, looking at Godefroid, whose cheeks were beaded with glittering tears, "have you, like me, studied life from blood-stained pages? What can you have to weep for, at your age?"

"Alas!" said Godefroid, "I regret a land more beautiful than any land on earth—a land I never saw and yet remember. Oh, if I could but cleave the air on beating wings, I would fly——"

"Whither?" asked the exile.

"Up there," replied the boy.

On hearing this answer, the stranger (Dante) seemed surprised; he looked darkly at the youth, who remained silent. They seemed to communicate by an unspeakable effusion of the spirit, hearing each other's yearnings in the teeming silence, and going forth side by side, like two doves sweeping the air on equal wing, till the boat, touching the strand of the island, roused them from their deep reverie.

Then, each lost in thought, they went together to the sergeant's house.

"And so the boy believes that he is an angel exiled from heaven!" thought the tall stranger. "Which of us all has a right to undeceive him? Not I—I, who am so often lifted by some magic spell so far above the earth; I who am dedicate to God; I who am a mystery to myself. Have I not already seen the fairest of the angels dwelling in this mire? Is this child more or less crazed than I am? Has he taken a bolder step in the way of faith?

He believes, and his belief no doubt will lead him into some path of light like that in which I walk. But though he is as beautiful as an angel, is he not too feeble to stand fast in such a struggle?"

Young Emerson Speaks, p.132
Ralph Waldo Emerson
Houghton Mifflin Co. Boston 1938

We are sad aliens from the heavenly life, we grievously break the commandments, if we are thus strangers to Him . . . Why should you make the happiness in the world, less?

Ibid. p.162

Ah, brethren. I fear we are strangers to ourselves. Amid the clamors of our passions, amid the din of the world's affairs, we do not heed the thunder call of a Superior Nature which pleads and warns us from within. . . . Let me exhort you then to lend an ear to all the good promptings that hitherto you have withstood, . . .

Good-bye, Stanza I.
Ralph Waldo Emerson, [1803-1882]

Good-bye proud world! I'm going home:
Thou art not my friend and I'm not thine.

George W. Russell ("AE"), [1867-1935].

To those who cry out against romance – I would say "you yourself are romance – you are the last prince, herding obscurely among the swine. The romance of your spirit is the most marvellous of stories. Your wanderings have been greater than Ulysses."

Hermes Trismegistus Vol. II
1884 Trans. from the Greek by
Dr. Anna Kingsford and Edward Maitland
Pub. Wizard's Bookshelf
Box 6600 San Diego CA., 92106

In a note appended to Thomas Taylor's Dissertations, Dr. Wilder quotes from Cocker's Greek Philosophy the following excellent reflections :

"The allegory of the Chariot and Winged Steeds, in Plato's *Phaedrus,* represents the lower or inferior part of man's nature (Adam or the body) as dragging the Soul down to the earth, and subjecting it to the slavery of corporeal conditions. Out of these conditions arise numerous evils that disorder the mind and becloud the reason, for evil is inherent to the condition of finite and multiform existence into which we have fallen. The earthly life is a fall. The soul is now dwelling in the grave which we call the body. . . . . . We resemble those 'captives chained in a subterraneous cave,' so poetically described in the seventh book of *The Republic*; their backs turned to the light, so that they see but the shadows of the objects which pass behind them, and 'to these shadows they attribute a perfect reality.' Their sojurn upon earth is thus a dark imprisonment in the body, a dreamy exile from their proper home." A.K.

p. 53 Hermes to Asclepios: "But I will speak to you of the consciousness and all that belongs to it, when I come to the exposition of the mind. For man alone is a dual creature. One of the two parts of which he consists is single and as the Greeks say essential; that is, formed after the divine likeness. The part which the Greeks call Kosmic–that is belonging to the world–is quadruple, and constitutes the body, which in man, serves as an envelope to the divine principle. This divine principle, and that which belongs to it, the perceptions of the pure intelligence conceal themselves behind the rampart of the body."

The Trickster
A Study in American Indian Mythology
Paul Radin, (1956)
Pub. Philosophical Library

[Comment: The Trickster is obviously the animal soul of man without control. His characteristics are those described elsewhere in these references and texts. His actions are understood by all men.]

Prefatory note by Paul Radin:

The Trickster myth is found in clearly recognizable form among the simplest aboriginal tribes and among the complex. We encounter it among the ancient Greeks, the Chinese, the Japanese and in the Semitic world. . . . Manifestly we are here in the presence of a figure and a theme or themes which have had an unusual attraction for mankind from the very beginnings of civilization.

He (the Trickster) wills nothing consciously. At all times he is constrained to behave from impulses over which he has no control.

Is this a *speculum mentis* wherein is depicted man's struggle with himself and with a world into which he has been thrust without his volition and consent? . . .

On the basis of very extensive data which we have today from aboriginal tribes it is not only a reasonable but, indeed, almost a verifiable hypothesis that we are here actually in the presence of such an archaic *speculum mentis.*

[Trickster's left arm quarrels with his right arm until the right arm cuts the left leaving it bleeding to the chagrin of the Trickster. He proceeds on a journey in an irrational way. All manner of abominable acts are committed by him but at times he shows man new and efficacious ways to do things that pertain to his material world.]

(C. G. Jung commentary *On the Psychology of the Trickster Figure.* pp. 200-206)

When, therefore, a primitive or barbarous consciousness forms a picture of itself on a much earlier level of development and continues to do so for hundreds or even thousands of years, undeterred by the contamination of its archaic qualities with differentiated, highly developed mental products, then the causal explanation is that the older the archaic qualities are, the more conservative and pertinacious is their behaviour. One simply cannot shake off the memory image of things as they were, and drags it along like a senseless appendage. . . .

The only question that would need answering is whether such personified reflections exist at all in empirical psychology. As a matter of fact they do, and these experiences of split or double personality actually form the core of the earliest psychopathological investigations. . . .

Here the trickster is represented by countertendencies in the unconscious, and in certain cases by a sort of second personality, of a puerile and inferior character, not unlike the personalities who announce themselves at spiritualistic seances and cause all those ineffably childish phenomena so typical of poltergeists. I have, I think, found a suitable designation for this character component when I called it the *shadow** . . . .

Anyone who belongs to a sphere of culture that seeks the perfect state somewhere in the past must feel very queerly indeed when confronted by the figure of the trickster. He is a forerunner of the saviour, and, like him, God, man, and animal at once. He is both subhuman and superhuman, a bestial and divine being, whose chief and most alarming characteristic is his unconsciousness. . . .

On the other hand he is in many respects stupider than the animals, and gets into one ridiculous scrape after another. Al-

*The same idea can be found in the Church Father Irenaeus, who calls it the 'umbra'. *Advers. Haer.* I, ii, 1.

though he is not really evil he does the most atrocious things from sheer unconsciousness and unrelatedness. . . .

This process of neutralization, as the history of the trickster motif shows, lasts a very long time, so that one can still find traces of it even at a high level of civilization. Its longevity could also be explained by the strength and vitality of the state of consciousness described in the myth, and by the secret attraction and fascination this has for the conscious mind. Although purely causal hypotheses in the biological sphere are not as a rule very satisfactory, due weight must nevertheless be given to the fact that in the case of the trickster a higher level of consciousness has covered up a lower one, and that the latter was already in retreat. His recollection, however, is mainly due to the interest which the conscious mind brings to bear on him, the inevitable concomitant being, as we have seen, the gradual civilizing, i.e. assimilation, of a primitive daemonic figure who was originally autonomous and even capable of causing possession.

But if the conscious should find itself in a critical or doubtful situation, then it soon becomes apparent that the shadow has not dissolved into nothing but is only waiting for a favourable opportunity to reappear as a projection upon one's neighbour. If this trick is successful, then immediately there is created between them that world of primordial darkness where everything that is characteristic of the trickster can happen—even on the highest plane of civilization. The best examples of these 'monkey tricks', as popular speech aptly and truthfully sums up this state of affairs in which everything goes wrong and nothing intelligent happens except by mistake at the last moment, are naturally to be found in politics.

The so-called civilized man has forgotten the trickster. He remembers him only figuratively and metaphorically, when, irritated by his own ineptitude, he speaks of fate playing tricks on him or of things being bewitched. He never suspects that his own hidden and apparently harmless shadow has qualities whose dangerousness exceeds his wildest dreams. As soon as people get together in masses and submerge the individual, the shadow is mobilized, and, as history shows, may even be personified and incarnated.

[Comment: See also *The Winnebago Tribe* by Paul Radin on p. 167.]

Etruscan Places (Viking Penguin 1932). p. 53.
D. H. Lawrence.

In the open room upon the courtyard of the Palazzo Vitelleschi lie a few sarcophagi of stone, with the effigies carved on top, something as the dead crusaders in English churches. And here, in Tarquinia, the effigies are more like crusaders than usual, for some lie flat on their backs, and have a dog at their feet;

[Comment: In the middle ages of Europe figures in stone were placed on the top of sarcophagi of knights and rulers. At their feet there is invariably a dog, a small lion, or a serpent. Sometimes these animals were even at the feet of upright statues of knights. The foot is depicted as always being on top of the animal. At times the animal is bristly and fierce but nearly always as placid and peaceful.

This custom undoubtedly stems from the statues of the saints and religious figures such as St. George, St. Margaret, St. Jerome, and the Virgin Mary where all manner of animals—serpents, dragons, lions, monkeys, boars, and dogs—are often found under the feet of the statue. Many of the animals are imaginary beasts.

All this signifies that the person involved has struggled with his animal nature (soul) and disciplined it. Where the animal is fierce he has failed. In those days the fight of a man against the devil and evil things was of paramount importance. The rages and passions were always identified with animals. (See pp. 292-93.)]

Ibid. pp. 92-93.

Every real discovery made, every serious and significant decision ever reached, was reached and made by divination. . . .

Facts are fitted around afterwards.

Ibid. p. 178.

Fascinating are the scenes of departures, journeyings in covered wagons drawn by two or more horses, accompanied by driver on foot and friend on horseback, and dogs, and met by other horsemen coming down the road. Under the arched tarpaulin tilt of the wagon reclines a man or a woman, or a whole family; and all moves forward along the highway with wonderful slow surge. And the wagon, as far as I saw, is always drawn by horses, not by oxen.

This is surely the journey of the soul. It is said to represent even the funeral procession, the ash-chest being borne away to the cemetery, to be laid in the tomb. But the *memory* in the scene seems much deeper than that. It gives so strongly the feeling of a people who have trekked in wagons, like the Boers, or the Mormons, from one land to another. . . .

Altogether the feeling of the Volterran scenes is peculiar. There is a great sense of *journeying*; as of a people which remembers its migrations, by sea as well as by land. And there is a curious restlessness, unlike the dancing surety of southern Etruria—a touch of the Gothic.

[The idea that the soul is on a long and dangerous journey is a theme of most myths and religions. Even children's fairy tales are stories of people going out to right a wrong, seek a fortune, or accomplish new goals. The soul journeys take place not only through the centuries but are actually urged during a life on earth to test our abilities to handle difficult situations and to teach our two entities new lessons. (See p. 307 and p. 326).]

L is for limbo

During the Renaissance artists devoted a great deal of their time to depicting their version of the Bible stories. Another theme was to draw figures to form the alphabet. Two such artists working approximately 300 years apart made their representations of man in the same way. Meister E.S. was one of the outstanding artists of the late 1400s while the other drawing came from the letters of St. Jerome in the 12th century. The churches dominated Western civilization at that time. The battle between good and evil was a serious daily subject. Devils, sins, dragons and evil crea-

tures of all kinds were fended off by guardian angels and the glorious host of heaven.

St. George, St. Margaret and St. Jerome were celebrated for the defeat of fierce beasts and dragons which they then trained to serve them. This was really a representation of a man's conflict with the animal within him. Thus drawings like the two shown here represent man as having an animal at his feet, a guardian angel above his head accompanied by a griffin which has always been the symbol of the messenger to God.

The Undiscovered Self
Carl G. Jung 1959.
Mentor Books.
Little Brown & Co. N.Y. N.Y.

[C. G. Jung has here explored the inner nature of man. As in the review of his life's work in *Man And His Symbols,* he divides the inner man into three parts:—

1. The Conscious Mind (the ego which reasons and carries out the general operations of the day, the thinker).
2. The Shadow (the dark side of man, the animal nature, the instincts, and those characteristics called demonism).
3. The Soul (Self, archetypal images, intuitions, subliminal guide, numinosity, conscience, redeemer.)

The last two he calls the psyche or the unconscious. Mitchell defines psyche as man's lower instinctive nature only. Phenomena above this he termed nous (from the Greek). It was his view that we must learn to clearly discriminate between soul or Self and the shadow. Until we do we cannot properly utilize the redeeming characteristic of the higher soul.

Jung's greatest efforts were devoted to the exploration of the shadow—the great opposer. He felt that most men are unaware of the unconscious but what man is not aware of the continual argument that goes on between his conscience and that part of him which argues for more of the sensual life—the comforts, the animal desires and appetites, and evil thoughts.

Mitchell would join Jung when he speaks of the dual nature of man and the psychological and psychotic explosions that take place when the conflict of these two becomes overwhelming.

While Jung never goes so far as to call the shadow a second soul, at one point he does go so far as to call it "the other person in us." His theme is – ignore the shadow at your own peril.]

[In speaking of the practising psychologist, Jung sees his patient as a human but he also sees a subhuman entity bound to him like an animal. Such statements have entered into the parlance of the day when the alcoholic or addict speaks about "the monkey on his back". This indeed gets very close to Mitchell's animal soul that must be redeemed by the higher divine soul or Self.] J.L.D.

Man and His Symbols
Carl G. Jung, Pub. 1964.
Doubleday & Co. Inc. Garden City, N.Y.

[Carl G. Jung made giant steps in psychology research. His work on the unconscious parallels the Eastern religions to a remarkable degree. He adheres to Western terms and the only way it is possible to compare them is to watch the definitions and characteristics he attaches to his terms.

His "unconscious" consists of many aspects of the inner man and covers both the lowest attributes of man and the highest spiritual attributes. Both are indeed in an unconscious world of which the conscious mind of man is dimly aware. However the Eastern Mystic separates the two by placing the lowest attributes below the conscious mind and the highest attributes above the conscious mind. See Mitchell table on p. 106.

Jung is quite blunt about the presence in each man of two personalities (p.23). Mitchell divides these two entities into the ego (or conscious mind) and the unconscious entity (or animal soul).

It is a curious fact that dreams* are the communication method of both Self (or higher soul) and the Shadow (or Mitchell's animal soul). This may be the reason why Jung placed them both into the category of the unconscious. Such a classification creates confusion because the conscious mind has a difficult

*See *The Divine Spirit Within Man* by John L. Davenport, CSA Press. Ga.

time discriminating between the dreams of the Self and the Shadow. Mitchell gives the student methods of discrimination.

Roy Mitchell would have called Jung's archetypal memories the reminiscence concept of Socrates (see *Meno* or *Phaedo*). It is the memory of the reincarnating soul which is a master of all knowledge (Plato). These memories can be invoked by the conscious mind through intuitions but more often take place in dreams if the person is alert to them and learns how to read them.

Jung concludes that life is a battleground between two inexorable opposites. Whitman speaks of "a war fight-out between myself and this contentious soul of mine." The Hindu bible (*The Bhagavad Gita*) describes the field of battle between man's upper Self and his lower self. The Moslem says there are two kinds of war. The war that goes on between men are minor wars. The major war is the one that goes on within each man. Mitchell's description of this conflict between higher soul attributes and the animal soul is a masterpiece.

Jung defines the "anima" as the unconscious feminine part of each man. It participates in an upper or godlike character and a lower or witchlike character. In the same way he describes an unconscious male part of each woman with an upper and lower character called the "animus".

These terms are reminiscent (at least in their spiritual aspects) of a figure in Chinese Buddhism called Avalokitesvara which has a female aspect and a male aspect. The female aspect is known as Kuan Yin and the male aspect as Kuan-shi-Yin. Kuan Yin is worshipped as the goddess of Compassion and Knowledge. Women pray to her for sons; others pray for relief from unendurable hardship.

It would be well to clarify Jung's terms with those of Roy Mitchell. This can be done with a table.

Jung	Mitchell
	Supreme Spirit (unknowable)
	Soul, Self,Divine Spirit in man
Conscious mind, ego	Conscious mind, ego, nous
Unconscious–psyche consisting of the following:	Animal soul, shadow
Shadow–selfishness to evil	Vital essence, breath, Prana
Anima and Animus	Astral body, psyche
Self, Soul, Archetypal images	Gross body
Dreamer	

Thus Mitchell and Jung's functions of the inner constitution of man can be related except that Jung says "shadow" and "archetypal memories"and Mitchell boldly says "no, two souls –an animal soul and an all-knowing, spiritual soul sent here time and time again to redeem the animal soul until finally it is purified and cleansed of its gross characteristics." Jung also speaks of a redeeming feature of the Self but he does not tie in the concept of reincarnation to give enough time to complete the task of purification.] J.L.D.

Analytical Psychology
Its Theory and Practice. p. 80-82.
C. G. Jung
Published by Routledge & Kegan Paul Ltd. 1968.

Ladies and Gentlemen, that leads me to something very important–the fact that a complex with its given tension or energy has the tendency to form a little personality of itself. It has a sort of body, a certain amount of its own physiology. It can upset the stomach. It upsets the breathing, it disturbs the heart–in short, it behaves like a partial personality. For instance, when you want to say or do something and unfortunately a complex interferes with this intention, then you say or do something different from what you intended. You are simply interrupted, and your best intention gets upset by the complex, exactly as if you had been interfered with by a human being or by circumstances from outside. Under those conditions we really are forced to speak of the tendencies of complexes to act as if they were characterized by a certain amount of will-power. When you speak of will-power you naturally ask about the ego. Where then is the ego that belongs to the will-power of the complexes? We know our own ego-complex, which is supposed to be in full possession of the body. It is not, but let us assume that it is a centre in full possession of the body, that there is a focus which we call the ego, and that the ego has a will and can do something with its components. The ego also is an agglomeration of highly toned contents, so that in principle there is no difference between the ego-complex and any other complex.

Because complexes have a certain will-power, a sort of ego, we find that in a schizophrenic condition they emancipate themselves from conscious control to such an extent that they become visible and audible. They appear as visions, they speak in voices which are like the voices of definite people. This personification of complexes is not in itself necessarily a pathological condition. In dreams, for instance, our complexes often appear in a personified form. And one can train oneself to such an extent that they become visible or audible also in a waking condition. It is part of a certain yoga training to split up consciousness into its components, each of which appears as a specific personality. In the psychology of our unconscious there are typical figures that have a definite life of their own.*

All this is explained by the fact that the so-called unity of consciousness is an illusion. It is really a wish-dream. We like to think that we are one; but we are not, most decidedly not. We

*For example, the figures of *anima* and *animus*. [See *Two Essays on Analytical Psychology* (C. W., vol. 7), pars. 296ff.]

are not really masters in our house. We like to believe in our will-power and in our energy and in what we can do; but when it comes to a real show-down we find that we can do it only to a certain extent, because we are hampered by those little devils the complexes. Complexes are autonomous groups of associations that have a tendency to move by themselves, to live their own life apart from our intentions. I hold that our personal unconscious, as well as the collective unconscious, consists of an indefinite, because unknown, number of complexes or fragmentary personalities.

This idea explains a lot. It explains, for instance, the simple fact that a poet has the capacity to dramatize and personify his mental contents. When he creates a character on the stage, or in his poem or drama or novel, he thinks it is merely a product of his imagination; but that character in a certain secret way has made itself. Any novelist or writer will deny that these characters have a psychological meaning, but as a matter of fact you know as well as I do that they have one. Therefore you can read a writer's mind when you study the characters he creates.

The complexes, then, are partial or fragmentary personalities. When we speak of the ego-complex, we naturally assume that it has a consciousness, because the relationship of the various contents to the centre, in other words to the ego, is called consciousness. But we also have a grouping of contents about a centre, a sort of nucleus, in other complexes. So we may ask the question: Do complexes have a consciousness of their own? If you study spiritualism, you must admit that the so-called spirits manifested in automatic writing or through the voice of a medium do indeed have a sort of consciousness of their own. Therefore unprejudiced people are inclined to believe that the spirits are the ghosts of a deceased aunt or grandfather or something of the kind, just on account of the more or less distinct personality which can be traced in these manifestations. Of course, when we are dealing with a case of insanity we are less inclined to assume that we have to do with ghosts. We call it pathological then.

A Dictionary of Symbols
J. E. Cirlot.
Published 1962 by Philosophical Library, Inc.
New York 10016.

Angel A symbol of invisible forces, of the powers ascending and descending between the Source-of-Life and the world of phenomena (50). Here, as in other cases (such as the Cross), the symbolic fact does not modify the real fact. In alchemy, the angel symbolizes sublimation, i.e. the ascension of a volatile (spiritual) principle, as in the figures of the *Viatorium spagyricum*. The parallelism between angelic orders and astral worlds has been traced with singular precision by Rudolf Steiner in *Les Hierarchies spirituelles*, following the treatise on the celestial hierarchies by the Pseudo-Dionysius. . . .

Animals Of the utmost importance in symbolism, both in connexion with their distinguishing features, their movement, shapes and colours, and becaue of their relationship with man. The origins of animal symbolism are closely linked with totemism and animal worship. The symbolism of any given animal varies according to its position in the symbolic pattern, and to the attitude and context in which it is depicted. Thus the frequent symbol of the 'tamed animal' can signify the reversal of those symbolic meanings associated with the same animal when wild. In the struggle between a knight and a wild or fabulous animal —one of the most frequent themes in symbolism—the knight's victory can consist either in the death or the taming of the animal. In Chretien de Troyes' medieval romance, Yvain, the hero is assisted by a lion. In the legend of St. George, the conquered dragon serves its conqueror. . . . In Assyrian and Persian bas-reliefs, the victory of a higher over a lower animal always stands for the victory of the higher life over the lower instincts. A similar case is in the characteristic struggle of the eagle with the snake as found in pre-Columbian America. The victory of the lion over the bull usually signifies the victory of Day over

Night and, by analogy, Light triumphing over Darkness and Good over Evil. . . . For the purposes of symbolic art, animals are subdivided into two categories: *natural* (often in antithetical pairs: toad/ frog, owl/eagle, etc.) and *fabulous*. Within the cosmic order, the latter occupy an intermediate position between the world of fully differentiated beings and the world of formless matter (50). They may have been suggested by the discovery of skeletons of antediluvian animals, and also by certain beings which, though natural, are ambiguous in appearance (carnivorous plants, sea urchins, flying fish, bats), and thus stand for flux and transformism, and also for purposeful evolution towards new forms. In any event, fabulous animals are powerful instruments of psychological projection. The most important fabulous animals are: chimaera, sphinx, lamia, minotaur, siren, triton, hydra, unicorn, griffin, harpy, winged horse, hippogryph, dragon, etc. In some of these the transmutation is a simple one, and clearly positive in character–such as Pegasus' wings (the spiritualization of a lower force)–but more often the symbol is a consequence of a more complex and ambiguous process of the imagination. The result is a range of highly ambivalent symbols, whose significance is heightened by the ingrained belief in the great powers exercised by such beings as well as in the magic importance of abnormality and deformity. In addition, there are animals which, while hardly or not at all fabulous in appearance, are credited with non-existential or supernatural qualities as the result of a symbolic projection (for example, the pelican, phoenix, salamander). There is a fragment by Callimachus on the Age of Saturn, in which animals have the power of speech (this being a symbol of the Golden Age which preceded the emergence of the intellect–Man–when the blind forces of Nature, not yet subject to the *logos,* were endowed with all sorts of extraordinary and exalted qualities). Hebrew and Islamic traditions also include references to 'speaking animals' (35). Another interesting classification is that of 'lunar animals', embracing all those animals whose life-span includes some kind of cyclic alternation, with periodic appearances and disappearances (18). The symbolism of such animals includes, in addition to the animal's specific symbolic significance, a whole range of lunar meanings. Schneider also mentions a very curious primitive belief: namely, that the voice of those animals which can be said to serve as symbols of heaven is high-pitched if the animal is large (the elephant, for example), but low-pitched if the animal is small (as the bee); while the converse is true of earth-symbol animals. Some animals, in particular the eagle and the lion, seem to embody certain qualities, such as beauty and the fighting spirit, to such an extent that they have come to be universally accepted as the allegorical representations of these qualities. The emblematic animals of Roman *signa* were: eagle, wolf, bull, horse and wild boar. In symbolism, whenever animals (or any other symbolic elements) are brought together in a system, the order of arrangement is always highly significant, implying either hierarchical precedence or relative position in space. In alchemy, the descending order or precedence is symbolized by different animals, thus: the phoenix (the culmination of the alchemical *opus*), the unicorn, the lion (the necessary qualities), the dragon (prime matter) (32). . . .The importance in Christianity of the symbols of the dove, the lamb and the fish is well known. The significance of the attitudes in which symbolic animals are depicted is usually self-evident: the counterbalancing of two identical—or two different—animals, so common in heraldry, stands for balance (i.e. justice and order, as symbolized for instance by the two snakes of the caduceus); the animals are usually shown supporting a shield or surmounting the crest of a helmet. Jung supports this interpretation with his observation that the counterbalancing of the lion and the unicorn in Britain's coat of arms stands for the inner stress of balanced opposites finding their equilibrium in the centre (32). . . .According to Jung, the animal stands for the non-human psyche, for the world of subhuman instincts, and for the unconscious areas of the psyche. The more primitive the animal, the deeper the stratum of which it is an expression. As in all symbolism, the greater the number of objects depicted, the baser and the more primitive is the meaning (56). Identifying oneself with animals represents integration of the unconscious and sometimes—like immersion in the primal waters—rejuvenation through bathing in the sources of life itself (32). . . .

Breathing Symbolically, to breathe is to assimilate spiritual power. Yoga exercises place particular emphasis upon breathing, since it enables man to absorb not only air but also the light of the sun. Concerning solar light, the alchemists had this to say: 'It is a fiery substance, a continuous emanation of solar corpuscles which, owing to the movement of the sun and the astral bodies, is in a perpetual state of flux and change, filling all the universe. . . . We breathe this astral gold continuously.' The two movements—positive and negative—of breathing are connected with the circulation of the blood and with the important symbolic paths of involution and evolution (3). Difficulty in breathing may therefore symbolize difficulty in assimilating the principles of the spirit and of the cosmos. The 'proper rhythm' of Yoga-breathing is associated with the 'proper voice' demanded by the Egyptians for the ritual reading of the sacred texts. Both are founded upon imitation of the rhythms of the universe.

Bucentaur A monster, half-man and half-ox or bull. In some monuments Hercules is shown fighting a bucentaur or smothering it in his arms. Like the centaur, this mythic animal is symbolic of the essential duality of man, but, in this case, stressing the baser—or animal—part. Hercules' struggle with the bucentaur is the archetype of all mythic combat: Theseus and the Minotaur, Siegfried and the dragon, etc. (8).

Butterfly Among the ancients, an emblem of the soul and of unconscious attraction towards the light (8). The purification of the soul by fire, represented in Romanesque art by the burning ember placed by the angel in the prophet's mouth, is visually portrayed on a small Mattei urn by means of an image of love holding a butterfly close to a flame (8). The Angel of Death was represented by the Gnostics as a winged foot crushing a butterfly, from which we may deduce that the butterfly was equated with life rather than with the soul in the sense of the spirit or transcendent being (36). This also explains why psychoanalysis regards the butterfly as a symbol of rebirth (56). In China, it has the secondary meanings of joy and conjugal bliss (5).

Caduceus A wand with two serpents twined round it, surmounted by two small wings or a winged helmet. The rational and historical explanation is the supposed intervention of Mercury in a fight between two serpents who thereupon curled themselves around his wand. For the Romans, the caduceus served as a symbol of moral equilibrium and of good conduct. The wand represents power: the two snakes wisdom; the wings diligence (8); and the helmet is an emblem of lofty thoughts. To-day the caduceus is the insignia of the Catholic bishop in the Ukraine. The caduceus also signifies the integration of the four elements, the wand corresponding to earth, the wings to air, the serpents to fire and water (by analogy with the undulating movement of waves and flames) (56). This symbol is very ancient, and is to be found for example in India engraved upon stone tablets called *nagakals,* a kind of votive offering placed at the entrance to temples. Heinrich Zimmer traces the caduceus back to Mesopotamia, detecting it in the design of the sacrificial cup of king Gudea of Lagash (2600 B.C.). Zimmer even goes so far as to state that the symbol probably dates back beyond this period, for the Mesopotamians considered the intertwining serpents as a symbol of the god who cures all illness, a meaning which passed into Greek culture and is still preserved in emblems of our day (60). According to esoteric Buddhism, the wand of the caduceus corresponds to the axis of the world and the serpents refer to the force called Kundalini, which, in Tantrist teaching, sleeps coiled up at the base of the backbone—a symbol of the evolutive power of pure energy (40). Schneider maintains that the two S-shapes of the serpents correspond to illness and convalescence (51). In reality, what defines the essence of the caduceus is the nature and meaning not so much of its individual elements as of the composite whole. The precisely symmetrical and bilateral arrangement, as in the balance of Libra, or in the tri-unity of heraldry (a shield between two supporters), is always expressive of the same idea of active equilibrium, of opposing forces balancing one another in such a way as to create a higher, static form. In the caduceus, this balanced duality is twice stated: in the serpents and in the wings, thereby emphasizing that supreme state of strength and self-control (and consequently of health) which can be achieved both on the lower plane of the instincts (symbolized by the serpents) and on the higher level of the spirit (represented by the wings).

Circle At times it is synonymous with the circumference, just as the circumference is often equated with circular movement.

Chinese Yang-Yin, surrounded by the eight trigrams.

But although its general meaning embraces both aspects, there are some further details which it is important to emphasize. The circle or disk is, very frequently, an emblem of the sun (and indisputably so when it is surrounded by rays). It also bears a certain relationship to the number ten (symbolizing the return to unity from multiplicity) (40), when it comes to stand for heaven and perfection (4) and sometimes eternity as well (20). There are profound psychological implications in this particular concept of perfection. As Jung observes, the square, representing the lowest of the composite and factorial numbers, symbolizes the pluralist state of man who has not achieved inner unity (perfection) whilst the circle would correspond to this ultimate state of Oneness. The octagon is the intermediate state between the square and the circle. Representations of the relationship between the circle and the square are very common in the universal and spiritual world of morphology, notably in the mandalas of India and Tibet and in Chinese emblems. Indeed, according to Chochod, in China, activity, or the masculine principle (*Yang*), is represented by a white circle (depicting heaven), whereas passivity, the feminine principle (*Yin*) is denoted by a black square (portraying earth). The white circle stands for energy and celestial influences and the black square for telluric forces. The interaction implicit in dualism is represented by the famous symbol of the Yang-Yin, a circle divided into two equal sections by a sigmoid line across the diameter, the white section *(Yang)* having a black spot within it, and the black *(Yin)* a white spot. These two spots signify that there is always something of the feminine in the masculine and something of the masculine in the feminine. The sigmoid line is a symbol of the movement of communication and serves the purpose of implying—like the swastika—the idea of rotation, so imparting a dynamic and complementary character to this bipartite symbol. The law of polarity has been the subject of much thought among Chinese philosophers, who have deduced from this bipolar symbol a series of principles of unquestionable value, which we here trancribe: (*a*) the quantity of energy distributed throughout the universe is invariable; (*b*) it consists of the sum of two equal amounts of energy, one positive and active in kind and the other negative and passive; (*c*) the nature of cosmic phenomena is characterized by the varying proportions of the two modes of energy involved in their creation. In the twelve months of the year, for example, there is a given quantity of energy drawn from six parts of *Yang* and six of *Yin*, in varying proportions (13). We must also point to the relationship between the circle and the sphere, which is a symbol of the All.

Journey From the spiritual point of view, the journey is never merely a passage through space, but rather an expression of the urgent desire for discovery and change that underlies the actual movement and experience of travelling. Hence, to study, to inquire, to seek or to live with intensity through new and profound experiences are all modes of travelling or, to put it another way, spiritual and symbolic equivalents of the journey. Heroes are always travellers, in that they are restless. Travelling, Jung observes, is an image of aspiration, of an unsatisfied longing that never finds its goal, seek where it may (31). He goes on to point out that this goal is in fact the lost Mother; but this is a moot point, for we might equally well say that, on the contrary, its journey is a flight from the Mother. Flying, swimming and running are other activities which may be equated with travelling; and so also are dreaming, day-dreaming and imagining. Crossing a ford marks the decisive stage in the passage from one state to another (56). There is a connexion between the symbolism of the journey, in its cosmic sense, and the symbolism of the essential landscape of megalithic cults (or that seen by the shamans in their visions). Travelling may also be related to the complete cycle of the year or to the attempt to escape from it, depending upon certain secondary characteristics of the journey. But the true Journey is neither acquiescence nor escape—it is evolution. For this reason Guenon has suggested that ordeals of initiation frequently take the form of 'symbolic journeys' representing a quest that starts in the darkness of the profane world (or of the unconscious—the mother) and gropes towards the light. Such ordeals or trials—like the stages in a journey—are rites of purification (29). The archetype of the journey is the pilgrimage to the 'Centre' or the holyland—or the way out of the maze. The Night Sea-Crossing, equivalent to the Journey into Hell, illustrates certain basic aspects of journey-symbolism which still call for elucidation. Primarily, to travel is to seek. The Turkish Kalenderi sect require their initiates to travel ceaselessly, since, as we have suggested, travelling is often invested with a higher, sublimatory significance.

Yang-Yin A Chinese symbol of the dual distribution of forces, comprising the active or masculine principle (**Yang**) and the passive or feminine principle (*Yin*). It takes the form of a circle bisected by a sigmoid line, and the two parts so formed are invested with a dynamic tendency which would be wanting if the division were by a diameter. The light half represents the *Yang* force and the dark half denotes *Yin*; however, each half includes an arc cut out of the middle of the opposing half, to symbolize that every mode must contain within it the germ of its antithesis. Guenon considers that the Yang-Yin is a helicoidal symbol, that is, that it is a section of the universal whirlwind which brings opposites together and engenders perpetual motion, metamorphosis and continuity in situations characterized by contradiction. The entrance to and exit from this movement lie outside the movement itself, in the same way that birth and death stand apart from the life of the individual in so far as it is conscious and self-determined. The vertical axis through the centre of the Yang-Yin constitutes the 'unvarying mean' or, in other words, the mystic 'Centre' where there is no rotation, no restlessness, no impulse, nor any suffering of any kind. It corresponds to the central zone of the Wheel of Transformations in Hindu symbolism, and the centre or the way out of the labyrinth in Egyptian and western symbolism. It is also expressive of the two counterbalancing tendencies of evolution and involution (25).

Larousse *World Mythology.*
p. 204.
J. de Menasce.

Manichaeism . . . is radically dualistic. . . and above all, the good that matter (evil) has invaded and subjugated is much more than a creation; it is an emanation, an evocation which, proceeding from the Father of Grandeurs, bears his image and yearns for return to his principle. The part played by matter is not only to divide and disperse the light particles as far as possible, but also to stamp out and extinguish their own awareness of their exile. Revelation, or a series of revelations, will on the contrary recall the soul to its original state, which is also its destiny. This is an awakening commanding the whole of salvation, and has qualified Manichaeism as a religion of the saviour-saved, a corollary of its initial pantheism.

Indonesian Dance.
Directed by Chap Rhosody.
Performed aboard the SS VEENDAM
January 26, 1981.

[In the Indonesian island of Bali the religion has remained Hindu despite the fact that most of the islands have adopted the Moslem religion. From Bali comes a widely performed dance called Rangda and Baris.

The dance opens in a dim light with the entrance of a large fearful figure with long scraggly hair hanging to the waist—the very epitome of evil. With outstretched arms it shakes its hands with extremely long fingernails. It glares from the masked face in all directions as it circumvents the dance floor accompanied by shrieks and wild music. Following at his back is a native holding a knife in one hand and clasping the shoulder of the ghost or Evil One with the other hand as he keeps in step. They pass out of the room.

In the next scene a brilliantly colored figure enters with metallic clothing and a bright semi-circular headdress like an aura around his head. To the sound of music this knight also passes around the room and at length sinks on his knees in prayer. The ghost re-enters and comes toward the knight and seems unable to harm the kneeling figure with his sword. The native watches this and as the knight rises to engage the Evil One in battle, he at first helps the ghost against the knight but he soon changes sides and together amid much clatter and stabbing, they slowly drive the ghost back until he finally runs away.

Prolonged applause from the audience followed the skillful performance. To one aware of the Hindu beliefs the meaning was clear. The three figures represented the threefold nature of the man. The native was the individual man with his god head and his "shadow" or animal soul. At first he follows a gross life like the prodigal son. Then through religious effort gradually casts off his evil companions and returns to his god.

The audience undoubtedly did not know the sacred story and yet they had an inner understanding that brought forth the remarkable response.]

Leaves of Grass.
Song of Myself.
Walt Whitman, 1819–1892.

These are really the thoughts of all men in all ages and lands,
    they are not original with me,
If they are not yours as much as mine they are nothing, or next
    to nothing,
If they are not the riddle and the untying of the riddle they
    are nothing,
If they are not just as close as they are distant they are nothing.

"Bout lures out the beast"
Bob Rubin
The Miami Herald
September 18, 1981

I was screaming along with everyone else in the room as Sugar Ray Leonard tried to put away Thomas Hearns late in the bout. My wife Ol' Penski, whose fight experience pretty much had been limited to stinging backseat jabs at my driving, was surprised and somewhat abashed to find herself gripped by the action, too.

My petite ball and chain and I caught the fight on two large TV screens graciously provided at the Doral Country Club by ON-TV, the Fort Lauderdale cable company that broadcast the fight locally. To my amazement and amusement, Ol' Penski was mesmerized by the sight of a man trying to tear off another's head.

Afterward, she was troubled by her emotions because they revealed a savage lurking inside she didn't know existed. She had thought she was more civilized. She always had found boxing primitive and cruel. She wouldn't go to fights because the sight of blood made her sick, and so did the pleasure people took in watching it being shed.

Intellectually, I agree with her. Emotionally, I was shrieking for Leonard to belt Hearns to Reno. Nothing against Hearns. I had no particular rooting interest. Had the situation been reversed and Hearns been the stalker, I'd have been screaming for him to pulverize Leonard. The object was the kill.

The difference between OP and me is that I long ago recognized the schizophrenia within, concluded it was incurable and decided to let the caveman emerge now and then.

He emerged Wednesday night, club in hand. It was a heck of a fight and a heck of a telecast, thanks to the moonlighting NBC crew in charge, headed by producer Mike Weisman. Ubiquitous Ferdie Pacheco and Marv Albert of NBC's regular fight crew did the commentary, along with the venerable Don Dunphy, but most of the time it was impossible to hear them over the frenzied crowd.

The reversal of tactics and roles by the fighters as the bout progressed was as fascinating as the action. Boxer turned into stalker; Hitman became the hunted. Damned if I know why so many people only like to watch heavyweights. Sure, there's the explosive power of the big guys, but by the sixth round they're usually hanging all over each other like beached whales.

There may have been a clinch, I can't recall. I do know there was enough drama and savagery to summon the Cro-Magnon in me and the Cro-Magness in Ol' Penski. Now she throws combinations off her jabs at my driving.

The Inner Game of Tennis. p. 25-26.
W. Timothy Gallwey.
Random House, New York. 1974.

We're interested in what is happening inside the player's mind. Who is telling who what? Most players are talking to themselves on the court all the time. "Get up for the ball." "Keep it to his backhand." "Keep your eyes on the ball." "Bend your knees." The commands are endless. For some, it's like hearing a tape recording of the last lesson playing inside their head. Then, after the shot is made, another thought flashes through the mind and might be expressed as follows: "You clumsy ox, your grandmother could play better!" One day I was wondering who was talking to whom. Who was scolding and who being scolded. "I'm talking to myself," say most people. But just who is this "I" and who the "myself"?

Obviously, the "I" and the "myself" are separate entities or there would be no conversation, so one could say that within each player there are two "selves." One, the "I," seems to give instructions; the other, "myself," seems to perform the action. Then "I" returns with an evaluation of the action. For clarity let's call the "teller" Self 1 and the "doer" Self 2.

Now we are ready for the first major postulate of the Inner Game: within each player the kind of relationship that exists between Self 1 and Self 2 is the prime factor in determining one's ability to translate his knowledge of technique into effective action. In other words, the key to better tennis—or better anything—lies in improving the relationship between the conscious teller, Self 1 and the doer, Self 2.

Imagine that instead of being parts of the same person, Self 1 (teller) and Self 2 (doer) are two separate persons. How would you characterize their relationship after witnessing the following conversation between them? The player on the court is trying to make a stroke improvement. "Okay, dammit, keep your stupid wrist firm," he orders. Then as ball after ball comes over the net, Self 1 reminds Self 2, "Keep it firm. Keep it firm. Keep it firm!" Monotonous? Think how Self 2 must feel! It seems as though Self 1 doesn't think Self 2 hears well, or has a short memory, or is stupid. The truth is, of course, that Self 2, which includes the unconscious mind and nervous system, hears everything, never forgets anything, and is anything but stupid. After hitting the ball firmly once, he knows forever which muscles to contract to do it again. That's his nature.

And what's going on during the hit itself? If you look closely at the face of the player, you will see that his cheek muscles are tightening and his lips are pursed in effort and attempted concentration. But face muscles aren't required to hit the backhand, nor do they help concentration. Who's initiating that effort? Self 1, of course. But why? He's supposed to be the teller, not the doer, but it seems he doesn't really trust 2 to do the job or else he wouldn't have to do all the work himself. This is the nub of the problem: Self 1 does not trust Self 2, even though the unconscious, automatic self is extremely competent.

Back to our player. His muscles tense in over-effort, contact is made with the ball, there is a slight flick of the wrist, and the ball hits the back fence. "You bum, you'll never learn how to hit a backhand," Self 1 complains. By thinking too much and trying too hard, Self 1 has produced tension and muscle conflict in the body. He is responsible for the error, but he heaps the blame on Self 2 and then, by condemning it further, undermines his own confidence in Self 2. As a result the stroke grows worse and frustration builds.

The Doctrine of the Subtle Body
in Western Tradition
G.R.S. Mead M.A. (Cantab)
2nd Edition, London
Stuart & Watkins, 1967

[Comment: G.R.S. Mead has sought the origins of the Subtle Body which he attributes to the Chaldeans, Mithriaca and the philosophers of The Later Platonic school. He speaks of its superior and inferior aspects. In the Mitchell table the inferior Subtle Body is called Astral Body or Linga or Psyche (see p.106). The superior aspect or Radiant Body of Mead is called Spiritual Vehicle, or Buddhi by Mitchell.

Mead deals first with the inferior aspect and applies such names as the spirit body of the physical form; spirituous body; the vehicle of the shadow; vehicle of the irrational or animal soul. The Germans have applied the name doppelganger which is defined as a ghostly counterpart and companion of a person.

The characteristics of the spirit body are not explored too well by Mead. The Eastern mystics state that it is the mould of the physical body around which the atoms form. At death it stays close to the body until the body disintegrates when it also disappears. It is said this is the vaporous form so often reported at grave sites.

There follows a chapter on the Radiant Body. This is the subtle body of the Superior soul; the celestial or luciform body; organon of light; the astrocides or augoeites; sidereal body; prime essence; aethereal body. It should be remembered that all "bodies" mentioned above are not visible unless they are mentioned as physical.]

[The recent death of Sir Hans Krebs terminated his wish to do something about present day criminal violence and vandalism. He felt that men of science should seek ways to solve this urgent problem. In long talks with J.L.D. he examined the long lost thesis of this book. He was impressed by Roy Mitchell's work and the unusual support from the literature of the ages.]

On the Dark Side of Man.
Sir Hans Krebs.
Discoverer of the Krebs Cycle.
Executive Health. Vol. XV, No. 10. July, 1979.

Man is a social animal and the health of the individual is therefore interlinked with the health of the society of which the individual is a member. Hence the state of health of our society is of concern to every family.

The societies of western civilizations are today beset with grave health problems. Criminality is ever increasing. Violent muggings make it risky to be in lonely places during the hours of darkness. Major robberies are reported daily. Pilfering in stores by customers and employees has reached enormous dimensions. (In 1970, it was estimated at one and one-half billion dollars in Britain alone and it is increasing every year.)

Vandals and hooligans wantonly destroy trees, lamp-posts, signposts, smash windows, and slash the tires of parked cars. Drug addiction is increasing. Our national economies grow more precarious, at least in part because of reckless unofficial strikes, irresponsible absenteeism, and inefficiency. Pollution deteriorates the environment, and in spite of many warnings we still carelessly exploit natural resources without regard for long-term effects.

These problems have been extensively discussed in the press and other media and in books. There is a lot of descriptive material, including statistics, and there is also a lot of speculation about the causes of the troubles. But most of the speculation, alas, is rather wild, falling short of the criteria which a scientist would impose upon his hypotheses.

A scientist is not satisfied with an hypothesis if it merely offers a *plausible* explanation. He insists upon an hypothesis which can be tested, either by observation or by experiment and *the test cannot aim at proving the hypothesis, but only at disproving, falsifying, it. If suitable tests do not disprove the hypothesis it strengthens the hypothesis. The all-important point is to abandon an hypothesis when the test (or experience) suggests that it may be wrong.* Present day sociological, educational and economic subjects are riddled with hypotheses which do not stand up to the criteria of acceptable scientific hypotheses. There is testimony to that effect by one of the most distinguished economists of our day, the Nobel Laureate F. A. von Hayek, who chose as the title of his Nobel Lecture (1974) *"The Pretence of Knowledge."* But in spite of their short-comings, such hypotheses are nowadays used as a basis for action in education, in economics, and in the handling of offenders.

What I propose, to repeat, is to look at the malaise I have described from the standpoint of the biologist and the medical scientist–as opposed to a legal, moral, or sociological point of view.

On the animal in man . . .

We pay too little attention to the fact that man is not only a rationally thinking and poetically feeling being, *he is also driven, guided, and motivated by those subconscious principles of behaviour that we see throughout the animal kingdom. The question is whether, and to what extent, the current sickness of society springs from a failure to understand human nature, especially the animal in man. In other words, have we neglected what biology can teach us?*

For example, *unless life is constantly renewed by hard effort, it runs down.* The individual must eat and drink, and he must protect himself against the environment with clothing and shelter. In a highly developed society, he has to earn money so that he can buy food, clothing, and shelter; and to earn means that he must render a service for which someone is willing to pay. He who does not render such service has to be carried by others.

Further, *Homo sapiens*, like all other species, does not work unless he has an incentive, such as the need for food and shelter or a desire for pleasure. In the last analysis, these are all to be had for money, and for the great majority of *Homo sapiens,* money is the greatest single incentive for overcoming natural laziness. Laziness in this context is not necessarily doing nothing at all, but the unwillingness to do something that serves society and for which society is willing to pay. Up to a point, the well-being and power of individuals and of society depend on having money, inasmuch as all the other contributory factors to well-being are useless without money.

What do these considerations mean in terms of practical politics? *If productive work is one of the bases on which the well-being and strength of society rests, the laws and the social organization should do everything to encourage it. Amazingly, a situation has developed during this century, in countries of our Western civilization, where laws all too often do exactly the opposite.* Unless this is recognized and acted upon, our Western civilization is likely to grow weaker and weaker. Taxes take away so much of our earnings that people do not find it worthwhile to work at their optimum capacity. Tax laws deter people from saving by high taxes on interest from savings. These laws prevent many highly trained, professional married women from working, because, absurdly enough, they cannot afford it: it would cost more to hire domestic help in England, for example, than the net income that a married doctor or teacher, for instance, would produce.

Many people believe that work is unhealthy and should be reduced to a minimum. Some hold that the average number of working hours may progressively decrease, perhaps to 20 hours per week, and that eventually most of man's time will be free for leisure pursuits. Such forecasts are neither realistic nor desirable.

The proper aim is to remove the drudgeries of hard, physical work, to remove the unpleasantness of work by providing a clean, congenial setting, to remove the boredom of repetitive work, and to make work as interesting, enjoyable and satisfying as possible—*but work it remains.*

But this is only one of the reasons why a continued decrease in the number of working hours is an unrealistic, utopian dream. *The survival of a nation is, alas, a matter of fierce competition with other nations. An ineffectual or lazy nation is weak in competing for world trade, because the goods it produces are likely to be expensive. It is also slow in making weapons to defend itself against harder-working nations. Thus, it may be starved out or destroyed.*

But if work is essential for the well-being of society, not every kind of work for which people are willing to pay is good for society. Work may well be lucrative for the individual but unproductive and even damaging to the country, either directly or through its side effects, such as pollution or the destruction of the countryside. It can be directly damaging when the work done, looked at from the national point of view, is futile and a waste of labour.

I have in mind some aspects of the advertising trade and of the deceptive, aggressive, persuasive, doorstep salesmanship that misinforms people so that they buy things they do not want or cannot afford. And are there not excessive numbers of civil servants and other administrators? Is the manufacture and advertising of cigarettes—which kill endless thousands of people per annum and make many more ill—a desirable form of work?

It follows then that we must plan and direct our available manpower resources into channels that are fruitful from the national point of view.

The unalterable criminal

Another problem concerns human conduct more directly. There is powerful evidence in the form of hard-core *recidivism,** that antisocial and criminal behaviour is very often so deeply ingrained that it has the character of an incurable disease—incurable for two reasons. It may be *inborn*, like inborn errors of metabolism, and therefore cannot be eradicated, though its effect might be alleviated. Or it may have become so deeply "*imprinted*" through environmental experiences that it has become as resistant to eradication as are inborn defects.

Evidence indicating that criminality can have genetic origins comes from studies of identical twins, who, though they grew up in different environments after early separation, became criminals at about the same time of their lives and committed the same type of crimes. In addition, there are many case reports that suggest, though they do not prove, a genetic factor. For example, we read a report from Columbus, Ohio: "Lee Arthur Henry (23) was 18 months old when his father was executed for murdering his mother—the last execution in Arkansas. Today his lawyers are trying to save him from the same fate. He has been sentenced for the murder of a shop attendant."

Crime reports in the press very frequently illustrate incorrigible recidivism. Thus, we read, "A man freed after serving nine years of a 14-year prison sentence for strangling his girl friend, committed an almost identical crime." We read that a murderer who had been on parole for only 48 hours, broke into the house of a woman social worker who had not responded to his advances, and when he was disturbed by her father, he shot the father and then killed himself.

James Griffiths of Glasgow, who began his criminal career when he was nine and spent most of the next 24 years in prison,

*Hardcore recidivism: the chronic tendency toward repetition of criminal or anti-social behavior patterns.

described his frame of mind: "When I get out of here, I shall either get money and live very well in South America for the rest of my life . . . or get buried. I don't get out with the intention of committing violence. But if it means either I get caught and put in prison or I whack someone over the head and they die, that's just their hard luck." He died at age 34 in a gun battle with Glasgow police.

In such cases, it is impossible to decide whether genetic factors or a bad environment are responsible for criminality. However, *for the purposes I have in mind, this distinction is not important. What matters is whether or not antisocial conduct can have a virtually unalterable, biological basis—unalterable as a result of either inherited or deeply ingrained traits—and whether this can be diagnosed. I submit that it can be diagnosed, the symptom of such a biological basis being recidivism. Innumerable case reports of recidivists make it clear that often neither good-will nor sympathy nor advice nor "punishment" will prevent them from pursuing their odd career.*

The problem of vandalism

A particularly disturbing disease of society is the rapid spread of vandalism—the wilful destruction without material benefit to the evildoer. This is essentially a juvenile aberration. A lawyer or educationalist is liable to look upon it as an evil trait arising from a lack of "moral quality," and he is at a loss as to how to cope with it. *A medical scientist, before trying to cope with it, would first make an effort to understand the nature and pathogenesis of the ailment. In the case of human diseases, especially those of the mind, we cannot explore the nature of the trouble by laboratory experiments and we must therefore proceed by another way. So efforts to understand vandalism must begin by formulating an hypothesis about its origins, based on observations. Once we have an hypothesis, we can use it as a basis for action in the form of social and educational measures and criti-*

cally observe the effects of their application. Junenile anti-social behaviour—in the form of vandalism, break-ins, mugging, violence, hooliganism—was rare 30 years ago. Scientific logic leads to the question: what environmental factors affecting the development of personality have changed over the last 30 years.

One such factor is the parent-child relationship, as the result of the increasing number of mothers who take up full-time employment. The absence of the mother or a parent from the home can seriously diminish the normal close affectionate contact between parent and child, as John Bowlby pointed out some time ago. *Maternal Care in Mental Health*, 1951; and *Attachment and Loss*, 1969 and 1973.

Parents may sense that they fail to give their children sufficient love and a sufficient feeling of security, and they compensate for their failure by spoiling the child with presents and by allowing them excess freedom. This is not what the child needs most. It needs disciplining of a kind which only a loving parent can provide because the child must sense that behind the disciplining there is the loving care of the parent. It is essential for the child's normal development that it is trained early to recognize firm limits as well as firm duties and challenging tasks. It is the loving parents' natural responsibility to instill this recognition of limits and duties. If this influence is lacking the child subconsciously goes on playfully to explore the limits to which it must go before it is restrained. Some children appear to find great pleasure in destructive activities, and if they are allowed to get away with it we get vandalism. Disciplining in this context means, of course, instilling considerateness towards others, but beyond this the child derives a sense of security and gratification from living in a meaningful order. Professor Hinde in his book (1974) *Biological Basis of Human Social Behaviour* has discussed the subject on the basis of work on animals where the problems are analogous.

A second major change during the recent decades is the increased "cultural deprivation." Education has become ineffectual for too many children. Not long ago the Prime Minister of Britain referred to the deterioration in the teaching of the three R's (to which a fourth R—religion—may be added). *Those who do not read with ease and pleasure are deprived of the accumulated experience and wisdom of humanity. Those who do not know Holy Books are deprived of guidelines and yardsticks of conduct.* Worse still, these old-established educational influences are replaced by other, often unhelpful, if not corrupt, influences of the mass-media. *Radio and television give semi-illiterate people information about crime and violence.*

Another source of cultural deprivation is *rootlessness.* Attracted by jobs people get uprooted and in their new communities they have no feeling of belonging, no pride in belonging and no links with the local society.

It is said that deprivation lies at the root of criminal behaviour. This is true but deprivation must not be understood only in its material sense. What offenders often lack is quality of character, "moral fibre," something which has to do with poor upbringing and poor education.

Action

What should be done to counteract the recent trends? First, extensive discussions are needed of the points I have raised.

I have already hinted at a few specific directions which follow from the diagnoses of the causes of the troubles. We must find ways and means of providing incentives for productive work, of protecting society from hard-core recidivist criminals, of rehabilitating curable offenders by intense active treatment, by introducing educational measures to instill self-discipline.

We must make use of the methodology of science because the methodology of the social subjects has proved insufficient. This means, above all, that we must get away from the *dogmatic* hypotheses of the social subjects and of party politics and *replace them as a basis for action by hypotheses which can be tested in the form of social, educational and economic measures. In the light of the results we must be ready to modify action.*

We must impress upon individuals that there are limits to personal freedom; that the practice of freedom by the individual must never interfere with the freedom of the next individual. We must try to achieve this by insisting on good discipline at home and at school and by a realistic enforcement of the law. *The recent relaxation of discipline at home and at school and the relaxation of law enforcement may have been an over-reaction against the exaggerated discipline of earlier days, but it must be recognized that the experiment of over-relaxation has had disastrous effects.*

We must aim at educating the public about the causes of crime and vandalism, especially about the importance of family upbringing. The subject of the biology of parenthood should be introduced into the high school curriculum, being no less important than sex education. We must provide better opportunities for young people to embark on constructive, purposeful activities, especially during leisure time. Vandalism may often be an expression of, and a reaction against, boredom in the absence of challenging tasks. We must stop the pernicious effects of the demonstration of crime on the television screen.

Some may argue that rigid proof of my diagnoses is still lacking. I would reply that in *this field of societal ailments, exactly as in clinical medicine, we must often act long before concepts about remedies have been rigidly tested and proved. The sick patient, be it a single individual or society, needs action based on the best available, but not necessarily conclusive, information. A patient would not be satisfied with a doctor's answer "I do not know of an absolutely reliable cure"; he would beg the doctor to try a treatment which might* possibly *help. Much of the present clinical therapeutics is of this kind. So I suggest that there is enough sound basic information about the causes of society's ailment to explore, by tests, new ways and means of combatting the troubles.*

Leaves of Grass.
Walt Whitman.
Comprehensive Reader's Edition, 1965.
Harold W. Blodgett and Sculley Bradley, Editors.

[Scattered throughout *Leaves of Grass* there are countless words, lines and poems that are straight out of the world of mysticism. These are acknowledged by the many scholars of Whitman but have not been brought into a system of his thoughts and beliefs. Maybe they never will be. A careful comparison of *Leaves of Grass* and *The Exile of the Soul* will show an incredible number of similarities. Mitchell had the highest esteem for Whitman and could quote long passages from *Leaves of Grass.*
Whitman had a plan for the placing of his mystical poetry. Those who strove to know his hidden meanings would be obliged to undergo a long initiation.] .

Whoever you are holding me now in hand,
Without one thing all will be useless,
I give you fair warning before you attempt me further,
I am not what you supposed, but far different.

Who is he that would become my follower?
Who would sign himself a candidate for my affections?

The way is suspicious, the result uncertain,
 perhaps destructive,
You would have to give up all else, I alone would expect
 to be your sole and exclusive standard,
Your novitiate would even then be long and exhausting,
The whole past theory of your life and all conformity
 to the lives around you would have to be abandon'd,
Therefore release me now before troubling yourself any
 further, let go your hand from my shoulders,
Put me down and depart on your way. . . . p. 115.

For it is not for what I have put into it that I
    have written this book,
Nor is it by reading it you will acquire it,
Nor do those know me best who admire me and
    vauntingly praise me,
Nor will the candidates for my love (unless at most
    a very few) prove victorious,
Nor will my poems do good only, they will do just
    as much evil, perhaps more,
For all is useless without that which you may
    guess at many times and not hit, that which
    I hinted at;
Therefore release me and depart on your way. . . . p. 116.

[Whitman believed that the soul is on a long journey from ages far in the past to ages far in the future, until after thousands of returns to earth, its task of purification of the "contentious soul" is complete. On completion the soul is freed of these cycles.]

I tramp a perpetual journey, (come listen all!) . . . p. 83.

The soul,
Forever and forever—longer than soil is brown and
    solid—longer than water ebbs and flows. . . . p. 18.

This day before dawn I ascended a hill and look'd
    at the crowded heaven,
And I said to my spirit *When we become the enfolders*
    of those orbs, and the pleasure and knowledge of
    every thing in them, shall we be fill'd and
    satisfied then?
And my spirit said *No, we but level that lift to*
    pass and continue beyond. . . . p. 83.

To gather the minds of men out of their brains as you
encounter them, to gather the love out of their
hearts,
To take your lovers on the road with you, for all that
you leave them behind you,
To know the universe itself as a road, as many roads,
as roads for traveling souls.

All parts away for the progress of souls,
All religion, all solid things, arts, governments—all that
was or is apparent upon this globe or any globe, falls
into niches and corners before the processions of souls
along the grand roads of the universe.

Of the progress of the souls of men and women along
the grand roads of the universe, all other progress
is the needed emblem and sustenance. . . . p. 157

Forever alive, forever forward,
Stately, solemn, sad, withdrawn, baffled, mad,
turbulent, feeble, dissatisfied,
Desperate, proud, fond, sick, accepted by men,
rejected by men,
They go! they go! I know that they go, but I know not
where they go,
But I know that they go toward the best—toward
something great.

Whoever you are, come forth! or man or woman come
forth!
You must not stay sleeping and dallying there in the
house, though you built it, or though it has been
built for you.

Out of the dark confinement! out from behind the
screen!
It is useless to protest, I know all and expose it.

Behold through you as bad as the rest,
Through the laughter, dancing, dining, supping, of
people,
Inside of dresses and ornaments, inside of those wash'd
and trimm'd faces,
Behold a secret silent loathing and despair.

No husband, no wife, no friend, trusted to hear the
confession,
Another self, a duplicate of every one, skulking and
hiding it goes,
Formless and wordless through the streets of the cities,
polite and bland in the parlors,
In the cars of railroads, in steamboats, in the public
assembly,
Home to the houses of men and women, at the table,
in the bedroom, everywhere,
Smartly attired, countenance smiling, form upright,
death under the breast-bones, hell under the
skull-bones,
Under the broadcloth and gloves, under the ribbons
and artificial flowers,
Keeping fair with the customs, speaking not a syllable
of itself,
Speaking of any thing else but never of itself.

Allons! through struggles and wars!
The goal that was named cannot be countermanded.

Have the past struggles succeeded?
What has succeeded? yourself? your nation? Nature?
Now understand me well–it is provided in the essence
of things that from any fruition of success, no
matter what, shall come forth something to make
a greater struggle necessary.

My call is the call of battle, I nourish active rebellion,
He going with me must go well arm'd,
He going with me goes often with spare diet, poverty,
angry enemies, desertions. . . . p. 157–158.

I am the poet of the Body and I am the poet of the Soul,
The pleasures of heaven are with me and the pains of
hell are with me,
The first I graft and increase upon myself, the latter I
translate into a new tongue. . . . p. 48.

Through me forbidden voices,
Voices of sexes and lusts, voices veil'd and I remove the
veil,
Voices indecent by me clarified and
transfigur'd. . . . p. 53.

I do not think seventy years is the time of a man or
woman,
Nor that seventy millions of years is the time of a man
or woman,
Nor that years will ever stop the existence of me, or
any one else. . . . p. 394.

Believing I shall come again upon the earth after five
thousand years,
Waiting responses from oracles, honoring the gods,
saluting the sun, . . . p. 78.

And whether I come to my own to-day or in ten
thousand or in ten million years,
I can cheerfully take it now, or with equal cheerfulness
I can wait. . . . p. 48.

And as to you Life I reckon you are the leavings of
many deaths,
(No doubt I have died myself ten thousand times
before.) . . . p. 87.

I see Hermes, unsuspected, dying, well-belov'd, saying
to the people *Do not weep for me,*
This is not my true country, I have lived banish'd
from my true country, I now go back there,
I return to the celestial sphere where every one goes
in his turn. . . . p. 142.

[Whitman speaks of himself as Body and Soul (a duality), also as I, Soul, and Body (a trinity).
The use of "spirit" is manifold, sometimes as the highest, all encompassing God, (similar to *the one* of Parmenides in *Plato's Dialogues*), and at other times as the soul in which he speaks with authority and again as spirit of the army or the country.
When Whitman refers to the body he is nearly always referring to an active, demanding, emotional entity, or in Mitchell's parlance "the animal soul". Indeed a few times Whitman himself refers to this entity as a soul—a soul in conflict with the higher soul. He also refers to this entity as "son", "camerado", "mate" and "My Fancy".
The following will illustrate these thoughts:—]

Come, said my soul,
Such verses for my Body let us write, (for we are one,)

That should I after death invisibly return,
Or, long, long hence, in other spheres,
There to some group of mates the chants resuming,
(Tallying Earth's soil, trees, winds, tumultuous waves,)
Ever with pleas'd smile I may keep on,
Ever and ever yet the verses owning–as, first, I here
and now,
Signing for Soul and Body, set to them my
name, . . . (Title page epigraph).

I too with my soul and body,
We, a curious trio, picking, wandering on our way,
Through these shores amid the shadows, with the
apparitions pressing,
Pioneers! O pioneers! . . . p. 231.

[Spirit]

Santa Spirita, breather, life,
Beyond the light, lighter than light,
Beyond the flames of hell, joyous, leaping easily
above hell,
Beyond Paradise, perfumed solely with mine own
perfume,
Including all life on earth, touching, including God,
including Saviour and Satan,
Ethereal, pervading all, (for without me what were
all? what were God?)
Essence of forms, life of the real identities, permanent,
positive, (namely the unseen,)
Life of the great round world, the sun and stars, and
of man, I, the general soul,
Here the square finishing, the solid, I the most solid,
Breathe my breath also through these songs. . . . p. 445.

[The higher and lower souls of man]

Adieu to a Soldier

Adieu O soldier,
You of the rude campaigning, (which we shared,)
The rapid march, the life of the camp,
The hot contention of opposing fronts, the long
manœuvre,
Red battles with their slaughter, the stimulus, the
strong terrific game,
Spell of all brave and manly hearts, the trains of time
through you and like of you all fill'd,
With war and war's expression.

Adieu dear comrade,
Your mission is fulfill'd–but I, more warlike,
Myself and this contentious soul of mine,
Still on our own campaigning bound,
Through untried roads with ambushes opponents
lined,
Through many a sharp defeat and many a crisis, often
baffled,
Here marching, ever marching on, a war fight out–aye
here,
To fiercer, weightier battles give expression. . . . p. 325.

[The above is remarkably similar to a report given by Ronald Eyre on a T.V. series, *The Long Search*–"The Moslem says there are two kinds of war. The wars between men are minor wars; the major war is the one that goes on within each man." Whitman also describes this war in the next poem and ends with the promise that finally this war will be won by the "real self" The Higher Soul.]

Ah poverties, wincings, and sulky retreats,
Ah you foes that in conflict have overcome me,
(For what is my life or any man's life but a conflict
with foes, the old, the incessant war?)
You degradations, you tussle with passions and
appetites,
You smarts from dissatisfied friendships, (ah wounds
the sharpest of all!)
You toil of painful and choked articulations, you
meannesses,
You shallow tongue-talks at tables, (my tongue the
shallowest of any;)
You broken resolutions, you racking angers, you
smother'd ennuis!
Ah think not you finally triumph, my real self has yet
to come forth,
It shall yet march forth o'ermastering, till all lies
beneath me,
It shall yet stand up the soldier of ultimate
victory. . . . p. 479.

As I ponder'd in silence,
Returning upon my poems, considering, lingering
long,
A Phantom arose before me with distrustful aspect,
Terrible in beauty, age, and power,
The genius of poets of old lands,
As to me directing like flame its eyes,
With finger pointing to many immortal songs,
And menacing voice, *What singest thou?* it said,
*Know'st thou not there is but one theme for ever-
enduring bards?*
And that is the theme of War, the fortune of battles,
The making of perfect soldiers.

Be it so, then I answer'd,
I too haughty Shade also sing war, and a longer and
greater one than any,
Waged in my book with varying fortune, with flight,
advance and retreat, victory deferr'd and wavering,
(Yet methinks certain, or as good as certain, at the last,)
the field the world,
For life and death, for the Body and for the eternal
Soul,
Lo, I too am come, chanting the chant of battles,
I above all promote brave soldiers. . . . p. 1.

[Whitman pictures the Higher Soul as sending forth bridges to connect with the lower self in the following remarkable poem.]

A noiseless patient spider,
I mark'd where on a little promontory it stood isolated,
Mark'd how to explore the vacant vast surrounding,
It launch'd forth filament, filament, filament, out of
itself,
Ever unreeling them, ever tirelessly speeding them.

And you O my soul where you stand,
Surrounded, detached, in measureless oceans of space,
Ceaselessly musing, venturing, throwing, seeking the
spheres to connect them,
Till the bridge you will need be form'd, till the ductile
anchor hold,
Till the gossamer thread you fling catch somewhere,
O my soul. . . . p. 450.

[It is rare for Whitman to refer to the lower self as a "soul" but he does slip it in here and there.]

By the city dead-house by the gate,
As idly sauntering wending my way from the clangor,
I curious pause, for lo, an outcast form, a poor dead
prostitute brought,
Her corpse they deposit unclaim'd, it lies on the damp
brick pavement,
The divine woman, her body, I see the body, I look on
it alone,
That house once full of passion and beauty, all else I
notice not,
Nor stillness so cold, nor running water from faucet,
nor odors morbific impress me,
But the house alone—that wondrous house—that
delicate fair house—that ruin!
That immortal house more than all the rows of
dwellings ever built!
Or white-domed capitol with majectic figure
surmounted, or all the old high-spired cathedrals,
That little house alone more than them all—poor,
desperate house!
Fair, fearful wreck—tenement of a soul—*itself a soul,* *
Unclaim'd, avoided house—take one breath from my
tremulous lips,
Take one tear dropt aside as I go for thought of you,
Dead house of love—house of madness and sin,
crumbled, crush'd,
House of life, erewhile talking and laughing—but ah,
poor house, dead even then,
Months, years, an echoing, garnish'd house—but dead,
dead, dead. . . . p. 367.
*[italics ours]

From *Leaves of Grass*
Walt Whitman

AFTERWORD

These are the ideas that the philosophers, the mystics, the poets and the sages of Eastern religious traditions have brought to us. Men of high esteem, they have invoked their gifts of reasoning, intuition and spiritual insight for their contributions to our heritage. By and large humanity has passed them by except for periods of renaissance, when the stature of certain communities has risen to great heights of perception.

And now, at last, in the 20th century, scientific research is supplying the corroboration of the dual entities in each man. These researchers—the neurosurgeons and the psychologists during the last two decades—have validated what the philosophers of long ago had been saying.

While the researchers have not said each man has two souls, they fully support the presence of two individuals existing in every man who do not act alike nor think alike. Indeed, they often work at cross purposes with one another. Furthermore, the two individuals bear a striking resemblance to the two entities in man which have been described by the wise men and philosophers for over two thousand years. The characteristics given to each entity by the scientists are almost identical to that of the philosophers.

All this came about when the neurosurgeons and the psychologists stepped into the picture by describing their observations of patients with brains damaged on one side or the other. The brain is divided into a right hemisphere and a left hemisphere. If the left hemisphere is badly damaged, by accident or disease, the right side of the patient is paralysed. He cannot read, write or speak except for an incoherent jargon. If it is the right hemisphere that is damaged the left side of the patient is paralysed. The patient retains his speech and literary qualities but loses the unusual powers of the right brain.

When a patient has epilepsy and all efforts to stop or reduce the attacks become futile, the neurosurgeon sometimes severs the bundle of nerve fibers which connect the two hemispheres. This bundle consisting of many thousands of fibers is known as the *corpus callosum* and provides the means for the two hemispheres to communicate and cooperate with one another, thus giving the impression of being a single person. The epilepsy is completely terminated but dramatic things happen to the patient. It is soon apparent to the researchers that they are dealing with two persons who behave and think differently. Often they are in conflict with one another. If one hand of the patient tries to carry out certain actions the other hand tries to undo what has been done. The left hemisphere which has dominated all its life gets a good deal of opposition and loses the complete control it had formerly.

While the severing of the *corpus callosum* had been carried out prior to 1950, it was the brilliant research in the early 1960s of Dr. Roger Sperry and his students, Michael Gazzaniga and Jerre Levy, which was responsible for opening new approaches to duality in man and which has now become the most highly favored sector of psychological research. A massive bibliography has taken place and Dr. Sperry's work has been rewarded with his selection for a Nobel prize.

Left handed people sometimes switch brain hemispheres in strange ways and are not dealt with here. Suffice it to say they do not escape being dual personalities.

The phenomena of dualism do not occur in animals. While they have two hemispheres of the brain, if one hemisphere is damaged the other side can take over equally well.

From the tests of a large number of patients many of the characteristics of each hemisphere have now been described. Except for a few small differences, each side of the brain is physically the same, both qualitatively and quantitatively, but their characteristics are far different. A brief delineation of these characteristics follow:

Left Hemisphere Traits

It is the dominant hemisphere, providing leadership in all fields of endeavor and acts as a throttle of emotional outbursts of the right hemisphere.

It is the hemisphere we know the best. It is the seat of the thinking activity.

It is concerned with speaking, writing and reading, analysis, programming and logic.

It deals with intellectual studies and planning and has the ability to generalize a series of phenomena into a principle.

By rational thought it can establish laws and codes of ethics and morals.

It is responsible for making and keeping records including history. It also has a memory for this activity,

It controls the conscience, knowing good from evil.

It acts in the field of behavioral judgments and is capable of temperance, sincerity, noble ideals, humanism, honesty and loyalty.

The right eye is connected to the left hemisphere.

It communicates through language.

Right Hemisphere Traits

It usually follows instructions of the dominant side but can disagree and object. It is the gremlin who interferes with planned work.

It is the seat of the emotions, anger, hate, sensuality, jealousy, impatience and arrogance.

It is selfish, fearful, insecure and suspicious. It is "the child within" mentioned by Socrates in the *Phaedo*.

Its behavior is animal-like tending to be rough, irreverent and irrational.

It works by "feel" in the field of the five senses.

Personality traits develop in this hemisphere.

It is unable to think and to generalize.

It is highly sensitive to visual perception, recognizes configurations, faces and shapes. In this respect it is superior to the left hemisphere. It is also superior in art and music being highly skilful with rhythm.

It is the seat of a very accurate memory.

It is Gallwey's No. 2 Self in sports (see p. 312).

It communicates in images.

The scientists in brain research have not yet asked the most important question. Why should man be inhabited by two persons? what is the purpose of these universal phenomena? If they will but go to the philosopher* they will tap a large fund of helpful information. The philosopher in turn will be grateful to know about the physical attributes of this vehicle of his animal soul and how it operates. The knowledge gained by the scientist will produce great benefits as he goes about the problem of how he can best teach this mute and troublesome entity. The philosopher affirms this activity is the Great Task of the thinking ego. Let us hope they will work hand in hand and advance from what they agree upon and not shout differences at each other.

*Philosopher as here used does not necessarily refer to all philosophers but to leaders like Socrates, Plato, Plotinus, Porphyry, Proclus, Paracelsus, Emerson and his New England group, and the leaders in Eastern and Mid-eastern religions including those of India, China, Egypt, and the Hebrews.